KU-023-644

THE
CONDITION
OF CREATURES

Agere & pati fortia.

Emblem from Claude Paradin, *Devises Heroïques,* 1557,
reproduced by permission of the Folger Shakespeare Library.

The

Condition of

Creatures

SUFFERING AND ACTION IN CHAUCER AND SPENSER

Georgia Ronan Crampton

New Haven and London, Yale University Press, 1974

Copyright © 1974 by Yale University.
All rights reserved. This book may not be
reproduced, in whole or in part, in any form
(except by reviewers for the public press),
without written permission from the publishers.
Library of Congress catalog card number: 73-93281
International standard book number: 0-300-01382-5

Designed by Sally Sullivan
and set in Baskerville type.
Printed in the United States of America by
Vail-Ballou Press, Inc., Binghamton, N.Y.

Published in Great Britain, Europe, and Africa by
Yale University Press, Ltd., London.
Distributed in Latin America by Kaiman & Polon,
Inc., New York City; in Australasia and Southeast
Asia by John Wiley & Sons Australasia Pty. Ltd.,
Sydney; in India by UBS Publishers' Distributors Pvt.,
Ltd., Delhi; in Japan by John Weatherhill, Inc., Tokyo.

For J. A. C.

Contents

Acknowledgments

In writing this book, I have been much helped. The stimulation and example of Stanley B. Greenfield as teacher, critic, and friend is my largest single debt. He read the manuscript at an early stage, and this represents a fraction of what I owe to his learning and to his generous interest and encouragement. Waldo F. McNeir made discriminating comments on the Spenser chapters. Others who suggested, corroborated, or corrected include Charles Chamberlain, Maria Oden, H. C. Kim, Jenny Clay, Miriam and Ben Rosenfeld, A. H. Travis, W. F. Bolton, Daniel J. Taylor, Phyllis G. Lewis, Thomas Doulis, and Rev. Thomas A. Kelley, C.S.C. John A. Crampton made suggestions on style. Patricia Cooper read page proofs discerningly. DeeAnne Westbrook helped with the index.

Librarians and library staffs gave the kind, efficient aid typical of their courteous guild at the Folger Shakespeare Library, the Henry E. Huntington Library, Cambridge University Library, the British Museum Reading Room, Northwestern University Library, University of Oregon Library, University of Washington Library, University of Portland Library, and Marylhurst College Library. Special thanks are due Louise Gerity of Lewis and Clark College library.

I thank the Folger Shakespeare Library and the University of Portland for grant support.

Virginia Meadows, Kathleen Moeller, and Patricia Knott typed the final manuscript. At Yale University Press I wish to acknowledge the early interest of Merle Spiegel and the final editing of Ellen Graham.

Note on Texts

Unless otherwise noted, the Loeb Classical Library editions (Cambridge, Mass.: Harvard University Press; London: Heinemann) are used for all classical texts. The following editions are used for Chaucer and Spenser:

The Works of Geoffrey Chaucer. Edited by F. N. Robinson. 2d ed. Boston: Houghton-Mifflin, 1957.
The Works of Edmund Spenser, a Variorum Edition. Edited by Edwin Greenlaw, Charles G. Osgood, Frederick M. Padelford, and others. Baltimore: Johns Hopkins University Press, 1932–57. I have altered the scribal *i* and *u*.

1

Agere et Pati:

Deed and Pathos

A hero weeps when he hears a poet sing. Odysseus, feasted in the palace of Alcinous, listens as Demodocus entertains. Then the guest congratulates the harper who has sung truly of the fate of the Achaeans, of what things they did (ὅσσ' ἔρξαν) and suffered (τ' ἔπαθόν) under the walls of Troy.[1] Thus Homer introduces the topos *agere et pati,* to do and to suffer, as western literature begins. I propose to examine suffering in its relation to action as a protagonistic ideal and as a formal element in literature, using Chaucer's Knight's Tale and parts of Spenser's *Faerie Queene* as examples, if not the most obvious ones. Following chapters treat the *agere-et-pati* topos as a shaping force in the dynamics of the poems, as one aspect of form. But first some account of the topic before it reached English poets is due.

Homer's line makes its pedigree as old and as honorable as possible. He uses it fundamentally. In the speech of Odysseus,

---

1. *Odyssey* 8.490. The human preference for being an agent rather than a patient emerges as Odysseus goes to request that Demodocus sing of the wooden horse. In that exploit, of course, Odysseus is the wily agent, not a patient.

the words *do* and *suffer* denote and connote that which the formula radically implies: in their involvement with events, men do things or they suffer them. In this sense "to suffer" is to have something done to one—the verb carries the philosophical meaning "manner of being acted upon." In this quite special sense, one may "suffer" a delight as well as a hardship, although this fact is not especially relevant in describing the reaction of Odysseus to the song of Demodocus and the special sense is rare in the poems to be discussed. But though suffering a joy is usually a benign, if unrealized, possibility in our poems, the implications of *suffer* are wider than the familiar meaning of experiencing pain or anguish. They are in fact those implied by the passive voice in grammar—the subject is acted upon—or those indicated when a noun is not a subject but a direct or indirect object.[2]

Some common pairs of English words by which writers have indicated this relationship, with or without the same root as *agere* (or *facere*) *et pati*, are *act* and *suffer, agent* and *patient, inflict* and *endure, active* and *passive, exact* and *yield, give* and *receive, doer* and *sufferer, do* and *bear;* more remotely, *ethos* and *pathos;* more occasionally, *action* and *passion.* Of course any noun may be converted into a special application: *user* and *used, master* and *mastered, cook* and *cooked, leader* and *led, eater* and *eaten, seller* and *sold.* Such examples say

2. Homer's frequent use of *pascho* refers to undergoing something grievous, according to Gottlieb C. Crusius in *A Complete Greek and English Lexicon of the Poems of Homer and the Homeridae,* trans. Henry Smith (Hartford, Conn.: H. Huntington, 1844), p. 401. Chaucer sometimes used the neutral meaning. In *The Book of the Duchess* the Black Knight says of himself and his lady, "ylyche they suffred thoo / Oo blysse, and eke oo sorwe bothe . . ." (1292–93). In *Piers Plowman* the dreamer is told that the road that will bring him to learn the nature of "Dowel" lies through "Suffre- / Bothe-wel-and-wo." See *The Vision of William Concerning Piers the Plowman,* ed. Walter W. Skeat (London: Oxford, 1886, 1968), B.X. 157–58 (1 : 296); this edition is cited throughout. St. Thomas, in defining passivity, explains that "not only he who is ill is said to be passive, but also he who is healed; not only he that is sad, but also he that is joyful; or whatever way he be altered or moved." *Summa theologica,* trans. Fathers of the English Dominican Province, 1st complete American ed., 3 vols. (New York: Benziger Brothers, 1947–48), pt. 1, q. 79, art. 2 (1 : 397); unless otherwise noted, references in English are to this edition and are cited *ST*, Dominican Fathers.

that the difference between noun or past participle may be crucial indeed to the referent. Sometimes it is difficult to tell whether the seminal topos is behind some conventional doublets. For instance, a favorite of Spenser is "labours and pains"; sometimes the labors are specifically deeds, actions, and the pains are clearly inflictions endured. At other times *pains* is merely a synonym for *labours,* a tautology in the line.

Ernst R. Curtius notes that although originally topoi were thought of mainly as helps in composing orations they penetrated all genres, and he observes that in late antiquity the new ethos of Christianity gave birth to new topics.[3] He considers as topoi motifs ranging from such an archetype as the *puer senex* to a formula of ideal excellence like *fortitudo et sapientia.*

To trace any one such topic exhaustively would be a work of years. It seems sufficient to establish that the formulation *to act* and *to suffer* existed, that its use was rich and manifold by the fourteenth century, and that it was known to Chaucer and Spenser; and this can most simply be done through contexts in works which Chaucer and Spenser might have known and in ones that the common reader is apt still to encounter. In these preliminaries it is advisable to cite texts where the formulation is explicit and to call attention only to immediate implications. Later, in discussions of Chaucer and Spenser, more complex situations and more substantial issues will be explored.

The topos may have appeared originally in Homer or it may have been already traditional. In any case, Odysseus uses it in his compliment to Demodocus without ethical emphasis. The hero weeps because the story is familiar, because it is his story, but he does not sense that the Achaeans suffered at Troy *because* of what they did there. Men act and suffer, that is what it is to be human, and when the actions and sufferings are dire and one's own, one weeps to hear them recalled.[4]

3. Ernst R. Curtius, *European Literature and the Latin Middle Ages* (1948), trans. Willard R. Trask (New York: Harper Torchbooks, 1963), pp. 79–105.

4. Homer's view of the relationship may be wider than that of Odysseus. Long after the music of Demodocus, Odysseus is the entertainer and

However, in Aeschylus the formula is instinct with personal, thematic, and moral significance. Clytemnestra justifies the murder of Agamemnon with her own, dramatically appropriate mirroring of the author's interest in limits, in justice. She tells the Argive elders that *because* her lord did certain things once he is now fittingly suffering these things "ἄξια δράσας ἄξια πάσχων." And the chorus takes up her words, looking forward, perhaps, to a vengeance upon the queen rather than endorsing a current murder when it says: "He remains, and so long as Zeus remains on the throne the doer suffers, for it is right" (μίμνει δὲ μίμνοντος ἐν θρόνῳ Διὸς / παθεῖν τὸν ἔρξαντα. θέσμιον γάρ).[5]

It is worth pausing to notice the qualities and intent of the Aeschylean use of the topic. In Homer the phrase is narratively summary and allusive, but morally neutral; however, the playwright makes it bear new implications. He suggests that there may be a reciprocal relation between doing and suffering. Clytemnestra reminds her chief subjects that if Agamemnon is suffering now he was a doer once and that the altars at Aulis smoked because of his action. Of course the queen rationalizes, her statement of the matter may be judged interested; but the chorus accepts her rationalization as tenable if not clearly and necessarily applicable to her own case. For the chorus, the rela-

---

Penelope does not close her eyes until he finishes all the story of ὅσα κήδε' ἔθηκεν ἀνθρώποις ὅσα τ᾽ αὐτὸς ὀϊζύσας ἐμόγησε, πάντ᾽ ἔλεγ' (23. 306–08, "whatever miseries he put upon men and whatever suffering he himself endured"). Syntactical parallelism makes the antithesis surely deliberate. G. E. Dimock, Jr., has put forth the suggestion that the very name *Odysseus* means one who causes pain and that from the time when as a boy the hero kills the boar and is himself scarred he bears a full identity as doer and sufferer. Dimock cites the puns on the name; see "The Name of Odysseus," *Hudson Review* 9 (1956) : 52–70. The epithet of the first line, *polytropon* 'many-turning,' 'crafty,' as against the frequent epithet, *polytlas* 'much-enduring,' might be cited in support of Dimock. See also 4. 242, 4. 271, and 5. 223, and *Iliad* 23. 607; I owe Charles Chamberlain thanks for his kind help with these further examples. Clearly, however, the expression is not only less frequent in Homer than in Aeschylus but without his moral shading, the link with justice.

5. Aeschylus *Agamemnon* 1527 and 1563–64. See also *Agamemnon* 533; *The Libation-Bearers* 313; and frag. 456 in *Tragicorum Graecorum fragmenta*, ed. Augustus Nauck, 2d ed. (Leipzig: B. G. Teubner, 1889), p. 126. I am indebted to Mrs. Jenny Clay for references to the tragic fragments and to Pindar cited below.

tion becomes a maxim—the doer suffers, "for it is right" or it is "the law" (sometimes translated "an ordinance") and will be, while Zeus remains on the throne. If it should ever be true that a man may do with impunity, without suffering, the world is without order, without Zeus. The chorus therefore implies not only that the relation between doing and suffering is morally reciprocal but, beyond this, that it *should* be so; that it should be so is of the permanent order of things.

The text also yields information on the progress of the phrase. Whereas Odysseus' speech might be his personal, felicitous phrasing, Clytemnestra's dramatic situation lets us see that by the time of Aeschylus *agere et pati* is already established *as* a topic. Clytemnestra uses it in what resembles an appeal to a jury, a received type of oration. And it has communal cachet. For she uses it in a kind of apologia to the chorus (one that speaks for her policy as well as her nerve), confident that they will understand the basis, at least, for her claim to have executed justice; and the chorus in return repeats the phrase, with what irony we cannot surely say. (Of course the exchange would seem ironical to the audience, who could hardly help reflecting that one day Orestes would act and Clytemnestra suffer on that impending day precisely because of her act now.) In sum, the context intimates that the *agere-et-pati* linking is part of the common store of ideas in legendary Argos, and it may be presumed that it was also a part of the audience's ideas.[6]

With Sophocles in *Oedipus the King* comes another original emphasis, and he introduces a consideration that was recurrently afterwards to be implicated with discussion of human actions and sufferings. Sophocles is interested in the problem of free will and destiny, and he suggests the possibility of divine responsibility for particular acts of men. His use of the topos then, like that of Aeschylus, is thematic, heavy with particular meaning for its own setting. And as with Clytem-

6. Pindar's Nemean Ode 4. 31–32 indicates, in fact, that the idea is proverbial: "Unversed in battles would he plainly be who knoweth not the proverb that in truth 'tis fitting that whoso doeth aught should suffer also." The ode is assigned to 473 B.C., a quarter century before the *Agamemnon.*

nestra's speech, the use is dramatically appropriate. The situation, however, is more complex. When the chorus addresses sightless Oedipus in awe as "you who have done terrible things" (ὦ δεινὰ δράσας), asking him how he dared actually to wipe out his own sight, Oedipus replies: "Apollo it was, Apollo, friends, who brought to pass these my sufferings [πάθεα] but I myself was the doer [τλάμων]" (1327–31). Oedipus thus combines acknowledgment of a fateful divinity with an assertion of his own human responsibility for the act that entails the suffering. Sophocles uses the strongest possible word for one who acts, τλάμων, which may be translated *one who dares,* the more usual word for act being δράν. A more orthodox and exactly antithetic wording comes earlier (1272), when the messenger describes Oedipus telling his sightless eyes that they now shall no more behold such horrors as he suffered (ἔπασχεν) or such things, such evils, as he did (ἔδρα).[7]

The topos also appears in philosophical writing. Plato evinces considerable fondness for it. As in Aeschylus, in the *Laws* it is attached to the idea of justice (9. 872E). In the *Symposium,* Agathon's praise of the *arête* of the love god is based in part on the premise that the god can neither do nor suffer wrong: "his greatest glory is that he can neither do nor suffer wrong to or from any god or any man; for he suffers not by force if he suffers; force comes not near him, neither when he acts does he act by force. For all men in all things serve him of their own free will."[8] Here, two new notes are worth attention. First, Agathon connects the notion of action with freedom from force; he who serves Eros *freely* does not suffer in the sense of being passively imposed upon; accordingly, no wrong is done to him. And if Eros appears to suffer, in an important sense he does not, because "force comes not near

7. Cf. *Antigone* 927–28, and Sophocles frag. 209, Nauck, p. 179.

8. *Symposium* 196C. I have used the Loeb text but the translation of B. Jowett in *Dialogues of Plato,* ed. J. D. Kaplan (New York: Washington Square Press, 1951). Unless otherwise noted, this is the source of subsequent translations of Plato. The first "do and suffer" does not exist in the Greek text although the radical relation does. The Greek is *adikei* 'wrongs' and *adikeitai* 'is wronged'; however, the second occurrence is literal: *paschei* 'suffers' and *poiei* 'does.'

him"—the gods are impassible. What is here clear-cut and simple becomes more complicated in a consideration of the meaning of freedom. All were not to agree that all men serve Eros freely, witness the legions of Elizabethans who declared themselves will-less thralls when struck by an arrow from their ladies' eyes. But still Agathon's remark proposes a stipulation which will be useful in determining tentative distinctions between actor and sufferer. If the human agent has undertaken a freely chosen task, he is in some radical sense an actor, even if he appears to be undergoing trials in its accomplishment. And even if the human actor seems to be engaging in triumphant derring-do (daring-to-do), he becomes a sufferer, a patient, if in fact an external force (or an interior one which has not the sanction of what may anachronistically be called his ego) compels him to "do" what he is doing.

In the *Phaedo* an innovation again occurs—the extension of the concepts of action and suffering beyond the human sphere. Still antithetic and complementary, action and suffering are general states which may apply to inanimate things. In refuting Simmias, who had proposed the view that the human soul is a harmony, Socrates indicates that being, doing, and suffering are three basic states of all the elements of the cosmos. Can Simmias imagine, Socrates demands, that a harmony can be in any other state than that of the elements of which it is made, or do or suffer anything other than they do or suffer? Later Socrates again uses this concept; if anyone wanted to know the cause of existence, of generation, and of destruction, Socrates had supposed, such a seeker must find out what state of being or suffering ($\pi\acute{a}\sigma\chi\epsilon\iota\nu$) or doing ($\pi o\iota\epsilon\hat{\iota}\nu$) was best for that thing. He once expected of Anaxagoras, Socrates says, information about the sun and the moon and the stars and their various states, active and passive ($\pi o\iota\epsilon\hat{\iota}\nu$ and $\pi\acute{a}\sigma\chi\epsilon\iota\nu$), but alas, Anaxagoras was not so wise as he had supposed (*Phaedo* 93, 97–98).

One of the greatest of *The Republic*'s passages, the vision of Er, is laced with plays upon the action-suffering distinction, and it appears in its classic formulation in the grave admonition which is the fruit of the vision: "A man must take with him into the world below an adamantine faith in truth and right, that there too he may be undazzled by the desire of wealth or the other allurements of evil, lest, coming upon tyrannies and similar villainies, he do irremediable wrongs to others [πράξεις] and suffer [πάθη] yet worse himself" (10. 15. 619).

This selected and superficial profile of the topos in Greek texts indicates that from earliest times it carried a considerable range of statement and of implication. In the example from the *Odyssey* the words themselves are used simply and directly, although enhanced emotionally by their context which is nothing less than the reader's memory of all the action and the passion of the *Iliad*. In Aeschylus, the words acquire an ethical sophistication, a moral valuation, the statements in which they appear suggesting a normative and causal relation between action and suffering in human life. The context adds a thematic concern, justice, and an intense effect, dramatic irony. In Sophocles, theology becomes involved: the statement of Oedipus joins himself and Apollo, man and the divine, as agent. In his deepest humiliation and impotence when he must seem to all who view him an archetypal sufferer, Oedipus perseveres in his drive for clarity, for analytic distinctions, and claims an apotheosis in heroic assertion: "I myself was the doer." In the *Symposium,* Plato in part supplies, in part assumes, a causal analysis of doing and suffering. The element of free will defines the actor. Implied in that text too is the vulnerable human's perception of what it is to be a god—the gods are impassible, that is, not subject to suffering. In the *Phaedo,* doing and suffering are detached from any human sphere, neutralized, stripped; they are operational modes in the physical, inanimate world, fundamental relations in processes. In the vision of Er the terms reappear in a specifically religious context. In classical times, then, the usefulness of the topos became established. Early it proved its adaptability to technical, humane, and aesthetic uses, proved its capacity for projecting new and personal meanings while bearing still the radical meaning it carries in Homer.

Latin literature used *agere et pati* in contexts similar to these Greek examples, and the scholars of late antiquity and the Latin Middle Ages transmitted it in most of the kinds of

literature that they wrote. Wherever the medieval clerk looked
from his schoolboy days on, an *agere et pati* would confront
him, handily presenting what he needed to know about grammar, logic, rhetoric, religion, philosophy, and the sciences—
cosmography, physiology, or alchemy. It was a verbal pack-
aging, a formula which would convey quite dissimilar matters
in terms of reassuring familiarity. The antithesis of doing and
suffering would be impressed upon the medieval man by most
of the authorities he regarded and through most of the intellectual perspectives from which he viewed life. He would find
it in the Bible.[9] He might hear it in the confessional as the
priest absolved him from his sins:

> Passio Domini nostri Jesu Christi, merita beatae Mariae Virginis,
> et omnium Sanctorum, quidquid boni feceris, et mali sustinueris,
> sint tibi in remissionem peccatorum, augmentum gratiae, et
> praemium vitae aeternae. Amen.

> [May the passion of our Lord Jesus Christ, the merits of the
> blessed Virgin Mary and of all the saints, whatever good you
> do, and evil you endure, be to you the remission of your sins,
> the increase of grace, and the reward of everlasting life.
> Amen.] [10]

No doubt other formulations moved more largely in the
common imagination. *Agere et pati* is not summed up in a

9. Typical *agere-et-pati* combinations appear in the Vulgate Bible, perhaps the most read book of the Middle Ages, and the antithesis is the
crux of both the *lex talionis* and the golden rule. See Lev. 24 : 19–20,
Tob. 4 : 16, Prov. 24 : 29, Matt. 7 : 12, and Luke 6 : 31. For these, varying
forms of the same verb generally suffice, as in "sicut fecit, sic fiet ei" ("as
he has done, so shall it be done to him") in Lev. 24 : 19. However, con-
trasting forms may be used: "eye for eye, tooth for tooth, shall he restore.
What blemish he inflicted, the like shall he be compelled to bear" ("qualem
inflixerit maculam, talem sustinere cogetur") in Lev. 24 : 20. Other
citations include Gen. 21 : 23 and 50 : 15, Deut. 19 : 18–19, Judges 1 : 7
and 15 : 11, Judith 8 : 26 ("non ulciscamur nos pro his quae patimur"),
1 Kings 28 : 18, Esther 2 : 1, 2 Cor. 7 : 12. See also 1 Peter 2 : 20. The
golden rule appears twice in the *Rule* of St. Benedict, where "The Tools
of Good Works" include "Honorare omnes homines. Et quod sibi quis
fieri non vult, alio ne faciat"; and, again, "Injuriam non facere, sed et
factas patienter sufferre." *The Rule of Saint Benedict*, ed. Abbot Justin
McCann (Westminster, Md.: Newman, 1952, 1960), chap. 4, pp. 26, 28.
10. "Absolutionis Forma Communis," *Rituale Romanum* (New York:
Benziger Brothers, 1945), p. 80. My translation.

magnificent metaphor as a total and integrated universe is summed up in the great chain of being, nor in a single icon like the wheel of fortune. It had plastic expressions and analogues, but remained chiefly a classification, a verbal construct. Impressed into service so various, inevitably the concept became complicated, sometimes confused, with other distinctions convenient to the medieval grasp of the universe. Before sorting out these overlappings we should have at hand a sampling of texts to illustrate versatility and transmission.

What must have made the formula most familiar was its place in grammar. The grammar of Donatus (fl. ca. A.D. 350) was the one used by far most frequently between 400 and 1500; almost all of the book lists for institutional and private libraries in the Middle Ages name it under one title or another. "Donat" or "donet" came to mean the rudiments not only of grammar but also of any study or craft. In England as late as 1443 Reginald Pecock called his introduction to Christian fundamentals *The Donet,* explaining,

> And siþen it is so, þat þis book beriþ him silf toward þe hool
> ful kunnyng of goddis lawe, even as þe comoun donet in latyn
> beriþ him silf toward þe hool ful kunnyng of grammer, as it is
> wel knowun of clerkis in latyn, þerfore þis present dialog myȝte
> wel and convenientli be clepid þe "donet" or "key" of goddis
> lawe, or ellis þe "donet" or "key" of cristen religioun.[11]

Through the Middle Ages grammar was the first study of the trivium. The schoolboy memorizing his "donet" would chant:

> Verbum quid est? Pars orationis cum tempore et persona sine
> casu aut agere aliquid aut pati aut neutrum significans.

> [What is a verb? A part of speech with tense and person, without
> case, meaning to do something or to suffer something or nei-
> ther.] [12]

In Priscian, who shared with Donatus the distinction of being carved under the figure of Grammar in medieval cathedral

11. Reginald Pecock, *The Donet,* ed. Elsie Vaughan Hitchcock, EETS, OS no. 156 (London: Oxford, 1921), p. 3. I alter the scribal *i* and *u* of early texts.

12. Wayland Johnson Chase, *The Ars Minor of Donatus,* University of Wisconsin Studies in the Social Sciences and History, no. 11 (Madison: University of Wisconsin, 1926), p. 38. Chase provides an introduction, text, and translation of this shorter version. In the *Paradiso,* 12. 137–38,

representations of the liberal arts, the language is virtually the same.[13]

Thus the definition of the verb was handed forward through the Middle Ages, and beyond, in terms of acting and suffering, for in *Martin Chuzzlewit* Mark Tapley declares that "a Werb [*sic*] is a word as signifies to be, to do, or to suffer (which is all the grammar and enough, too, as ever I wos taught)." This shaping of the definition was not inevitable; Aristotle had considered grammar, but although he used *facere et pati* often and innovatively, he defined the verb less confidently, attaching it to the notion of time.[14] Grammar follows poetry: in their appropriation, the grammarians made a brilliant adaptation; to have so defined the verb *ex nihilo* would have been an astonishing analysis.

But chiefly the presence of *agere et pati* in the donet is important because it so became a classification that would come

---

Dante salutes "quel Donato / ch 'alla prim' arte degnò por la mano" ("that Donatus / who gladly turned his hand to the first art"); and he places the grammarian in the circle of the sun. The Temple Classics *Divine Comedy* is used for the Italian text (London: Dent, 1899; frequently reprinted), with the English translations of John Ciardi (New York: New American Library Mentor, 1970).

13. *Grammatici, Omnia opera* (Florence, 1554), book 8 (p. 97); see also Isidore of Seville, *Etymologiarum sive originum*, ed. W. M. Lindsay, 2 vols. (Oxford: Clarendon, 1911; reprinted 1962), book 1. 9; See Emile Mâle, *The Gothic Image: Religious Art in France of the Thirteenth Century*, 1st French ed. 1913, trans. Dora Nussey from 3d French ed. (New York: Harper Torchbooks, 1958), p. 87.

14. *On Interpretation* 3. 16b and *Poetics* 20. 9. The definition of the verb in terms of *facere et pati* can be traced back to Dionysius Thrax, pupil of Aristarchus (2d century B.C.), who established the Greek system of eight classes. The definition of Dionysius may be translated "The verb [*rhema*] is a part of speech [*lexis*] without case-inflection, admitting inflections of tense, person and number, signifying an activity [*energeian*] or a being acted on [*pathos*]." *Dionysii Thracis ars grammatica*, ed. Gustavus Uhlig (Leipzig: B. G. Teubner, 1883; reprinted in *Grammatici Graeci*, Hildesheim: Georg Olms, 1965), 1. 1. 46, sec. 13 (15b). The translation of R. H. Robins, *Ancient & Mediaeval Grammatical Theory in Europe* (London: G. Bell, 1951), p. 40, is used. Cf. Robins's "The Development of the Word Class System of the European Grammatical Tradition," *Foundations of Language* 2 (1966): 3–19, and "Dionysius Thrax and the Western Grammatical Tradition," *Transactions of the Philological Society,* 1957 (Oxford: Basil Blackwell, 1958), pp. 67–106. Prof. Daniel J. Taylor kindly called my attention to *facere et pati* formulations in grammarians before Donatus and Priscian.

fluently, a cliché. It was one of the first things people had learned when first they began to learn. Macrobius is concerned that this predominance might be confusing. He cautions against mistaking the grammatical form with life-states of action and suffering. As he argues that the soul is self-moved, he discriminates: passivity is indicated "not by the words used but by what is involved," and the passive voice may mislead:

> Do not be puzzled at the fact that the verb *to be moved* is in the passive voice; nor should you think, because in the verb *to be cut* there are two things involved, that which cuts and that which is cut . . . that there are also two things meant here, that which moves and that which is moved. The verbs *to be cut* and *to be held* denote passivity and therefore include consideration of both the agent and the thing acted upon [*facientis* & *patientis*]; the verb *to be moved*, when referring to those things which are moved by something else, also presents two aspects; but when the verb *to be moved* refers to something which is self-moved so that it is *autokinetos*, since it is moved by itself and not by something else, it can have no suggestion of passivity about it.[15]

Macrobius carefully distinguishes grammatical phenomena from living modes.

On the other hand, Alanus de Insulis lavishly exploits grammar in the criticism of life. In *De planctu naturae,* a source for Chaucer's *The Parlement of Foules,* he deplores homosexuality thus:

> Activi generis sexus, se turpiter horret
> Sic in passivum degenerare genus.
> Femina vir factus, sexus denigrat honorem,
> Ars magicae Veneris hermaphroditat eum.

---

15. Macrobius, *Commentarius ex Cicerone in somnium Scipionis, opera,* 9th ed. (London: T. Dring and C. Harper, 1694), 2. 15. 120. The translation is from *Commentary on the Dream of Scipio,* trans. William Harris Stahl (New York: Columbia, 1952), p. 235. As Macrobius is a source for Chaucer, it is worth noting that a *facere-pati* phrase appears in the *Commentary* in classic form in a classification of *somnium* (1. 3. 11). The "personal" somnium occurs when the dreamer dreams he is himself doing or suffering something ("Proprium est; cum se quis facientem patientemve aliquid somniat").

Praedicat et subjicit, fit duplex terminus idem,
Grammaticae leges ampliat ille nimis.

[The sex of active nature trembles shamefully at the way in
which it declines into passive nature. Man is made woman, he
blackens the honor of his sex, the craft of magic Venus makes
him of double gender. He is both predicate and subject, he
becomes likewise of two declensions, he pushes the laws of
grammar too far.] [16]

In proceeding from grammar to logic, the student would again
find *agere* and *pati,* this time listed as basic categories or predicaments. Such writers as Isidore handed on the Aristotilean
categories: *Etymologies II* gives *substantia, quantitas, qualitas,
relatio, situs, locus, tempus, habitus, agere et pati.*[17] Poets
trained as schoolboys in logic and rhetoric would use the
"common places" of these disciplines as a matter of course in
their "invention." Thus "manner of acting" and "manner of
suffering" would be among those ways in which poets would
deliberately appraise any subject they worked with.[18]

Writers on medieval natural science also thought in these
terms. Macrobius and Alanus were known to Chaucer; and
possibly so was the popular thirteenth-century encyclopaedia
of Bartholomaeus Anglicus which John Trevisa Englished.
De proprietatibus rerum begins with the Trinity and proceeds
downward through a discussion of angels, men, astronomy,

16. Alanus de Insulis, *Liber de planctu naturae, in Patrologiae cursus
completus. Series latina,* ed. J.-P. Migne (Paris, 1855), vol. 210, col. 431,
met. 1. Subsequent references to the series are cited *PL.* The translation
is that of Douglas M. Moffat, *The Complaint of Nature by Alain de Lille,*
Yale Studies in English, 36 (New York: Holt, 1908), p. 3.

17. Aristotle *Categories* 4. 1b25. Cf. *Posterior Analytics* 1. 22. 83b and
1. 22. 83a. See Isidore *Etymologiarum* 2. 26. *Agere et pati* also appears in
Isidore's chapter "De Ethopeia" 2. 14. They are also given virtually un-
changed by Martianus Capella, *De nuptiis Philologiae et Mercurii libri
viiii,* ed. Adolfus Dick (Stuttgart: B. G. Teubner, 1969), book 4 (pp. 167–
68); by Boethius, *In categorias Aristotelis,* in *PL,* vol. 64, col. 180, with a
brief discussion of *facere et pati,* cols. 261–62; and by Cassiodorus, *De
dialectica, Opera omnia quae extant* (Geneva: Philippus Gamonetus, 1650),
p. 535.

18. Rosemond Tuve, *Elizabethan and Metaphysical Imagery* (University
of Chicago, 1947), pp. 281–99.

jewels, geography, animals, musical instruments, odors, and colors. Bartholomaeus thus describes qualities of the elements and humors:

> Two of these qualitees benne called Active, able to werke, hotte and coldenesse. The other two be dry and wetenesse, and ben called Passive, able to suffre. And so as these qualitees prevayle and have maistry, the elementes bene called active and passyve able to do and suffre.[19]

Such distinctions frequently inform the work; and Bartholomaeus himself points out how conventional his "boystous" compendium is.

If grammarians, rhetoricians, logicians, and compilers found the *agere-et-pati* distinction apt, so did philosophers. *Agere et pati* is a general and a quasi-technical term for them from late antiquity through and beyond the High Middle Ages. St. Augustine explains to his disciple Laurentius how well-merited is the punishment meted out to the wicked:

> Ad iram quippe Dei pertinet justam, quidquid caeca et indomita concupiscentia faciunt libenter mali, et quidquid manifestis opertisque poenis patiuntur inviti.
>
> [For whatever the wicked freely do through blind and unbridled lust, and whatever they suffer against their will in the way of open punishment, this all evidently pertains to the just wrath of God.] [20]

One would expect the rhetor of Carthage (contemporary of Donatus, rhetor of Rome) to revert easily to the classical term. Augustine here implies, as do Agathon's speech in Plato and the absolution formula given above, that people *do* freely but *suffer* against their wills, under duress.

19. *De proprietatibus rerum* (London: Thomae Bertheleti, 1535), 4. 1. 22.
20. *Enchiridion de fide, spe et charitate*, in *PL*, vol. 40, col. 245. The translation is from Rev. Marcus Dods, ed., *The Works of Aurelius Augustine, Bishop of Hippo* (Edinburgh: T. & T. Clark, 1873), 9 : 195. St. Augustine used *facere et pati* frequently, at least seven times in varied contexts of the *Confessions* alone, in passages allusive of the golden rule (1. 18 and 1. 19); in reference to Aristotle's categories (4. 16); in examinations of his own motives in everyday life and in spiritual crisis (5. 12 and 8. 5); in theological argument (7. 3), and in cosmic speculations on creation and Creator (12. 28). *Confessionum libri tredecim*, ex recognitione P. Knöll (Leipzig: B. G. Teubner, 1898).

Somewhat later Boethius uses various versions of *agere et pati* in the *Consolation of Philosophy*. It would be difficult to name a more influential book through the Middle Ages, a more likely conduit. I excerpt from Chaucer's translation of book 4, prose 4, in which the *agere-et-pati* distinction is especially prominent. Chaucer almost invariably translates the varied expressions of Boethius narrowly as *do* and *suffer*, once using *resceyveth* and *dooth* where Boethius uses *accipientis* and *inferentis*, but sticking elsewhere to the most ordinary terms. Here Lady Philosophy concludes an important argument:

> "Thanne semeth it," quod sche, "that *the doere* of wrong is more wrecche than *he that hath suffrid wrong?*"
> "That folweth wel," quod I.
> "Than," quod sche, "by thise causes and by othere causes that ben enforced by the same roote, that filthe or synne be the propre nature of it maketh man wrecches; and it scheweth wel that the wrong that man doon nis nat the wrecchidnesse of *hym that resceyveth* the wrong, but wrecchidnesse of *hym that dooth* the wrong." [243–54; my italics]

Lady Philosophy even argues that wicked men ("schrewes") are more happy punished than they would be in evading punishment (a Platonic refinement).[21] Perhaps it is this paradoxical insistence which here gives the Lady her rather peremptory, didactic manner. As with the definition of a verb, what once seemed fresh has become piety, so one must pause a bit to realize the perspective. A quick way to begin is to try imagining any Homeric hero saying that it is better to suffer wrong than to do it. Such a notion would strike any of them as a preposterous perversion of common sense and natural feeling. The vogue of revenge tragedy shows that even a thousand years after Boethius acceptance of such hard sayings did not come easily to Christians. Nonetheless, in a Christian era, the Platonic and Christian propositions of Lady Philosophy had

21. *Gorgias*, ed. E. R. Dodds (Oxford: Clarendon, 1959), 469–80. The guiding translation is that of W. Hamilton (Baltimore: Penguin, 1960). Polos displays the average commonsensical attitude toward this view by laughing heartily before he finally yields to Socrates' opinion.

great éclat, judging by the frequency with which she was quoted.

Throughout the Middle Ages, writers continued to think of doing and suffering as summary headings for the intimate flow of experience just as Odysseus had. And simultaneously in philosophy and theology *agere et pati* acquired specialized uses and came to overlap with certain other organizing foci of medieval thought, with, in particular, distinctions between act and potency, between matter and form, between the passions and reason, and between change and impassibility. To see how this is so, it is helpful to consider these scholastic (and not only scholastic) terms in a series under the heads of action and suffering. (See the accompanying chart; the definitions

ACTION	SUFFERING
I. Act (L. *ag-ere,* to drive, carry on, do)	Potency (L. *potentia,* power)
To put in motion, move to action, impel; to actuate, influence, animate. *Obs.*	Capability of active development; potentiality, inherent capability or possibility.
To bring into action, bring about, produce, perform, work, make, do. *Obs.*	Potential
	Possible as opposed to actual; existing *in posse* or in a latent or undeveloped state; capable of coming into being or action.
II. Form (L. *forma*)	Matter (L. *materia,* building material, timber, hence stuff of which a thing is made)
In the Scholastic philosophy: the essential determinant principle of a thing; that which makes anything (*matter*) a determinant species or kind of being; the essential creative quality.	Physical or corporeal substance in general . . . contradistinguished from immaterial or incorporeal substance (spirit, soul, mind), and from qualities, actions, or conditions.
	That component of the essence of any thing or being which has bare existence, but which requires the addition of a particular "form" . . . to constitute the thing or being as determinately existent.

ACTION	SUFFERING

III. Reason (L. *ration-em*)
That intellectual power or faculty (usually regarded as characteristic of mankind, but sometimes also attributed in a certain degree to the lower animals) which is ordinarily employed in adapting thought or action to some end.

Passion (L. *passion-em,* suffering; f. *pati, pass-,* to suffer)
The suffering of pain.
The fact of being acted upon, the being passive. (Late L. *passio,* used to render Gr. πάθος.)
An affection of the mind. . . . Any kind of feeling by which the mind is powerfully affected or moved; a vehement, commanding, or overpowering emotion. Sometimes personified.

IV. Impassibility (L. *impassibilitas;* tr. Gr. ἀπάθεια)
Incapability of, or exemption from, suffering; insusceptibility to injury.
Incapability of feeling or emotion; insensibility.

Passible (late L. *passibilis,* f. *pati,* to suffer)
Capable of suffering, liable to suffer; liable to impressions or feelings; susceptible of sensation or of emotion. Chiefly *Theol.*
Liable to suffer change or decay. *Obs.*

are adapted from the *Oxford English Dictionary*.) Within vertical columns, definitions tend to shade into one another. The topos functions as a kind of bridge among these sets of antithetic terms and has, indeed, through the shared root *pati,* an etymological link with three of the four "suffering" members. St. Thomas is a convenient locus for the first two pairs. From his discussion of the nature of God one can see how *act* and *form* came to be understood as virtually synonymous and how close in philosophical discourse was the relationship between suffering—passivity (potentiality)—and matter.

Act and potency, form and matter. St. Thomas defined God as "pure act" without any trace of potency.[22] *Potency* here should be glossed, obviously, not as *power* but as *potentiality;* that stuff has potentiality which can be made into something (and *must* be, to be anything; see II, Matter). To be in potency

22. *Compendium theologiae, Opuscula omnia,* ed. R. P. Petri Mandonnet (Paris: P. Lethielleux, 1927), vol. 2, chap. 10, p. 6. The translation is that of Cyril Vollert (St. Louis, Mo.: B. Herder, 1952), p. 15. Subsequent references are cited *CT* and are to these editions.

is to be that to which something can happen, that which can be moved. But God, as complete Act, is Mover and only Mover, never moved: "For everything that is moved is, to that extent, in potency [*potentia*], and whatever moves is in act [*actu*]." [23] In St. Thomas's terms, that which is most in potency, without any share in action, is prime matter. Matter is, as it were, the extreme opposite of God: on the one hand is God, fully act; on the other hand is prime matter, totally susceptible to "suffer" shaping. (Most beings, including man, lie between these extremes. For example, a tree is in *act* to the extent that it at the present moment stands, has grown, is bearing fruit, etc.; it is in *potency* to the extent that it may in the future grow further, put forth another crop of fruit, take a graft, be chopped down, be burnt, etc. Existentialists express somewhat comparable differences in the terms "necessity" vis-à-vis "contingency.") These concepts can perhaps be put most exactly by St. Thomas himself. Here the general context is an argu- ment that the power of God is infinite:

> Nam unumquodque quod est in potentia, secundum hoc habet virtutem receptivam et passivam, secundum vero quod actu est, habet virtutem activam. Quod igitur est in potentia tantum, scilicet materia prima, habet virtutem infinitam ad recipiendum, nihil de virtute activa participans: et supra ipsam quanto aliquid formalius est, tanto id abundat in virtute agendi. Propter quod ignis inter omnia elementa est maxime activus, Deus igitur qui est actus purus nihil potentialitatis permistum habens, in in- finitum abundat in virtute activa super alia.

> [Whatever is in potency, is thereby endowed with receptive and passive power; and so far as a thing is in act, it possesses active power. Hence what is exclusively in potency, namely, prime matter, has an unlimited power of receptivity, but has no part in active power. And in the scale of being above matter, the more a thing has of form, the more it abounds in the power of acting. This is why fire is the most active of all the elements. Therefore God, who is pure act without any admixture of potency, in- finitely abounds in active power above all things.] [24]

23. *CT*, chap. 4, p. 3; cf. chap. 9, p. 5; Vollert, pp. 10 and 14.
24. *CT*, chap. 19, pp. 10–11; Vollert, p. 22.

"The more a thing has of form, the more it abounds in the power of acting." For St. Thomas form was not structure (a play should have a beginning, middle, and end), but "that which makes a thing what it is." Form is "substantial form." Thus the human soul is the "substantial form" of the human body, the active, as opposed to the passive, constituent of man.[25] Form is shaping and active; matter receives action. Form "acts." Matter "suffers." Spenser was to furnish a late gloss: "For of the soule the bodie forme doth take: / For soule is forme, and doth the bodie make." Or again, "the soule doth rule the earthly masse, / And all the service of the bodie frame." [26] But while man remains in the body, he is not only the ruling, active soul, but also the slugggish body, "the earthly masse"; he is involved with matter and to that extent in potency. To be in potency is to be apt to suffer change, to be "passible"—and passionate.

Reason and passion. Here we need to invoke a third conflation, the antithesis of reason vis-à-vis the passions (quite apart from this bearing, a rich theme and ever self-division's cause). Medieval writers sometimes spoke of action in opposition not only to passion in its general definition of being-acted-upon, but also to its specific reference to the emotions. The etymological link, the shared root *pati,* is once more a trustworthy clue to an alliance. The passions were considered somehow to be a part of what man suffered, to contribute largely to his liability to being acted upon, to menace his possibilities for being an agent and creator. (The courts still take this into account; only murder committed "in cold blood" is first degree. When the murderer acts in a passion, he is to some extent a patient. That the defendant is patient, not agent, is also the rationale of the insanity plea.) To the medieval writer, man's passions were second only to his inexorably coming death as not the sign of his being a sufferer on this earth but the very

25. *ST, Dominican Fathers,* pt. 1. q. 76, art. 1 (1 : 370–71). The soul as the form or "act" of the body was the orthodox thirteenth-century view. See Bartholomaeus, 3. 24. 22. The source is Aristotle.

26. "An Hymne in Honour of Beautie," 132–33; also, *FQ* 4. 9. 2. I alter the scribal *i* and *u.*

predicament itself. God, St. Thomas remarked, has no passions.[27]

Now if to be in a passion was to be acted upon, to be reasonable was to control passion, to be, therefore, in a position to choose a goal and move to it, to act. Action and reason were alike opposites of passion; and thus action came to be held the prerogative of reason. Action need not then be physical nor expressed in a discernible project, it might be a movement of the spirit. Bartholomaeus on the reasonable soul is apposite: "Wherefore his [the soul's] principall acte and dede, that is intelligere, to understonde, is not dependant of the body. And it lyveth perfitely, and understondeth whan it is departed from the body" (3. 13. 13ᵛ).

Anatomies of the soul strengthened a steady equivalence of reason with action and of the passions with suffering. Philosophers, with slight variations in the scheme, assigned the passions to the appetitive part of the sensitive soul, which men shared with animals and which was closer to the bodily, inactive state of matter. This accounts, perhaps, for such curious biology as that of Alanus' *Complaint of Nature* in which, when the goddess approaches, "Fish swam out into the upper waters, in so far as the inactivity of their sensual existence permitted, and with joy and delight knew in advance the coming of their mistress" (Moffat trans., p. 20). This psychology may reinforce the iconology of the passions as beasts (sometimes overlapping with icons of the seven sins).

Passibility and impassibility. To the medieval man, activity, form, and reason seemed to belong together, to be opposed to and, quite simply, better than, passivity, matter, and the passions. The concepts related to action should exert "maystrey" over those allied with suffering, though life's chances might

---

27. *ST*, Dominican Fathers, 1.21.1 (1 : 118). But Thomas does allow that Christ in his human nature might experience sadness; see *CT*, Vollert, p. 281. In criticism of the Stoics he writes that they held that emotion diminishes an action's goodness, but that "it is better not merely to will good, but also to feel good about it." *ST*, in *St. Thomas Aquinas Philosophical Texts*, selected and trans. Thomas Gilby (New York: Oxford Galaxy Book, 1960), pt. 1 of pt. 2, q. 25, art. 3 (p. 297). This selection is hereafter cited as Gilby.

upset this proper order. The final set of terms we need to deal
with, the "passible" and the "impassible," became prominent
in the working vocabulary of an early dogmatic controversy.
The controversy was over no less a matter than the nature of
God. The crux for the Fathers was that God, fully actual, the
Mover unmoved, impassible by definition, became man, suffered, and died on the Cross. This paradox so terribly flouting
reason was the central event of Christianity. Did this really
happen? How could it have happened? How could this one
pure Act become one acted upon, a part matter, an item in
the lumber of the world? Was the Son in some way a lesser
God? Or was He only disguised as man so that God's death
truly was but a play? Christology is full of this discussion for
several hundred years. One of the more vivid debates at the
heart of the question was whether and how Christ suffered on
the Cross. Noetus of Smyrna in the second century taught that
as Christ was Almighty God and Father, the Father had taken
upon himself suffering and death in the flesh, a view which
brought Noetus excommunication and his followers their
name, *patripassians.*[28] On the other hand, Origen (d. ca. 253)
seems to have believed that the Logos used the body and soul
of Jesus without itself undergoing death.

Although with neither serenity nor finality, the issue got
settled during the fifth century. Early, Cyril pronounced an
anathema upon anyone who "does not confess that the Word
of God suffered in the flesh and was crucified in the flesh and
tasted death in the flesh, and became the first-born of the
dead."[29] The "tome" of Leo the Great (Twenty-Eighth Epistle

28. Wilhelm Moeller, *History of the Christian Church,* trans. Andrew
Rutherfurd, 2d ed. (London: Swan Sonnenschein; New York: Macmillan,
1898), I : 225.
29. E. R. Hardy, ed., *Christology of the Later Fathers,* The Library of
Christian Classics, vol. 3 (London: S.C.M. Press; Philadelphia: Westminster Press, 1954), p. 354. An article by Rosemary Woolf, "Doctrinal
Influences on 'The Dream of the Rood'," *Medium Aevum* 67 (1958) : 137–
53, contains bibliographical references on the dogmatic controversy. The
controversy is critically reviewed with a bibliography by Herbert Thurston, "Devotion to the Passion of Jesus Christ," *Catholic Encyclopedia*
(New York: Robert Appleton, 1911). See also Adolph Harnack, *History
of Dogma,* trans. E. B. Speirs and James Millar from the 3d German ed.,

or Epistle to Flavian) stated the solution, as dogmatists in the west came to see it, of the dilemma between an Impassible God and a Passible Christ in the formula of "two natures." Leo wrote to oppose Eutyches, who held, if Leo reports him rightly, that Christ had not "a body really derived from his mother's body." Leo's rebuttal exemplifies the tendency to divide the career of Jesus into *agere-et-pati* configurations, into an active life of preaching and miracles on the one hand and the passion (i.e. suffering) and death on the cross on the other. This accent and his use of "passibility" and impassibility" bear notice; I quote from two places rather widely separated in the text:

> . . . the Lord of the universe . . . took upon him the form of a servant: the impassible God did not disdain to become passible, and the immortal one to be subject to the laws of death. . . . the fact that the nativity of our Lord Jesus Christ is wonderful, in that he was born of a virgin's womb, does not imply that his nature is ·unlike ours. . . . For each "form" does the acts which belong to it, in communion with the other; the Word, that is, performing what belongs to the Word, and the flesh carrying out what belongs to the flesh. The one of these shines out in miracles; the other succumbs to injuries. . . . To hunger, to thirst, to be weary, and to sleep is evidently human. But to feed five thousand men with five loaves, and to bestow upon the woman of Samaria that living water, to drink of which can secure one from thirsting again; to walk on the surface of the sea with feet that sink not, and by rebuking the storm to bring down the "uplifted waves," is unquestionably divine. And then —to pass by many points—it does not belong to the same nature to weep with feelings of pity over a dead friend and, after the mass of stone had been removed from the grave where he had lain four days, by a voice of command to raise him up to life again; or to hang on the wood and to make all the elements tremble after daylight had been turned into night.

> On which mystery of the faith [the two natures of Christ and their unity] this Eutyches must be regarded as unhappily having no hold whatever. . . . Moreover, seeing he is blind as to the

Theological Translation Library, 7 vols. (London: Williams & Norgate, 1895–99), 4 : 190–226.

nature of Christ's body, he must needs be involved in the like
senseless blindness with regard to his Passion also. For if he
does not think the Lord's crucifixion to be unreal, . . . as he
believes in his death, let him acknowledge his flesh also, . . .
since to deny his true flesh is also to deny his bodily sufferings.[30]

Suppressed at Ephesus, the Tome was approved at Chalcedon
(451)—"Peter has spoken through Leo"—and Leo's formulation has remained, despite challenges, orthodoxy.[31]

Leo's insistence that Christ suffered in the body, even such a
body as have you and I, is firm; but there is no personal involvement with the passion. The only emotion projected is a
somewhat brisk scorn for the views of Eutyches. But, in time,
logical difficulty in reconciling passibility and impassibility
became a rhetorical advantage and then basis for a passionate
appeal. Later writers preached the paradox to impress the
marvel of that instant "quando patì la suprema possanza"
("when the supreme might suffered"), as Dante was to put it
(*Paradiso* 27. 36). That it was exactly by Christ's suffering
death that he wrought this great act, our salvation, called for
wondering gratitude, St. Bernard of Clairvaux (d. 1153)
pointed out that Christ took into his hands our heritage from
Adam, "laborem videlicet, et dolorem: laborem in actione,
dolorem in passione" ("labor and sorrow, labor in doing and
sorrow in bearing"), and went on to celebrate that Christ "in
vita passivam habuit actionem, et in morte passionem activam
sustinuit, dum salutem operaretur in medio terrae" ("had in
life a passive action and underwent in death an active passion,
doing the work of salvation on earth").[32] His more personal
Meditations gave a signal not for mere intellectual awe but for
an empathy that particularly characterized later medieval

30. Hardy, pp. 364–67. See also Moeller, 1 : 419–22, for background on
Leo's Tome.
31. P. T. Camelot, "Council of Chalcedon," *New Catholic Encyclopedia*
(New York: McGraw-Hill, 1967). The decree is printed in Hardy, pp.
371–74.
32. St. Bernard, "In feria IV hebdomadae sanctae sermo," *Opera omnia,*
in *PL,* vol. 183, cols. 268–69. Bernard's *labor-and-woe* approximation of
agere et pati is common. In Chaucer, see the Pardoner's Tale (505–07);
Legend of Good Women (F. 988); the Franklin's Tale (1106). Cf. "travaille
nor grame" of *T&C* (1. 372).

devotion. This work, frequently translated and paraphrased, remained popular into the seventeenth century.[33] (Whatever the authenticity of its attribution, it probably accounts for Cranach's woodcut of Bernard in his cell before a sharply detailed vision of Christ with the instruments of the Passion.)

Progressively through the Middle Ages this more urgently personal emphasis increased. Early crosses figured forth Christ's triumphing divinity, not his bodily, suffering humanity. Crosses were bare or carried a symbolic agnus dei. In the High Middle Ages, a strained body commonly appeared on life-size crosses. Some of the most powerful works combine motifs: Christ is represented bodily on the cross, crowned regally, not with thorns, yet with a severe, tense face. The body will be composed, not distorted with the out-thrust ribs of some later crucifixions. Sometimes the blood flows in ornamental tassels contributing, in a way that affects the modern viewer oddly, to an over-all stylization.[34]

The loneliness of the unaccompanied cross assumes some reverent and, sometimes, a corresponding aesthetic, distance. But with attention upon the Virgin, distance may diminish. Whatever the Virgin's position as mediatrix of grace, she with her women provides an aesthetic mediatrix. The praying onlooker may identify with these involved spectators as he dare

33. *A Meditation of S. Bernard, concerning the Passion of Jesus Christ* appears bound with *Saint Bernard, His Meditations: or Sighes, Sobbes, and Teares, upon Our Saviour's Passion*, trans. "W.P.," 2d ed. (London: Arthur Johnson, 1611). The second work is a selection from the *Meditations*, augmented, its compiler writes, "with such other Meditations, as it pleased God to infuse into my minde" (A3ᵛ). It is longer than the translation and decidedly more self-regarding, the writer continually berating himself for his failure to produce commensurate sighs, sobs, and tears.

34. In the Catalonian Museum of Fine Arts at Barcelona, several striking polychrome crucifixes are titled "Christ in Majesty." The head is regally crowned in many. Nails appear, but not necessarily in the appropriate places. The figure may be robed in red. In this museum titles of thirteenth-century crucifixes are about equally divided between *Cristo crucificado* and *Cristo majestad*, but the first title does not necessarily mean that the crown will be of thorns nor the latter that nails will be absent. On early images in England of Christ suffering on the cross, see Rosemary Woolf, *The English Religious Lyric in the Middle Ages* (Oxford: Clarendon, 1968), p. 22.

not with the God-man on the cross. Their function is choric, as a model audience mediating between the central horror and the viewers but also drawing them closer.[35] The Pietà, depositions, such hymns as the "Stabat Mater," such poems as "Quia amore langueo" nourish or express a newly close relationship between art object and audience; arousal is sought, for the Christian viewer is to feel compassion, experience empathy. Aesthetic constituents—audience, work, subject—tend to converge.

It is difficult to say whether commemoration of the Passion in its aspect as an execution is cause or effect of a wider growth toward the "creatural" in art, the trend toward realistic mimesis.[36] F. P. Pickering, in a many-faceted study of crucifixion iconography, has concluded that details often called realistic are in fact the product of a learned tradition based upon scriptural commentary and the habit of typology; for instance, Psalm 21, used in the Good Friday liturgy, with its verse 18— "They have pierced my hands and feet, they have numbered all my bones"—accounts for the strained corpses; interest in realism has little to do with it.[37] Nonetheless, wide differences between early and later treatments of the crucifixion remain.

Emile Mâle reproduces a photograph of a fifteenth-century statue found throughout France representative of this shift, "a figure which is like a sorrowful summing up of the whole Passion. Naked, exhausted, Christ is seated upon a hillock. His feet and His hands are bound. . . . The crown of thorns tears His forehead, and what blood is left in Him slowly oozes away. He seems to wait, and an unspeakable weariness fills the half-closed eyes." [38] The dominant, and extreme, note is powerlessness. This Christ *is* the subject, one to whom things may be, have been done. The hillock is a brilliant anti-image—if not

35. See Woolf, p. 241.

36. "Creatural" is from Erich Auerbach, *Mimesis* (1946), trans. Willard Trask (Garden City, N.Y.: Doubleday Anchor, 1957), pp. 216–19.

37. F. P. Pickering, *Literature & Art in the Middle Ages* (Coral Gables, Fla.: University of Miami, 1970; original version under the title *Literatur und darstellende Kunst im Mittelalter,* Berlin: Erich Schmidt, 1966), pp. 223–307.

38. *Religious Art from the Twelfth to the Eighteenth Century* (New York: Pantheon, 1949), p. 113.

a deliberate one—to the judgment throne of Christ in Majesty.[39]

Church historians confirm the evidence art furnishes that meditation on the Passion flourished especially in the late Middle Ages.[40] Perhaps exercises in meditation in which neophytes were instructed to recreate in imagination the details of a religious event helped to make such devotion and its artistic products so pronounced and creatural. For instance, the *Oculus sacerdotis* of William of Pagula was a wide-ranging manual for parish priests, including such secular matters as advice to expectant mothers (avoid heavy work). Into it William imported a fragment from the *Stimulus amoris* (a symptomatic title) in which the object of meditation is the wounds of Christ:

> . . . whenever you wish to bend God deeply towards you, bear in your heart the Wounds of Christ, and, sprinkled with His Blood, present yourself to the Father as His Only-begotten Son; and he will most sweetly and most fully provide for you.
> . . . Think deeply on these Wounds every day; they will be to you a refreshment and solace; and doubt not that if you imprint them well upon your heart, no temptation will weigh you down.[41]

39. G. Von der Osten, "Job and Christ: The Development of a Devotional Image," *Journal of the Warburg and Courtauld Institutes* 16 (1953): 153–58, comments on history and iconographical types of the *Christus im Elend* 'Christ in Distress' to which group Mâle's statues belong. Its details, he convincingly argues, are derived from representations of Job. See also Pickering, pp. 110–14, on the Christian meaning of *Sessio*.

40. W. A. Pantin, *The English Church in the Fourteenth Century* (Cambridge University, 1955), p. 190.

41. As quoted by Pantin, p. 201. The pseudo-Bonaventuran *Stimulus Amoris*, possibly written by James of Milan, thirteenth-century Franciscan, was extremely popular for several centuries. A preface to a seventeenth-century translation is an anthology of conventional tropes connected with the passion, among them Christ as the book, Christ as a wine-press, and *agere-et-pati* paradoxes, curiously mingled: "And in this *wine-presse Christ* was not onely a patient, but he was likewise an agent, he was not onely *pressed*, but he himselfe also *pressed*. . . . Do not marveile, that I make *Christ crucified* to be both the *Booke* and the *lesson*. . . . on the Crosse he both *offered* and *suffered*, he was both *agent* and *patient*, he was the *Sacrifice* and *Sacrificer*: and a great many other such like marveiles there are to be found in him." St. Bonaventura, *"Stimulus divini amoris": that is, "The Goade of Divine Love,"* trans. B. Lewis Augustine (at Doway by the widow of Marke Wyon, 1642), preface, unpaged.

Such an exercise makes emotional fluency a project, and it presumes not only a passible Christ but also a God the Father and a penitent alike with what Mâle has called the *goût de la pathétique*.

England was not behind in this devotional writing. Richard Rolle's *Meditations on the Passion* is made intense by a creatural rendering "of þe pynus and of þe schamus" that Christ suffers before "þe byschopus and maystres of þe lawe" (28–29) and the mob.[42] Scene-by-scene the speaker attempts, with special reference to Mary, to view each event from the Agony in the Garden to the entombment as if it were then before his eyes or were only tentatively sealed in the past. Descriptions are concrete: the body is "blody" and "bledderyd" (blistered). He addresses the dying Christ: "Now þei lede þe forthe nakyd os a worm" (55); "þi heere mevyth with þe wynde, clemyd with þe blood" (62); because of the "bolnyd" (swollen) face, "a mysel [leper] art þou lyckere þan a clene man" (67). The crowd along the way spurn Christ "with here feet os þou hadde been a dogge" (58–59). The detail is intended to move the deficient heart to tender and grateful devotion. As one poor in response, the speaker prays the Virgin to share her wealth of grief. If for some like Margery Kempe, adept "to cryyn ful lowde & wepyn ful sor" the recommended meditation furnished a release, for others it may have seemed a sorrowful obligation.[43] The author of the Middle English paraphrase of the pseudo-Bonaventuran *Meditationes vitae Christi* assumes a reluctant audience:

> Now crystyn creature, take goode hede,
> And do þyn herte for pyte to blede;
> Loþe þou nat hys sorowes to se,
> Þe whych hym loþed nat to suffre for þe.
>
> [297–300]

---

42. *English Writings of Richard Rolle*, ed. H. E. Allen (Oxford: Clarendon, 1931). Quotations are from text 1, pp. 20–24 passim.

43. *The Book of Margery Kempe*, ed. S. B. Meech and H. E. Allen, EETS no. 212 (London: Oxford, 1940), p. 148. See also *"Meditations on the Supper of Our Lord, and the Hours of the Passion" by Cardinal John Bonaventura, the Seraphic Doctor, Drawn into English Verse by Robert Manning of Brunne*, ed. J. M. Cowper, EETS no. 60 (London: N. Trübner, 1875).

The author improvises pathetic effects. As he says in describing Mary's grief over Christ's shaven head, "The evangelystys telle nat of þys doyng, / For þey myȝte nat wryte alle þyng" (967–68). (The remark that an episode is lacking in the accounts of the evangelists is usual in such devotional writings, Pickering says [p. 244].) One of these additions incorporates *agere et pati:* at the Agony in the Garden, Michael speaks to Christ: "Cumforte þe weyl and do manly; / Hyt ys semely to hym þat ys hyghest, / Grete þynges to do, and suffre mest" (398–400). Not even the Wakefield and York plays outdo the creaturalism of Christ's death throes in this work which strongly influenced the medieval passion plays.[44]

The plays allow us to see some ways in which *agere et pati* may become a formal element. Drama lends generic aptitudes to contrasts of agent and patient even when the material is not based on torture. But beyond necessary design inherent in the Crucifixion subject, and perhaps inherent in the nature of dramatic conflict, medieval playwrights managed their materials so as to set in boldest relief the suffering of Christ against cruel action. Further, the playwrights disposed gesture and dialogue ironically so as to imply Christ's larger area of action beyond the Crucifixion. In the York *Crucifixion,* dominant concentration is on the doers as they yank and strain at the body to meet misplaced bores on the wood and deliberately raise the cross so as to assure most pain—and so as most to harrow the audience:

> i Mil. Nowe raise hym nemely for þe nonys,
> And sette hym be þis mortas heere.
> And latte hym falle in alle at ones,
> For certis þat payne schall have no pere.
> iii Mil. Heve uppe!
>
> [219–23] [45]

If, as Pickering suggests (pp. 288 ff.), this detail originated in the image of the crucified one as God's harp and psalter (from

44. Waldo F. NcNeir in "The Corpus Christi Passion Plays as Dramatic Art," *SP* 48 (1951): 608n, notes the influence of this work on the medieval passion plays.

45. *York Plays: The Plays Performed by the Crafts or Mysteries of York on the Day of Corpus Christi in the 14th, 15th, and 16th Centuries,* ed. Lucy T. Smith (1885; New York: Russell & Russell, 1963), p. 356.

the Easter liturgy's use of Psalm 56 : 9 and commentary on it
by the fathers), dramatic enactment would make the suffering
seem not remote and allusive, but actual and excruciating.
To this, and to primitive jests—"Say, sir, howe likis þou nowe,
/ Þis werke þat we have wrought?"—Christ opposes a silence
broken by two speeches: one calls attention to his suffering at
the hands of human agents and asks his Father to forgive
them, thus at once acknowledging his role of victim and
claiming a range of action and insight larger than any they
know: "For-giffis þes men þat dois me pyne. / What þai wirke
wotte þai noght" (260–61). The Wakefield writer in *The
Scourging* also uses the protagonist's silence to put action as
against suffering in high relief. Here too the effect is not simply one of suffering protagonist and active scourgers, because
while they beat at Jesus they also recount "all thi warkys of
greatt mastry" (144).[46] While players "thrash" and "slash" at
the immobile, silent God, they remind an audience that he
had turned water to wine, commanded the elements so that he
could walk on the sea, healed lepers, made the blind see, and
raised the dead. Jesus has only one speech also in *The Buffet-
ing* where his patient silence (which is biblical) is contrasted
to the ragings of Caiaphas, perhaps played for comedy, whom
the more politic Annas just barely restrains from fisticuffs.
Christ's only speech, however, asserts his ultimate might in
action. When Annas asks whether he is the God of Heaven's
son as he is wont to avow, Jesus answers:

> So thou says by thy steven,
> And right so I am;
> ffor after this shall thou se / when that [I] do com downe
> In brightnes on he / in clowdys from abone.
>
> [251–54]

Passion lyrics contributed toward this sensibility and took
shape along avenues we have discussed, inclining toward the
visual, or toward the dramatic, or toward the meditative. An
imaginative participation in a realistic Passion is their fre-

46. *The Towneley Plays*, ed. George England with notes and intro. by
Alfred W. Pollard, EETS no. 71 (London: Oxford, 1897; reprinted 1925),
pp. 247, 236.

quent strategy. As in the plays, the concepts of doing and
suffering function aesthetically; this works in various ways.

For instance, they are important structurally and syntactically in the fourteenth-century "Popule meus quid feci tibi?",
organizing explicitly both rhetoric and content of that paraphrase of the reproaches for Good Friday's liturgy.[47] Through
the poem, Christ challenges his people: "Mi folk, nou answere
me, / an sey wat is my gilth." There follows a litany of God
the Father's actions counterpointed with the Son's sufferings,
alternating in an "I did this for you—you did that to me"
pattern. Regularly, the divine persona shifts from subject *I*
to direct object *me,* that is from actor to the one acted upon,
and as regularly Yahwe's action balances exactly Christ's
suffering:

> Out of Egipte i brouthte þe,
> þer þu wer in þi wo;
> & wikkedliche þu nome me,
> als i hadde ben þi fo.
>
> .   .   .   .
>
> Heilsum water i sente þe
> out of þe harde ston;
> & eysil & galle þu sentist me,
> oþer ȝef þu me non.

The pattern is sustained through eight stanzas, a lyrical
analogue of the dispute about the nature of Christ, its resolution identical to Leo's of one person, two natures. Old and
New Testament narratives, God the Father and God the Son,
action and passion speak together as "I."

Here the radical antithesis of action and pathos rigidly
governs design; it enters other lyrics with a less precise equity
but still affects the lyric's poise. In many, Christ speaks to an
imagined spectator; from the rood he may direct attention to
his wounds, his crown of thorns, his desolation. Such poems

47. *Religious Lyrics of the XIVth Century,* ed. Carleton Brown, 2d ed.
rev. by G. V. Smithers (Oxford: Clarendon, 1957), no. 72, pp. 88–89. This
is a text expanded from Micheas 6 : 3. Cf. no. 15, pp. 17–18. Unless otherwise stated, lyrics quoted are from this edition.

differ in effect from the unmitigated sense of Christ as sufferer
that the *Christus im Elend* and Rolle's meditations offer. For
in these lyrics, while Christ suffers, he also acts; he indicts and
reproves man. The title "Homo vide quid pro te patior" is
illustrative with its initial imperative verb introducing *patior.*
The longer poem of that title summarizes the life of Christ
even before the Passion in terms of passibility: "Twa &
thyrty ʒere & mare / I was for þe in travel sare / with hungyr,
thirst, hete, & calde"; but the speaker ends with an action,
issuing an imperative and a promise based on infinite
resources:

> Lufe þou me als þe wele aw,
> And fra syn þou þe draw,
> I gyf þe my body with woundes sare;
> And þare-to sall I gyf þe mare,
> Over all þis I-wysse,
> In erth mi grace, in heven my blysse.
>
> [No. 77, p. 93]

Stress is more apt to fall purely on suffering when the penitent
speaks, pouring out to Christ on the Cross his guilt, sympathy,
and rue. The language of profane love—"leman," "darling"—
may project the intimacy of the poet's sense of connection
with Christ in his Passion.

The view that the Passion itself is an action—which finds
masterly expression in the Old English "Dream of the Rood"
—dominates few Middle English lyrics. However, some do
take over the moving older image of Christ as youthful warrior
hero, and the effect is to make the Passion seem a deed, an
exploit—"I Am iesu, þat cum to fith / With-outen seld &
spere." [48] But "A Lament over the Passion" alludes to the

48. No. 63, p. 82. In the Old English "Christ III," another associated
theme appears. As Christ rebukes sinners, he distinguishes between the
chosen and the "unwillingly suffered":

. . .	More bitter to Me
The Cross of your sins	I unwillingly suffered
Than was that other	I ascended of old
Of My own will . . .	

This is quoted in a chapter on "Christ as Poetic Hero," by Stanley B.
Greenfield, *A Critical History of Old English Literature* (New York Uni-

heroic with an accentuation of pathos. The speaker-penitent moves among several appeals, the warrior image taking over in a deposition stanza, echoic of epic battlegrounds where loyal thanes mourned dead chieftains:

> My fender of my fose, sa fonden in þe felde,
> Sa lufly lyghtand at þe evensang tyde;
> Þi moder and hir menȝhe unlaced þi scheld—
> All weped þat þar were, þi woundes was sa wyde.
>
> [No. 79, pp. 94–95]

A late lyric divides exactly and stunningly between Christ passible and Christ triumphant:

> I Have laborede sore and suffered deyȝth,
> and now I Rest and draw my breyght;
> but I schall come and call Ryght sone
> hevene and erght and hell to dome;
> and than schall know both devyll and mane,
> What I was and what I ame.[49]

The writer locates his poem in a narrow time between Crucifixion and Harrowing, exactly at the pivot between the Passion and Divine Act. The final line's echo of the biblical "I am who am" gives resonance to the portent, almost ominous, of an oncoming, judging power. The "was" and "am" fuse, collapsing time to assert Christ's divine identity, an infinite power in an infinite present.

Formal effects aside, the passion plays and lyrics demonstrate that as the Christian Era gave birth to new topics, it newly focused the significance of ancient ones like *agere et pati* with important results for the ideals, expectations, and capacities for response of the audience. Secular narratives like the tales of Griselda and Constance give pointed and leisurely elaboration to pathos, indicating that what now seems a special, even suspect, taste was once general. There was a

versity, 1965), p. 132. This chapter, especially the discussion of "The Dream of the Rood," pp. 136–40, is relevant. Pickering, pp. 255–56, refers the concept of the crucifixion as a victory to the appropriation by the church of Cant. 7 : 8—*ascendam in palmam.*

49. *Religious Lyrics of the XVth Century*, ed. Carleton Brown (Oxford: Clarendon, 1939), no. 111, p. 177.

different way to be heroic: if to act was to express the image of
God the Father, Prime Mover, Pure Act, to suffer was to take
on the image of His Son, who suffered so extremely. The
strictly gratuitous vulnerability of Christ overgoes the classic
immunity of the antique gods who neither suffer change nor
die.

Not that suffering fully replaces action as a protagonistic
ideal. A hero still may perform great deeds. To act is the
human thing: "To be self-acting and self-conducting . . . is
proper to human nature. Irrational nature is rather acted on
or conducted." "To set oneself into activity is the noblest
mode of movement and the heart of life." [50] St. Thomas did
not forget that Aristotle had defined happiness as an *activity*
of the soul nor his observation that encomia are bestowed upon
acts.[51] Similar is the valuation of de Guilleville's angel: "al
þat is do with owt myght, it lakkith the dignite and the name
of the dede, and it is called passion." [52]

But the Passion of Christ did exert a powerful attraction as
an alternative heroic ideal. It was a model transcendent but
open to all, urged upon all, a prize for which mere Christian
wayfarers, too modest to set out for a golden fleece, might com-
pete. Patience, from the root *pati*, to suffer, took for its unique
exploit not the deed but the ordeal. One crystallization of this
modality, its relation to *agere et pati* obvious, was the victory
of patience. In earliest exegesis, unaffected by the intimate

50. The two quotations are from *ST*, pt. 1 of pt. 2, q. 1, art. 2, Gilby,
p. 264; and from *Opus.* 10, Exposition, *de Causis*, lect. 18, Gilby, p. 217.

51. *Nicomachean Ethics* 1.7.15–16, and 1.8.2–9, where the matter is
put this way: "virtue in active exercise cannot be inoperative—it will
of necessity act, and act well. And just as at the Olympic games the
wreaths of victory are not bestowed upon the handsomest and strongest
persons present, but on men who enter for the competitions—since it is
among these that the winners are found,—so it is those who *act* rightly
who carry off the prizes and good things of life."

52. "The Middle English *Pilgrimage of the Soul:* An Edition of MS.
Egerton 615," ed. Merrel Dare Clubb, Jr. (Ph.D. diss., University of Michigan, 1953), 5.26.103b (p. 331). Hamlet remarks that enterprises of great
pith and moment may "lose the name of action" (3.1), and, as Shakespeare frequently uses *agere et pati*, it could be argued, almost plausibly,
that Hamlet also means that his program of revenge has lapsed in time
and in[to] mere passion, so that he has let go the "important *acting*" of
his father's dread command (3.4; my italics).

identification with the Passion of Christ just under survey, praise of patience might naively retain rather more of the spirit of the Old Adam than the New. Some commend a cheerful patience as that posture best calculated to set an enemy's teeth on edge. So Tertullian notes what satisfaction the patient sufferer may glean in frustrating his oppressor:

> When therefore thou hast overthrown his gain by not being pained, he must himself needs be pained in missing his gain: and then thou wilt come off not only unhurt . . . but besides this both pleased by the disappointment of thine adversary, and avenged by his pain. Such is the profit and the pleasure of Patience.[53]

More subtle, but still, one imagines, sweet, is the victory Libertinus of Funda wins as St. Gregory tells the story. The monk's exemplary patience makes an abbot who has beaten him with a footstool one day leap suddenly from bed the next to embrace his feet for "presuming to offer unto so good and worthy a man so cruel and contumelious an injury. . . . And by this means, the Abbot was brought to great meekness; and the humility of the scholar became a teacher to the master." [54]

Though any might savor such a victory of patience, martyrs shared in Christ's victory in its most costly mode, by repeating its history. Recorders pointed out the victory as they recounted the passion—the *gloria passionis*.[55] As we have already seen with the passion lyrics above, the new ideal absorbed to itself language of the old, the new tenor claiming epic vehicles. Bede giving his bibliography tells of his care to set down in his Martyrology "all that I could find, and not only on what day, but also by what sort of combat [*quo genere certaminis*], or

53. "Of Patience," *Apologetic and Practical Treatises,* trans. Rev. C. Dodgson, A Library of the Fathers (Oxford: John Henry Parker; London: J.G.F. and J. Rivington, 1842), 1 : 338. Chaucer's Parson capaciously includes this endorsement of the virtue (661).

54. *The Dialogues of St. Gregory,* ed. E. G. Gardner of translation of 1608 by "P.W." (London: Medici Society, 1911), 1.2 (p. 13).

55. See "Gloria Passionis" in Erich Auerbach, *Literary Language & Its Public in Late Latin Antiquity and in the Middle Ages,* trans. Ralph Manheim from the German text of 1958, Bollingen Series 74 (New York: Pantheon, 1965), pp. 67–81.

under what judge they overcame the world [*mundum vi-cerint*]." [56] The motif of the victory of patience was a cliché of Chaucer's time. Witness Anima to the dreamer in *Piers Plowman:* "Ac he suffred in ensample that we shulde suffre also, / And seide to suche that suffre wolde that *pacientes vincunt*" (B, 15. 261–62). "Men seyn: 'the suffrant overcomith,' parde" (4. 1584), Criseyde tells Troilus. "Pacience is an heigh vertu, certeyn, / For it venquysseth, as thise clerkes seyn, / Thynges that rigour sholde nevere atteyne" (773–75), the franklin moralizes. Still in Spenser's time, *vincit qui patitur* was a popular tag, an emblematic commonplace. In the formal Renaissance *Triumph of Patience,* by Martin Heemskerk, Patience sits in a car to the rear of which is tied a blindfold Fortune with her wheel broken. Following plates depict devotees of Patience with their spoils, including Joseph with Invidia (a reference to his brothers), a nude (Potiphar's wife); Job with his wife, comforters, and Satan; St. Stephen on an elephant drags two men carrying stones, the instruments of his passion. Last comes Christ with the World, Sin, Death, and Tartarus led in captivity behind him.[57]

The Renaissance further saw that a patient heroism antedated the Passion of Christ. The admired Stoics had made it an ideal and a strategy; and perhaps under Stoic influence—with Homer furnishing justification in the epithet πολύτλας (much-enduring) for Odysseus—Renaissance readers spotted a model of suffering in the *Odyssey* to match that of action in the *Iliad.* Thus Castiglione's Ottaviano observes,

> e parmi che Omero, secondo che formò dui omini eccellentissimi per esempio della vita umana, l'uno nelle azioni, che fu Achille, l'altro nelle passioni e tolleranzie, che fu Ulisse, così volesse ancora formar un perfetto cortegiano, che fu quel Fenice.

56. Bede, *Ecclesiastical History of the English Nation,* trans. John Stevens, rev. Lionel C. Jane, Everyman's Library (London: Dent, 1951), p. 285; and *Anglo-Saxonis Historia Ecclesiastica,* in *PL,* vol. 95, col. 290 .The *acts and passions* of the martyrs, which might seem to refer to the topos, does not do so but refers to official proceedings as against other accounts of the martyrdom. See F. X. Murphy, "Passio," and M. J. Costelloe, "Acts of the Martyrs," in *New Catholic Encyclopedia,* 1967.

57. S. C. Chew, *The Pilgrimage of Life* (New Haven: Yale, 1962), pp. 121–22.

[And I can not see but Homer, as hee fashioned two most excellent personages for example of mans life, the one in practises, which was Achilles, the other in passions and sufferances, which was Ulisses: even so in like manner minded to fashion a perfect courtier (which was Phoenix).[58]

Chapman dedicates his translation of the *Odyssey* to the Earl of Somerset, Robert Carr, as an exemplar of the Ulyssean temper; and the antithesis of action and endurance as heroic ideals informs his comparison of the two epics:

> In one, Predominant Perturbation; in the other, over-ruling Wisedome; in one, the Bodie's fervour and fashion of outward Fortitude to all possible height of Heroicall Action; in the other, the Mind's inward, constant and unconquered Empire, unbroken, unalterd with any most insolent and tyrannous infliction.[59]

Milton, who used *agere et pati* frequently—during the debate in hell in *Paradise Lost* every major devil relies upon it in one form or another—is plainly aware of the alternative possibilities when he rejects "the wrath / Of stern *Achilles*" (9. 14–15) as less heroic than "the better fortitude / Of Patience and Heroic Martyrdom" (9. 31–32), though he inexactly says the second has been unsung.

Just how much the emphasis on the protagonist as sufferer

58. Baldesar Castiglione, *Il libro del cortegiano,* ed. Giulio Preti (Turin: Giulio Einaudi, 1960), 4. 57 (p. 407). The translation is Hoby's. *The Book of the Courtier,* trans. Sir Thomas Hoby, 1561, Everyman's Library (London: Dent, 1928), p. 299.

59. *Chapman's Homer: The Odyssey & The Lesser Homerica,* ed. Allardyce Nicoll, Bollingen Series 41 (New York: Pantheon, 1956), 2 : 4. The dedication is given on p. xii.

Earlier, with considerably less textual justification, Homer's heroes had been allegorized as the active and the contemplative life. Badius, an early commentator on Virgil, in pointing out the superiority of his author said that Homer described the contemplative life in Ulysses and the active life in the Trojan war, whereas Virgil had done both in one epic and fewer books. *P. Virgilli Maronis, Poetae Mantuani, Universum Poema: cum Absolvta Servii Honorati Mavri, Grammatici, & Badii Ascensii interpretatione* . . . (Venice: Joannem Mariam Bonellum, 1562), p. 124. Tasso repeats the identification of the Odyssey with the contemplative life in his essay on *Jerusalem Delivered.* For comment on these, see William Nelson, *The Poetry of Edmund Spenser* (New York: Columbia, 1965), pp. 118–20. Actually conflation of *agere et pati* with the distinction between active and contemplative lives was rare.

owes to Stoicism is a perplexed matter. Clearly, with Chapman and in the Jacobean drama generally the debt is certainly more to Seneca than to the saints.[60] (The Machiavel and the Stoic of late Jacobean drama may in fact be loosely placed as types of agent and patient then in vogue.) Even here there is a difference, for in antique Stoicism *what* was conquered by him who suffered was himself, his passions. The hero wins not battles, ladies, and preferment, but self-mastery. But the Jacobean hero may be a redoubtable soldier, lover, and court-ier, though items of his *vita* relating to the first tend to be furnished perfunctorily more or less as costuming. More im-portantly different, rather than governing his passions, he expresses them until the climactic time comes for him to dis-play eligibility for high and intense satisfactions by his con-tempt for suffering equally extreme. The celebration is not of Christian sufferance but of human endurance, behaving well under stress; and the flamboyant rhetoric of the hero about his dying stance both comprises and attests his victory. His act is to speak with style about his suffering while he suffers. Rather than the temperance that marked the antique Stoic and the faith that marked the Christian martyr, orgy, injury, and a smattering of Stoic theory prepared the Jacobean pro-tagonist for his climactic, disdainful passion. Just how far he might come from sharing Christ's cross is indicated by Web-ster's Flamineo, who as an infant broke the leg of the corpus on his mother's crucifix. Naturally, such differences did not escape attention, and sometimes playwrights carefully dis-tinguished a Stoic endurance from a Christian patience.[61] Any full typology of the protagonist as sufferer would have to reserve place for the Jacobean hero—and heroine—but Chaucer and Spenser offer no genuine cognates of his extreme, conventionalized passion.

The victory of patience has carried us past the Middle Ages

60. Senecan influence alone might account for what appears to be a sharp increase in the incidence of *facere et pati* in the drama from Elizabeth's time forward; it was a favorite Senecan locution. (See, for example, *Hercules Furens* 386–87, 735, and 1278; *Troades* 254; *Hippolytus* 723–24; and *Oedipus* 980 ff., esp. 983–84.)

61. Michael Higgins, "The Development of the 'Senecal Man': Chap-man's *Bussy D'Ambois* and Some Precursors," *RES* 23 (1947) : 24–33.

and beyond Spenser. This flow is unexceptional, for the new
learning did not relinquish medieval uses of *agere et pati*.
Further, from the Renaissance forward, English writers, at
least, exploited *agere-et-pati* formulas more frequently, deliberately, and cunningly than did their predecessors who wrote
in English. A sampling of texts from Renaissance figures in
overlapping generations may be taken as emblematic of, not
an identical, but an identity of tradition. (I give commonly
accepted birthdates.) Ficino (b. 1433) comprehensively regrets
that postlapsarian men live outside the order of first nature
and even, "O sorrow!—act and suffer [*agimus atque patimur*]
contrary to the order of nature." He illustrates the continued
association of suffering with the passions of the sensible soul
and with matter, referring to "the passions of matter" (*ma-
teriae passionibus*) and to "the beast in us, that is, sense" (*in
nobis bestiam nostram, id est, sensum*) and to "the true man
in us, that is, reason" (*homo vero noster, id est, ratio*).[62] Erasmus (b. 1466) commends the undertaking of such an enterprise
as his adages: who could do it, "unless he be a real Hercules
in mind, able to do and suffer anything for the sake of serving
others?" (*nisi si quis sit animo plane Herculeo, qui possit, alios
juvandi studio, quidvis & facere & pati?*).[63] Thomas Wilson
(b. 1525) illustrates the vitality of *agere-et-pati* formulations
in school disciplines. His logic lists the predicaments without
substitution and in their Aristotelian order and discusses
"*The maner of doyng, in Latine called* Actio. *Agere, seu
facere*" which is "when our labour is extended upon a weake
or lesse thyng" and "*Perpessio, called in Englishe a sufferyng.
Pati, fieri, sue accipere.*"[64] His rhetoric gives currency to
Boethian propositions, including in a supply of sentences

62. Ficino, *Epistolarum, Opera . . .* 2 vols. (Paris: Apud Dionysium
Bechet, 1641), book 2, no. 1 (1 : 661–62). I follow, but make more literal,
the translation of J. L. Burroughs which appears under the title "Five
Questions concerning the Mind," in *The Renaissance Philosophy of Man*
(1948), ed. Ernst Cassirer et al., Phoenix Books (University of Chicago,
1956, 1967), pp. 193 ff. The figure's source is Plato's *Republic* 9. 588–89.

63. Desiderius Erasmus, *Adagia, Opera omnia . . .* 10 vols. (Lyons:
Petri Vander Aa., 1703; repub. London: Gregg, 1962), vol. 2, col. 710.
The translation is by Margaret Mann Phillips, *The "Adages" of Erasmus:
A Study with Translations* (Cambridge University, 1964), p. 194.

64. *The Rule of Reason, conteinying the Art of Logike* (London: John
Kyngston, 1580), pp. 13–13ᵛ.

suitable to be "gathered or heaped together" on the subject of the evils of revenge the following: "He is more harmed that doeth wrong, then he that hath suffered wrong." [65] Justus Lipsius (b. 1547), very possibly a source for the mutability cantos, gives his approval: "Boethus spake wittilie [in original, "Acutè Boëthius"], The wicked that abide some punishment are happier, then if no rod of Justice did correct them." [66] Finally Fulke Greville (b. 1554), born two years after Spenser but long surviving him, describes Sir Philip Sidney telling the surgeons to cut and search his wounds to the bottom: "For besides his hope of health, he would make this farther profit of the pains which he must suffer, that they should bear witness, they had indeed a sensible natured man under their hands, yet one to whom a stronger Spirit had given power above himself, either to do or suffer." [67] It is appropriate to close this survey with so curious a compound of the antique, Christian, and Renaissance spirit.

This account of *agere et pati* in intellectual history is sufficient for present purposes. Tenacious, flexible, it kept identity over many centuries in contacts with three cultures. Any literate medieval or Renaissance man would know it from his schoolboy days. Chaucer resorted to it most conspicuously as a translator in his somewhat rigid reduction of the more resourceful vocabulary of Boethius to the verbs *do* and *suffer;* Spenser varied it freely.

Some Functions of the Topos

The topos has functioned in literature in many ways. It allowed a writer to connect his verse with the prestige of

65. *The Arte of Rhetorike* (London: George Robinson, 1584), p. 120.

66. *De Constantia* (Antwerp: [Plantin], 1599), 2. 10 (p. 57). The English is from *Two Bookes of Constancie* (1584), trans. Sir John Stradling, 1594, ed. Rudolf Kirk (New Brunswick, N.J.: Rutgers, 1939), p. 154. Stradling glosses, *"For this is in respect of the sufferer. That of the doer."* Lipsius uses *facere et pati* exactly when he writes of destiny, 1. 19 (p. 34), that it does not force or constrain, "sed ut quidque natum est facere aut pati, ita dirigit singula & flectit" ("But as everie thing is made to doe, or suffer, so it directeth and turneth all things" [Stradling, p. 119]).

67. *Life of Sir Philip Sidney,* vol. 4 of *The Works in Verse and Prose Complete of The Right Honourable Fulke Greville, Lord Brooke,* ed. A. B. Grosart (printed for private circulation, 1870), p. 131.

former art, with endeavors of old clerks. Virgil claims the old
as he marks out his new subject, a comprehensive hero, one
who both acts and suffers, who is both to *volvere casus* [68] and
adire labores:

> Musa, mihi causas memora, quo numine laeso
> quidve dolens regina deum tot volvere casus
> insignem pietate virum, tot adire labores
> impulerit.
>
> > [*Aeneid* 1. 8–11]

And Tasso carries on, in his way as pious as Aeneas, in an
attentive tribute to Virgilian nuances:

> Canto l'arme pietose e 'l capitano
> che 'l gran sepolcro liberò di Cristo:
> molto egli oprò co 'l senno e con la mano,
> molto suffrí nel glorïoso acquisto.
>
> > [1. 1]
>
> [The sacred armies and the godly knight
> That the great sepulchre of Christ did free
> I sing; much wrought his valor and foresight,
> And in that glorious war much suffer'd he.] [69]

And, not piously at all, an allusion might certify the wit of
characters while placing the moral tone of their milieu; witness an exchange in Jonson's *Catiline* as the "ladies' auxiliary"
rejoins male conspirators:

> *Sempronia.*   We ha' done;
> And now are fit for action.
> > *Longinus.*   Which is passion.
> There's your best activitie, lady.
> > *Sempronia.*   How
> Knowes your wise fatnesse that?

68. In school editions of Virgil, *volvere* is often glossed "undergo" or
"endure," and is frequently so translated. One undergoes chances, undertakes works.

69. *Gerusalemme liberata* (Milan: Feltrinelli, 1961), p. 3. The English
is from *Jerusalem Delivered,* trans. Edward Fairfax in 1600, introduced by
John Charles Nelson (New York: Capricorn Books, 1963), p. 2. Cf.
Dante, *Inferno* 2. 4–5: "the double war / of the journey and the pity."

> *Longinus.*   Your mothers daughter
> Did teach me, madame.
>
>   [3. 680–84] [70]

Agere et pati was ready to hand for parody as in Johnson's account of the antiquities in a hack writer's London garret:

> Such, Mr. Rambler, are the changes which have happened in the narrow space where my present fortune has fixed my residence. . . . and so just is the observation of Juvenal, that a single house will show what is done or suffered in the world.[71]

Agere et pati might be more than a local verbal event. If Rosemond Tuve is right about the influence of the logical "places" in the modus operandi of poets, the writer would also think about the "manner of suffering" and "manner of acting" of his subjects as he "invented" and "amplified." This might produce a happy analogy, an insight in characterization, a help for design, or determine the evolution of a trope. In the brief discussion of medieval plays and lyrics above, we have seen the concepts *agere et pati* functioning structurally.

For the reader, attention to action and passivity may be a way of coming at a poem, even when we cannot certainly know that an author used the tradition consciously. In any one scene of drama or of narrative, the relation between agent and patient may be shifting. This is clear in slapstick comedy when he who acts last may be that patient who first suffered a custard pie in the face. Cartoons, animated or strip, furnish joys almost wholly arising from severe articulation of actor-patient relationships in predictable patterns, and this articulation may also figure in densely compacted, sophisticated entertainments. Consider the bedroom scene in *Hamlet* (act 3, sc. 4). Three of its four participants enter upon it confident that they are actors in this situation, determined to carry things off with a high hand. Hamlet even fears he may go too far: "Let me be cruel, not unnatural; / I will speak daggers to her, but use none" (3. 2). Polonius: "Look you lay home to him; / Tell him

70. W. F. Bolton kindly called my attention to this passage from *Catiline*. Cf. 3. 858–59 and *Sejanus* 1. 293–98 and 4. 73–76.

71. *The Rambler*, Everyman's Library (London: Dent, 1953), no. 161, p. 252.

his pranks have been too broad to bear with." Gertrude: "I'll warrant you; fear me not. Withdraw, I hear him coming." Each is in a mood and, he thinks, a position to give orders, to carry his point. All end as patients; only the ghost, who might be considered to have the status of patient more assuredly than anyone, winds up having carried out his purpose unambiguously.

Thinking of scenic or narrative progression in terms of action and passion may sharpen attention to what is going on in the work before us, but still may tell next to nothing about qualitative texture. Before battle scenes, Shakespeare allows prospective agents and patients to appreciate dawns in comparable poetry. Having said a character is a patient, one must add something, for the patient may be exultant (Bussy), resigned (Becket), bored (Uncle Vanya). In longer works, a catena of images or other incremental effects may do much to establish and refine suffering and action.

It is possible that a structure of action and suffering is intrinsic to some genres and to the fundamental appeals of archetypal figures.[72] Undoubtedly seeing patient become agent is important to comedy and gratifying to the audience, while

72. Francis Fergusson in his introduction to Aristotle's *Poetics* (New York: Hill and Wang, 1961), pp. 8–13, explains how the action "to find the slayer" arises out of the pathos of fear originating in the suffering of Thebes under the plague. In *The Idea of a Theater* (1949; Garden City, N.Y.: Doubleday Anchor, 1953), he develops the concept of a total tragic rhythm of action consisting of purpose (an active phase), passion (roughly analogous to the Aristotelian "scene of suffering"), and emergence of a new perception. He cites (p. 31) Kenneth Burke's terms "Poiema," "Pathema," and "Mathema" in *A Grammar of Motives,* a dialectic the first two phases of which correspond to action and suffering. Cf. Burke in *The Philosophy of Literary Form* (1941; rev. ed. New York: Random Vintage, 1957), pp. 68*n*, 90*n*. John Lawlor in *The Tragic Sense in Shakespeare,* 1st American ed. (New York: Harcourt, Brace, 1960), pp. 45–73, uses the ideas of agent and patient in a commentary on *Hamlet.* Anthony Low in "Action and Suffering: *Samson Agonistes* and the Irony of Alternatives," *PMLA* 84 (1969) : 514–19, makes critical use of the concepts *agere et pati.* These concepts are at the heart of the discussion of Odysseus by G. E. Dimock, Jr., cited above, n. 4. There are other less systematic uses in criticism, such as the remarks of Maynard Mack, " 'We Come Crying Hither': An Essay on Some Characteristics of *King Lear,*" *Yale Review* 54 (1964) : 165, 177 et passim. (In particular drama seems to bring critics to terms approximating *agere et pati.*) Maud Bodkin in *Archetypal Patterns in Poetry* (1934; New York: Random Vintage, 1958),

seeing one who seems to be the actor turn out to be the patient (Oedipus) is horrifying to the audience and results, when stakes and characters are high, in tragedy. (The stripping of the pretender is an analogous effect in comedy, one never wholly free of its concomitance of tragic response.)

Perhaps the most rewarding consideration of *agere-et-pati* distinctions comes in narrative forms with their fuller mimesis of heroic, romantic, or realistic characters—epic, romance, novel, short fictions. As a critical gauge, its application is not limited to writers who know it as a classic cliché. Dickens, in fact, did so know it, but do-and-bear, inflict-endure, act-and-suffer combinations mostly come from the genteel lips of his duller characters. However, taut agent-patient relationships are crucial to the vitality at the heart of many of his novels. The relation among the rent collector Pancks, the tenants of Bleeding Heart Yard, and the apparently benevolent owner, Mr. Casby, who orders the collector to squeeze harder (as Mr. Pancks expresses it, "Pancks is only the Works: but here's the Winder!") demonstrates the glaring clarity with which Dickens perceived economic actors and sufferers (*Little Dorrit,* chap. 32). Even more important are agent-patient interactions in personal, affective bonds. The fact of one human being's desire to control another, the variety of that appetite and the forms of its embodiment are a continuous, almost an obsessive interest; the bullied child, the harsh school (*Dotheboys*), is par excellence the Dickensian expression of this concern, but does not exhaust it. It may be suspected that one of the more dubious sources of Dickens's complex appeal is the latent pulse of

---

pp. 234–38, verges upon the concepts of action and suffering in her analysis of Satan as hero. Coleridge is a standard critic who used *agere et pati* in analysis. It is a point of reference in his review of philosophy in *Biographia Literaria* (see chaps. 5 and 7) and in the discussion of "Venus and Adonis" (see chap. 15). In a comment on Spenser he noticed that the figure of Grief (*FQ* 3. 12. 16) represents both the grieved and the aggriever, for Grief is himself sadly hanging his head and carrying pincers with which he torments others. The confusion of agent and patient, Coleridge writes, occurs so frequently in Spenser that it must be inferred that the poet considered it within the legitimate principles of allegory; but Coleridge is clearly put off by it. *Coleridge's Miscellaneous Criticism,* ed. Thomas Middleton Raysor (Cambridge, Mass.: Harvard, 1936), p. 39.

diseased, potentially sadistic, fiercely frustrated, or inverse agent-patient relationships among characters: for example, in *Dombey and Son,* Dombey and his daughter; Carker and his younger brother; Carker and Dombey; Edith Dombey and Carker; Edith Dombey and her husband, even Carker and Rob the Grinder. Even when the history accounting for these relationships is benign, they are kept overtly tense, hidden, or half-revealed in sudden, naked gestures as when Jaggers forces Estella's mother to expose her wrists in *Great Expectations.* A fascinated interaction of fear and cruelty, on the one hand the will to dominate verging upon a will to destroy, on the other an intuition of threat to the self's integrity verging upon extinction—this provides much of the obscurely exciting, threatening vitality in interpersonal relations among Dickens's agents and patients.

Thinking of characters in terms of agency and patience may lead to appreciation of a character's individual psychology as well as to presented interpersonal relations. This too is most readily discerned in the larger narrative forms. The practical criticism in the following chapters engages such forms. In the Knight's Tale, I attempt a demonstration of *agere et pati* in its full relevance. To do this with Spenser would be both redundant and formidably long, so with him I am arbitrarily selective. These exercises do not constitute a study of influences, but are individual explications of narratives that, sharing a tradition, overlap in some rewarding ways for our understanding of action and passion in literature. In choosing poems for illustration it has been decidedly more interesting to work on those where the relation of action and suffering is qualified rather than too neatly dialectic. As a tale of suffering, Griselda's is exemplary, but the Knight's Tale is more satisfying. As an account of action in opposition to suffering, the legend of justice is full of event, of crisp and forceful reversals, but the quests of the Red Cross Knight, Guyon, and Britomart repay more richly, if with more dubiety, a consideration of the protagonist as agent and sufferer.

2

Theseus' Scene:

Action in

the Knight's Tale

With one exception, Chaucer presents the characters in the Knight's Tale as sufferers, almost as victims. This has become, in fact, a common reading.[1] Threaded through the perfor-

1. Opinions on the Knight's Tale range along a comedy-tragedy continuum. (Not that critics who place emphasis on comedy necessarily deny the tale philosophical claims nor that their opposite numbers deny its comedic elements.) Edward B. Ham, "Knight's Tale 38," *ELH* 17 (1950: 252–61, gives a convenient review of opinion before the fifties, presenting his own that the tale is one of courtoisie and levity. To Paull F. Baum, *Chaucer: A Critical Appreciation* (Durham, N.C.: Duke, 1958), p. 99, the tale's moral is that things somehow come right and that even passive love is triumphant. Robert A. Pratt, "'Joye after Wo' in the *Knight's Tale*," *JEGP* 57 (1958) : 416, notes "thoughtfulness and sadness" but thinks the treatment mostly "light-hearted and romantic." Richard Neuse in "The Knight: The First Mover in Chaucer's Human Comedy," *UTQ* 31 (1962) : 300, thinks the story the product of a knight "in an unbuttoned, holiday mood." Paul T. Thurston, *Artistic Ambivalence in Chaucer's Knight's Tale* (Gainesville: University of Florida, 1968), argues that the sophisticated reader is intended to take the tale as a satire of chivalric traditions, courtly allegory, and the romance. Robert O. Payne, *The Key of Remembrance* (New Haven: Yale, 1963), p. 163, had earlier

mance of Chaucer's first pilgrim is the motif of *Homo sapiens*
as a patient, the recipient of the gifts and slings of a Fortuna
sufficiently outrageous. Not only does fate impose upon its
heroes from the time they are presented, as much dead as alive,
at the bottom of a "taas" of bodies at Thebes. Not only is the
heroine bestowed, her wishes regardless, first on one and then
another of these two knights. Other aspects of the tale are
echoic of these inescapably prominent events in the plot.
Minor characters, the decor of the tale's fictive furnishings,
its most haunting images, and its most elaborately set senti-
ments, authorial and dramatic, present a world in which things
happen to people, in which people do not move events but
events befall people.

This does not come about because the characters are passive
psychologically, or because they are mere convenient labels for
mood or emotions. They struggle. Although idealized and
largely conventionalized (particularly Emily), they are not allegorical. The heroes do theorize about necessity: the thought
strikes Palamon that to the gods men may be no more than

---

suggested that the tale moved toward parody. Latterly, allegorically per-
suaded critics have offered a serio-moral version of a comic reading, taking note of Arcite and Palamon's regard for Emily as cupidinous: see
Richard L. Hoffman, *Ovid and the Canterbury Tales* (Philadelphia: University of Pennsylvania, 1966), pp. 46–48, 89–93, 96–98. In this vein see
also the tactful, attentive reading of W. F. Bolton, "The Topic of the
Knight's Tale," *Chaucer Review* 1 (1967) : 217–27.

Some readers have emphasized Boethian elements, among them R. E.
Kaske, "The Knight's Interruption of the Monk's Tale," *ELH* 24 (1957) :
249–68; R. M. Lumiansky, *Of Sondry Folk* (Austin: University of Texas,
1955), pp. 34 ff.; and E. T. Donaldson, *Chaucer's Poetry: An Anthology
for the Modern Reader* (New York: Ronald, 1958), pp. 901–05. Dale
Underwood, "The First of *The Canterbury Tales*," *ELH* 26 (1959) : 455–
69, is concerned with human and divine order in the poem. His account
refers to the view of Charles A. Muscatine, *Chaucer and the French Tradition* (Berkeley: University of California, 1957), pp. 175–90, who asserts
that order itself, which so characterizes the articulation of the poem, is
the core of its meaning, a high achievement, for the poem also discloses
the antagonistic chaos that threatens the order of the noble life. William
Frost, "An Interpretation of Chaucer's Knight's Tale," *RES* 25 (1949) :
289–304, holds that the tale's view of the human condition is a tragic
one. Cf. Elizabeth Salter, *Chaucer: The Knight's Tale and The Clerk's
Tale*, Studies in English Literature no. 5 (London: Edward Arnold, 1962).
This sampling is representative, not exhaustive.

items in the fauna; Arcite feels that his death was shaped before his shirt of flesh and is fatalistically submissive to the onset of love. They each consider that the grudge Juno holds against the race of Cadmus may be responsible for their lot and for that of their doomed city (1328–31, 1542–62). Their theories should immobilize them, but Palamon and Arcite are not so strictly logical as to act upon their expressed theories. They *do* as well as suffer, wish, and pray. Certainly they are pre-Oblomovian. To pick a comparison nearer to hand, neither resembles Troilus, whose *psychological* make-up is that of a sufferer, a patient. To be sure, to each the opportunities of the other are more distinct than are his own. Arcite, when he must leave prison, Athens, and Emily, says that as Palamon is a knight, "a worthy and an able," it is possible, with Fortune, that "Thow maist to thy desir somtyme atteyne" (1243). Palamon also couples individual action—Arcite may "make a werre" —and luck in reviewing his rival's clear advantages (see lines 1285–94). In fact Arcite raises no army, and it requires a dream message from the gods to bring him back to Athens in a more modest fashion than Palamon expects.

Apart from this laggard interval for Arcite and despite their necessitarian general views, the heroes keep an eager, healthy sense of possibility. Until Arcite's fall, in spite of their woes, they seem to be excellent types, promising, young, unburdened by legend even though they come from a fated city. Some of this impression comes from the reader's lazy optimism, the opinion, derived from literary experience, that characters who are prisoners in Fitt I always manage to get out by Fitt IV. The rest is validated because Chaucer sets before us not drifters, but choosing, striving beings whose actions are stultified, for all their being passionately pursued, and whose choices are vain, for all their being passionately willed.

The effectual exception, of course, is Theseus, who deserves detailed remark. Applying the topos *agere et pati* to analyze his position may refine our understanding of the poem's action, inner and overt. Not that commentary on Theseus is wanting. Although the differences and/or similarities between Palamon and Arcite absorbed most critical effort for many years, the importance of Theseus has always been acknowledged. To be sure, Stuart Robertson in an article on medieval realism in the poem included Theseus in his statement of complaint that the characters are not arresting: "It is true that the realism of the *Knight's Tale* is not upon the surface: the figures of the main characters, of Arcite and Palamon, of Theseus and Emily, do not stand before us with any great distinctness." [2] But Robertson's attitude toward the duke is friendly rather than not: Chaucer intends to surprise us at the "unmercenary" character of his duke who might have had ransom money in hand rather than the expense of supporting two prisoners. Since Stuart Robertson's article, if the impression of the duke's vividness has grown, that of his amiability has on the whole declined. The duke has been called harsh, "ignoble or cruel"; the epithet "noble" as applied to him may well be yet another flick of Chaucerian irony.[3] Richard Neuse sees (pp. 305–07) Theseus as a "political opportunist," whose watchword is "politics as usual" and whose mainspring of action is a will to power. In what I believe is a more balanced account, William Frost (pp. 297–98) has written:

> Theseus is the executant of destiny. . . . As a personality he is appropriately impressive: terrifying in action, philosophical in outlook; richly experienced yet detached in point of view; warmly sympathetic to misfortune yet mockingly ironical at the expense of youthful enthusiasm. From the moment when he gives orders that the captured knights be imprisoned to the moment when he arranges the final nuptials of Emelye and Palamon he dominates the plot.

He dominates the plot. In the beginning he undertakes and wins the campaign against Thebes, he decrees that there shall be no ransom for the royal kinsmen and damns them to prison perpetually, he decides to free Arcite and sets the limitations upon that freedom. In the middle, Theseus halts the fighting

---

2. Stuart Robertson, "Elements of Realism in the 'Knight's Tale,'" *JEGP* 14 (1915) : 226.

3. Henry J. Webb, "A Reinterpretation of Chaucer's Theseus," *RES* 23 (1947) : 289, 296.

between Palamon and Arcite and orders the issue to be decided by tournament. He then "gooth so bisily / To maken up the lystes roially." He fixes the terms of the contest. In the end, he arranges Arcite's funeral and he marries off Emily to the survivor. Throughout, he "gooth so bisily" to make up the crucial arrangements that condition most of the poem's events.

This career of decision, of action, almost balances the disposal of Palamon, Arcite, and Emily in all of their lives and in the death of one, the images of desolation, impotence, and imprisonment, and the lavish comment on the inescapability of destiny. If Theseus does not quite manage to tip thematic emphasis from the necessities and constrictions of suffering to the possibilities of virtuosity in action, still he is not only free and responsible but also often effectual. He is actor, not patient, an example not only of human possibility but also of human achievement. This statement must be qualified, but in the large he is a worthy exemplar of action as a protagonistic ideal. I propose to attend to the means by which Chaucer so establishes his Theseus, then to look at the limits he makes Theseus confront, and finally to consider what the poem's development records of alteration in his magisterial figure.

It has always been remarked that Chaucer gives much less of Theseus as an extrovert than was available to him. Boccaccio details the campaign against the Amazons and the rather brusque wooing that closes it. It is some time before Palamon and Arcita appear in the *Teseida*, which is so named for reason, if perhaps an insufficient one.[4] Chaucer has not only focused his story more sharply on the two knights; his interest in Theseus is of a different kind from Boccaccio's. Chaucer's Theseus is a warrior and a conqueror; a few firm strokes so define him, but the validating details are curtailed. What Boccaccio presents as scene, Chaucer gives in crisp summary. Without the speeches with which Boccaccio embellishes the meeting of Creon and Teseo, Theseus dispatches the tyrant:

4. An English summary of the *Teseida* with notations of parallels in Chaucer appears in *Sources and Analogues of Chaucer's Canterbury Tales* (1941), ed. W. F. Bryan and Germaine Dempster (New York: Humanities, 1958). There is no full English translation.

> With Creon, which that was of Thebes kyng,
> He faught, and slough hym manly as a knyght
> In pleyn bataille . . .

[986–88]

And this is all we have about Theseus in the field, because Chaucer is interested in Theseus not so much as a soldier but as a governor; and what attention he accords Theseus the soldier goes to the commander, not the swordsman. For Chaucer, Theseus is a man of action because he makes decisions and has the power and the will to enforce them. He is "this conqueror," and "this governor." Not only is Theseus physically (martially) and politically more powerful than the young princes, but also he is older and wiser than they; he is the rational man. And this also makes him an actor rather than a sufferer, one who does things rather than one to whom things are done.

The bases, then, that Chaucer provides Theseus as a protagonist of action are these: physical power, force (he won the war, Creon's knights did not); political power, the kingship; and a relative moral disinterestedness which comes to him not only because he is thoughtful and intelligent but also because, older than Palamon and Arcite, he is past susceptibility to most of their motives and cues for passion. The first two factors are apparent early. Quite apart from his mythic redolence which Chaucer mainly ignores, Theseus is no everyman. Only one side's warriors win the wars and only one man in a monarchial system—under any system, few in relation to the whole—may be duke and governor. But for all men it is true that the substantiation of decision in action depends upon power or, less purely, leverage of some kind—muscle, magic, or money, depending upon the cultural ambience—that permits men to jostle the rocks of their world or to set its wheels in motion. (Can one venture that the realm the Franklin's Tale inhabits is more advanced than that in the Knight's Tale because it requires expertise, that is magic and money, to move the rocks in the former, whereas the story in the Knight's Tale moves mainly at the instance of muscle, at least at the human level?) Action without power is stillborn as intention, does not become deed: "al þat is do with owt myght, it lakkith the dignite and the name of the dede, and it is called passion" (see above, p. 33). Chaucer emphasizes the most crude and brutal distinctions as functions of raw political power. Theseus is at the human apex of the poem's world, Palamon and Arcite at the bottom, first literally at the bottom of a pile of bodies, because he won and they lost. Theseus acts and the Theban princes suffer. He is free and they are unfree; so he lives in his castle and they live in his prison.

This iteration of the overt character of the action-suffering antithesis as between the tale's characters has for its excuse that Chaucer also insists upon it, as in the lines when the two barely-alive royal youths are carried to the tent of Theseus, and the duke disposes of them:

> . . . he ful soone hem sente
> To Atthenes, to dwellen in prisoun
> Perpetuelly,—he nolde no raunsoun.
> And whan this worthy duc hath thus ydon,
> He took his hoost, and hoom he rit anon
> With laurer crowned as a conquerour;
> And there he lyveth in joye and in honour
> Terme of his lyf; what nedeth wordes mo?
> And in a tour, in angwissh and in wo,
> This Palamon and his felawe Arcite
> For everemoore; ther may no gold hem quite.
>
> [1022–32]

The grammar and disposition of verse enforce the contrast. Chaucer makes the principal verb about Theseus—*lyveth*—serve also for the languishment of Palamon and Arcite.[5] The zeugma joins an antithesis of joy and honor and anguish and woe. Theseus "lyveth" in one way, the captive knights so completely in another. Affective nouns summarize a host of concrete, daily differences. The (apparent) permanence of their respective conditions is iterated and metrically balanced down to the syllable, each occurrence occupying the emphatic

5. Several MSS have "dwellen" in line 1031, erasing the zeugma—although not the contrast. See John M. Manly and Edith Rickert, eds., *The Text of the Canterbury Tales* (University of Chicago, 1940), 3 : 47 and 427n.

opening position in its verse: "Terme of his lyf," takes up the two feet before the caesura in the duke's line, and "Perpetuelly" and "For everemoore" take up the same breathing space in the flanking verses (1024 and 1032) devoted to Palamon and Arcite. These lines are completed with the same information, the refusal of ransom, first from the viewpoint of the duke ("he nolde no raunsoun") and then from that of the prisoners: "ther may no gold hem quite."

The surrounding context has also emphasized the power of the victor. Theseus "dide with al the contree as hym leste." As he takes his ease in the defeated city, his pillagers ransack it. The power and the impotence are strongly put. Active and passive verbs in the lines quoted above and those that immediately precede them correspond to agent-patient roles. In four of five references to the knights they are direct objects, grammatically as well as narratively receivers of the action. The two are "torn" from the heap of bodies by "pilours," and then carried to the tent of Theseus. Theseus, however, is the subject of the verbs "sente," "nolde," "ydon," "took," "rit," and "lyveth."

Chaucer's swift narration also emphasizes Theseus as actor, compressing what Boccaccio disperses over many stanzas into one syntactical sequence that in a spate of verbs tells of the duke's acts. "But shortly for to speken of this thyng" introduces a single sentence in which Theseus fights with Creon, kills him, puts the people to flight, wins the city by assault, rends "adoun bothe wall and sparre and rafter," and restores to the ladies the bones of their husbands:

> But shortly for to speken of this thyng,
> With Creon, which that was of Thebes kyng,
> He faught, and slough hym manly as a knyght
> In pleyn bataille, and putte the folk to flyght;
> And by assaut he wan the citee after,
> And rente adoun bothe wall and sparre and rafter;
> And to the ladyes he restored agayn
> The bones of hir housbondes that were slayn,
> To doon obsequies, as was tho the gyse.

[985–93]

The poet's briskness in relating the campaign becomes, for the reader, the dispatch of Theseus in fighting it.

Chaucer's alteration of Boccaccio to have Theseus take the city by assault and his mention of ransom have been cited as examples of medieval realism. They also help form the more ruthless picture Chaucer gives of the Theban campaign and of the duke, too; perhaps not so much of Theseus himself as of the situation of a military conqueror. For at this same point in the *Teseida,* Boccaccio's attention is more personal, has riveted upon Teseo as a heroic, conscientious individual. As he has fought Creon primarily for the impiety in the refusal to allow burial rites, Teseo himself takes care to gather up the bodies of the dead in *this* battle and properly to inter them. On his way back he stops at a temple to offer thanks for victory. Chaucer omits this homecoming, although it includes matter apt for pointed antithesis between action and suffering. But although Boccaccio makes the progress home a kind of Roman triumph with the young knights paraded as captives, he does not exploit this for pathos or emphasize the powerlessness of Palamon and Arcita. It is rather pageantry, a part of a sumptuously cere- monial return, a prelude to the greeting of the queen, the en- counter with Teseo's father, the rites paid the gods.[6] Boc- caccio later specifies that the captives, in deference to their "sangue reale" (2.99), are given handsome treatment in prison.

In Chaucer's poem as a whole the epithets applied to Theseus vis-à-vis those for the captives join their force to the effects of syntax and compression. Epithets and substantives of adjectival color throughout direct attention to the situa- tion, not the individual. Because they are prisoners, Palamon and Arcite are "woeful," "wrecched," and "sorrowful." (Arcite does garner a greater variety of personal epithets than Pala-

6. Boccaccio, *Teseida,* ed. Salvatore Battaglia (Florence: G. C. Sansoni, 1938), 2.92–93. All citations are from this edition; translations are my own. Perhaps Chaucer cuts the triumph because he wants to get more immediately to the love story. Boccaccio again refers to the triumph when he describes the frieze with which Palamon adorns a memorial temple to Arcita, and here there is emphasis on the wretchedness of captivity. This shift in disposition presumably is justified in that Arcita is the center of interest in the mural; in book 2, Boccaccio is still primarily telling the story of Teseo.

mon, who is "hardy" and "gentil," even "the gentil man."
Arcite is "yong," which Boccaccio also mentions several times,
"strong," "fierce," and, a new development when his death is
imminent, "goode," also said of him posthumously.) The
epithets and attributive substantives of the duke stress political
power. In the first part he is four times referred to as a "conqueror," called "worthy" three times, "noble" twice, and
"gentil," "governor," and "lord" once each. This word-
counting of itself offers little. Chaucer's treatment of complex
metaphoric and sustained imagery is skillful; his analytic
simple imagery (that represented by adjectives), if central and
sometimes brilliant, is more often conventional. But disposal
of epithets does second the contrast everywhere marked between the duke and the heroes.

In sum, Theseus projects his presence, firmness, and puissance as he comes triumphantly home to Athens, listens to the
appeal, and, sending his conquered queen home, turns aside
from Athens, riding directly to besiege Thebes, wins that war,
and disposes of the prisoners. Before refining upon the relation
of agent to patient, Chaucer gives a straightforward version of
it; before expressing the limits and illusions of action, he presents a narrative that tells at its outset chiefly of action on the
one hand and suffering, having actions done to one, on the
other. But the forthright victor, the conquering soldier of
part 1 we are to see further on as the bemused and sometimes
amused, the reflective, and finally saddened sovereign. One
linear movement of the Knight's Tale is the shaking of the
duke's confidence in purposeful action.

Some ambiguities of life as action rest implicit in the first
scene, the duke's brilliant processional home in triumph after
the Amazonian campaign with his captive bride and her shining young sister. As the Knight's Tale is the only one among
the *Canterbury Tales* with an epigraph (apart from sermonic
tales of Pardoner and Parson), let us begin there. The quota-
tion is from Statius, and the complete sentence of which
Chaucer gives the beginning is:

> Iamque domos patrias Scythicae post aspera gentis
> proelia laurigero subeuntem Thesea curru

laetifici plausus missusque ad sidera vulgi
clamor et emeritis hilaris tuba nuntiat armis.

[*Thebaid* 12. 519–22]

[And now Theseus, drawing near his native land in laurelled
chariot after bitter fighting with the Scythians, is heralded by
glad applause and the heaven-flung shout of the people and
the merry trump announces warfare ended.]

The knight begins with an equivalent fanfare-effect. Theseus
has just won a war, just married, and is bringing his bride
home with "muchel glorie and greet solempnytee" (870); they
ride toward Athens "with victorie and with melodye" (872), his
armed host riding beside him. For a reader who knew the
Thebaid the legend would redouble the victorious, festal note.
One who did not would be reassured: this is apparently an
established, fertile "olde felde." Obviously too, glamor and
magnitude of gesture are in the offing, for the very first thing
to happen seems to be some momentous victory.[7]

In Chaucer this mood, this élan, is quickly qualified. Although flushed "In al his wele and in his mooste pride," the
duke is aware, "as he caste his eye aside," of mourning ladies,
suppliants from another campaign which has nothing, as yet,
to do with him. With human egoism, he first thinks of them
from his own point of view. He wants to help, but who are
these women whose harsh cries disturb his feast? Do these
wailing ladies so much envy him? Here is the context:

This duc, of whom I make mencioun,
Whan he was come almoost unto the toun,
In al his wele and in his mooste pride,
He was war, as he caste his eye aside,
Where that ther kneled in the heighe weye
A compaignye of ladyes, tweye and tweye,
Ech after oother, clad in clothes blake;
But swich a cry and swich a wo they make
That in this world nys creature lyvynge
That herde swich another waymentynge;

7. Recent criticism has been attentive to Chaucer's fashioning of his
poems for oral delivery to a contemporary audience. Such an audience,
of course, would not attend to the resonance of an epigraph, and the
performer, even if he were Chaucer himself, might well omit to give it.

> And of this cry they nolde nevere stenten
> Til they the reynes of his brydel henten.
>   "What folk been ye, that at myn homcomynge
> Perturben so my feste with criynge?"
> Quod Theseus. "Have ye so greet envye
> Of myn honour, that thus compleyne and crye?
> Or who hath yow mysboden or offended?
> And telleth me if it may been amended,
> And why that ye been clothed thus in blak."
>
> [893–911]

Immediately, before he is forty lines into the poem, the reader is confronted with the close juxtaposition of nuptial and funeral, of victory and defeat, which is to lurk throughout. The antithesis between the kneeling, bereaved women and the mounted, victorious duke, they just widowed, he just married, seems complete. But Ypolita is there, and she is involved in both triumph and defeat. To be sure Chaucer's interest in Ypolita is not quick, but her case does suggest the complex interplay of action and suffering; and there is also a confusion that penetrates to the motivations of Theseus himself.

His situation apparently is that of any man on his most sunny day—still subliminally aware, if sensitive, of an area of shadow, of affliction on the margin of his glory, good feeling, or mere ease. Here, however, the sufferers are importunate, and they are strong enough to interrupt the combined triumph and wedding procession. They "the reynes of his brydel henten." And Theseus is different from the average man of middling good will in that he is in a position to do something about the suffering he sees. And he does. Theseus, then, is ostensibly the doer, the agent. The women are apparently sufferers. They receive injury from Creon, they receive redress from Theseus. But they have transformed the nature of this occasion, imposed their mourning upon his feast. Paradoxically it is their suffering which prompts his action. Which of course entails more suffering, this time to the heroes and, less prominently but still the narrator remarks the fact, to all the defeated Thebans. The hand on the bridle is a juncture where the roles between actor and sufferer may be seen almost visibly to pivot. (Traditional associations of horsemanship with command may underlie the gesture. One remembers the foreshadowing touch of Diomede's grasp upon the bridle of Criseyde's horse.)

The scene gives us grounds to infer that the relations of suffering to action are apt to be dynamic, not necessarily confinable, nor predictable, nor straightforward. They may or may not be reciprocal. An action may boomerang, and that, at least, might be poetic justice; but it may also ricochet (as in this episode), start a chain reaction, or spread its results messily about, like a stain in water.

That passion inhibits or deflects rational action was discovered to be a common medieval and Renaissance theme. Theseus is a case in point: the actor by every obvious criterion, he is in the opening scene in a more fundamental way the patient, the one who "suffers" the suffering of the troop of women. His own emotional nature, which makes him susceptible to the dissonantly mourning ladies, checks him. He possesses those qualities of the ruler summed up as *fortitudo et sapientia* (Chaucer's words are an equivalent "wysdom" and "chivalrie").[8] Still, not these, but his unfree passional nature, sets his choice: Pity, if not fear, enlists him to act. (One cannot discard the motive of fear, either, in Aristotle's sense, for the exposed bones of those that "whilom weren of so greet estaat" is, for Theseus the ruler, the spectacle of misfortune to those who are like himself.)

It may be objected that an argument should not lean heavily upon a scene that Chaucer so largely takes from Boccaccio. For Teseo also feels "greve duol" when he hears that sad story of death and dishonor to kings; he also responds tenderly to the bereaved women; and he is sobered by the imposing spectacle of pride leveled:

> L'abito oscuro e 'l piangere angoscioso,
> e 'l voi conoscer pe' vostri maggiori,
> e 'l ricordarmi il vostro esser pomposo,

8. "Chivalrie" could refer to a knight's personal qualities; to the military system; or to the body of soldiery. In the tale it most often appears to mean not so much the personal *fortitudo* of Theseus as his force as a leader of a body of troops.

gli agi e' diletti e' regni e' servidori
e de' re vostri il regnar glorioso,
hanno trovato ne' miei sommi onori
luogo a' vostri prieghi, e la mutata
fortuna trista di lieta tornata.

[2. 37]

[Your dark garments and painful weeping, what one knows of
your great ancestors, and remembers of your pride, your com-
forts, your pleasures, your kingdoms, your followers and of
your kings' glorious reign, have made me hear your appeals
and have changed your fortune from bad to good.]

Chaucer keeps details down to the suppliants' dark clothing.
Still the tone is different, the crucial change being that the narrator tells the response as *inward:*

This gentil duc doun from his courser sterte
With herte pitous, whan he herde hem speke.
Hym thoughte that his herte wolde breke,
Whan he saugh hem so pitous and so maat,
That whilom weren of so greet estaat.

[952–56]

Making internal what Teseo *announces* erases the faint aura
of histrionic, official sentiment. The scene, less dramatic, is
more felt and more authoritative. Furthermore, the response
of Theseus is not casual, merely a part of the given plot, but
is made characteristic and thematic. We are not allowed to
doubt that Theseus is the kind of man easily moved to pity nor
that intercessions may succeed. Chaucer will reinforce this
episode: an important intercession leads to Arcite's limited
freedom when Perotheus visits "his felawe" Theseus and re-
quests enfranchisement for his other friend; Theseus pities the
Theban women, his queen and her companions, and women
in general; Saturn, on request, will see that Venus gets her way.

The second variation may claim attention here, for it sets
forth firmly that third basis (beyond power on the field or in
the city) for the status of Theseus as agent—his rationality.

The scene is the duke's interruption of the fight between Palamon and Arcite. The case is more complicated than the first where the pity of Theseus is so quick and so lavish. When Theseus comes upon the battling knights and learns that one is an escaped prisoner and one a former prisoner who has insinuated himself into his household under a false name, he is furious. But then he stops to think, and Chaucer gives us an account of a mind in debate with itself. Although we apprehend the ratiocination of several characters, notably in the prayers before the tournament, these are characteristically the mental processes of persons intent on getting something they want or avoiding something not wanted. Their minds are made up. With Theseus, we see a mind making itself up.

It is virtually an interior monologue: turning from his fury, the duke considers how natural it is to help oneself in love or out of prison if one can; it occurs to him that a ruler should have clemency; and he is amused by the tumult over a girl who does not even know of "al this hoote fare"—it takes him back to when he was a servant of love; moreover, the queen, Emily, and the whole troop of ladies on the hunt beg him to pardon the two heroes. He regards Ipolyta, Emily, and the company of kneeling women, for he has a gentle heart, one quick to pity, and he is always compassionate of women. The immediate situation, the fact that both have flouted his authority, the appeal, memories that link him with the lovers, his convictions about what a ruler should be, his settled disposition—all these are presented in a natural and convincing account. Emotional and rational factors are both in play, and Theseus *chooses* his course—is more clearly the actor than in the scene with the Greek ladies where the physical action and its consequences are overt and dramatic.

Very little of this is from Boccaccio. There the women do not intervene (although Emilia, who finds the knights fighting, has summoned Teseo). There is no authorial comment that Teseo's ire accused and his reason excused the combatants, no reflections on the good ruler. Rather, a less deliberative, if rather more pious, duke says that to execute the men, as

Palamon has somewhat officiously counseled, would not be pleasing to God (5. 91). Further:

> Ma però, ch'io già innamorato fui
> e per amor sovente folleggiai,
> me' è caro molto il perdonare altrui.

[5. 92]

[Moreover, because I have been in love in my time and for love often did foolish things, it is the more fitting for me to pardon others.]

Teseo's past as a lover is what Chaucer keeps. This is important, too, for age—maturity—is one of the duke's advantages. He is past the importunities of courtly passion, though he remembers them. Both that he had this experience, and that it is over, make him free to be the rational man.

In Chaucer's considerable elaboration, the appeal of the women is most conspicuous. Critics pondering the interstices of the two narratives for clues to authorial intention or dating have found this to be a courtier's tribute to a queenly act, perhaps Queen Philippa's intervention on behalf of the six citizens of Calais, or Queen Anne's intercession for all offenders in 1382, or that to Gloucester in 1388 when she prayed, reportedly like Ipolyta on her knees, for the life of her husband's friend, Sir Simon Burley. Gloucester's callousness then would be an inverse model for Theseus.[9]

The acts of either queen may have been in Chaucer's mind. Such an allusion would enrich the poem topically. And the episode also contributes to defining model authority, adding political extension to the poem. Theseus' reflections on the lord "that wol have no mercy, / But been a leon, bothe in word and dede" are proximate. Does the Knight's Tale include a miniature mirror of a prince? Snippets about Theseus could be pieced into a sketch of what a prince should be: he will be fierce in war, but mild in peace; he will make sure his enemies cannot harm him, or he will oblige them so they will remain

---

9. See Robinson, p. 675, note on line 1748; John Matthews Manly, ed., *Canterbury Tales*, by Geoffrey Chaucer (New York: Henry Holt, 1928), pp. 548–49, note on line 1748; Johnstone Parr, "The Date and Revision of Chaucer's *Knight's Tale*," *PMLA* 60 (1945) : 317.

his friends; he will provide the populace with spectacular entertainments; he will build shrines to the gods; he will not
pursue a course mechanically, but will consider circumstances
and look to motives. ("That lord hath litel of discrecioun,/
That in swich cas kan no divisioun, / But weyeth pride and
humblesse after oon" [1779–81].)

But pressing for the historic parallel (even if it were possible
to make a certain identification) and canvassing general political interest are not the nearest ways to account for the variance
from Boccaccio. Whether the material came from life or not,
it strengthens the character of Theseus as he is introduced
and adds to that first impression one of a more sophisticated,
more considerate man; and it gives saliency to the motif of
intercession, referring back to the supplicating widows and the
Perotheus episode and pointing forward toward Saturn's
pliancy.

For Chaucer's anthropomorphic god is as susceptible as
Theseus is. Saturn does as a weeping Venus wants in contriv-
ing Arcite's fatal injury. In the *Teseida,* there is no appeal
to Saturn nor need for it. That Venus is quite able to manage
alone. When the jousting ends with Palamon's capture, she
informs Mars that his part is finished and then fetches Erines
to frighten Arcita's mount (11. 2–7). Venus does not do her
own dirty work, but there is no suggestion that she needs a
male strategist to plan it. Historic parallels help little with
this fourth, heavenly, scherzo version of intercession.

The version centering on Theseus furnishes a transition
from the duke as implacable victor to the ruler who mercifully
bans lethal weapons in a tournament, the duke as "swich a
lord, that is so good, / He wilneth no destruccion of blood!"
(2563–64). The first book presents primarily the destroyer of
Thebes; the last, the "gentil" lord. In the woods scene Theseus
seesaws between vengeance and mercy and opts for the latter.
I do not think Theseus changes here; rather, different circumstances call forth differing behaviors.

However, a significant change does occur in Theseus himself;
this begins a year later with the tournament and his ban on
lethal weapons. What is this change? The motives of the duke

in setting the tournament and in decreeing that it be fought
under restriction are good. When he stopped the savage duel
between Palamon and Arcite, he exercised mercy, empathy,
and discretion. When he decided to have the two fight in a
tournament, he did what perhaps is all that the wisest ruler
can do—set up the conditions for a free competition between
merits, that is, for the pursuit of happiness. Neatly, his building of the tournament theater, that marvelously elaborate
fictive architecture, gives the exact physical equivalent of what
his decision gives the Theban lovers—ordered space for clash
and resolution. If we suspend belief in the tale as fiction, if
we consider it as open-ended, we must grant that Theseus
might have resolved the conflict in a number of more conclusive, less modest ways. He might have awarded Emily to either
knight or neither, returned both to prison, executed both,
freed one and returned the other to prison, freed but exiled
both, etc. But the use of power is palpably restrained; Theseus
merely provides an arrangement so that "ech of yow shal have
his destynee / As hym is shape" (1842–43). He will give
"Emelya to wyve / To whom that Fortune yeveth so fair a
grace" (1860–61). At the tournament this impartiality continues. Promptly when Palamon is taken, Theseus stops the
fighting:

> . . . "Hoo! namoore, for it is doon!
> I wol be trewe juge, and no partie.
> Arcite of Thebes shal have Emelie,
> That by his fortune hath hire faire ywonne."
>
> [2656–59]

But as all readers know, Arcite of Thebes does not have Emily
because he is soon dead.

When events stultify well-intended policies it should give
pause. Theseus had wanted to save all the knights, but one of
the best dies. He had wanted to give his sister-in-law to the
winner, but the loser survives to receive her. And the tournament itself as an instrument for selection is suspect, for Arcite
himself did not take "unyolden" Palamon; that feat required
twenty good men. For merit there is little to choose between

the sides; and Theseus himself judges (though perhaps partly in tact) "The gree as wel of o syde as of oother." "Aventure" decides who wins. "Aventure" has been a recurrent motif, chiefly as regards the affairs of Palamon and Arcite. The word appears frequently—Palamon first sees Emily "by aventure or cas" (1074); Arcite refers to his love as "myn aventure" (1160) and advises Palamon that they must endure in prison, taking each his "aventure" (1186); when Arcite is freed, Palamon fears that "som aventure" will put his rival in position to gain Emily. "By aventure" Arcite goes to exactly that grove where Palamon is to find him (1506), and it is by "aventure" that "this Palamoun / Was in a bussh" nearby (1516–17). That Theseus arrives at their duel is yet another "aventure"— though the narrator here does not use the word, but talks rather of "destinee" (1663). "Aventure" settles the tournament, and so far Theseus must be amenable; then "aventure" un-settles the settlement: "For fallyng nys nat but an aventure" (2722). What does a ruler do if the world itself is random?

The ban on lethal weapons is for Theseus the moral climax of events that began when the suppliants interrupted his wedding feast. Up to the tournament he has been not only victorious but easily, stylishly so. Chaucer subordinates his legendary triumphs, but reminds us of the crowded, rich heroic life beside which the matter of Palamon and Arcite must seem a detail: the conquest of the "regne of Femenye," gratifyingly renewed in mind by the gracious presence of a human sou-venir, his queen; the leveling of Thebes, and an older victory over more primitive forces, commemorated in the embroidered image of the Minotaur on the golden gonfalon. He has always gotten what he wants. Now he wants "to shapen that they shal nat dye" (2541). Nonetheless, Arcite is killed.

Chaucer handles the decree scene in a tone curiously fluc-tuating toward bravura, a glancingly comic treatment that never steadies enough to make the reader's response secure. We know how disconcerting Chaucer's tone can be, the local risks he is willing to take. The account of Arcite's death, shift-ing between the narrator's brisk, assured nosography and the hero's bewildered, questioning philosophy is perhaps the most egregious example in the Knight's Tale. But the decree scene is also a little peculiar. The reader may heartily approve of the ban, he may feel he should go along with the enthusiastic populace in their admiration for Theseus; but Chaucer does not make him feel like doing so wholeheartedly. What Chaucer has somehow arranged is a scene that not only pictures a magnanimous Theseus as he appears to others—and as he quite sincerely is—but that also hints of a partly illusive self-image. To name what happens irony is technically inexact, for Chaucer is not saying one thing and meaning another. He is saying one thing and meaning it but also meaning something unsaid; and this further range of implication is what deflects, discourages slightly, the reader's proper, stereotyped reaction.

The early iteration of "conqueror"—innocent in each single context—works in the same way, making the reader feel that he is not only seeing in Theseus someone very splendid but also someone very aware that he is splendid. The duke's early illusion, and one events tend to confirm, is that he is an invincible dealer of death. His illusion in the decree scene is that he presides over life; but events do not conform. The references to Theseus as a conqueror disappear, but those to his will and power remain salient, coming with high frequency in the decree scene:

> Duc Theseus was at a wyndow set,
> Arrayed right as he were *a god in trone*.
> The peple preesseth thiderward ful soone
> Hym for to seen, and doon heigh reverence,
> And eek to herkne *his heste* and *his sentence*.
> And heraud on a scaffold made on "Oo!"
> Til al the noyse of peple was ydo,
> And whan he saugh the peple of noyse al stille,
> Tho shewed he *the myghty dukes wille*.
> "The lord hath of *his heigh discrecioun*
> Considered that it were destruccioun
> To gentil blood to fighten in the gyse
> Of mortal bataille now in this emprise.
> Wherfore, *to shapen* that they shal nat dye,
> He wol his firste purpos modifye."
>
> [2528–42; my italics]

Specific regulations on weapons follow, the herald concluding: "Gooth now youre wey, *this is the lordes wille*" (my italics). The applause is satisfactory:

> The voys of peple touchede the hevene,
> So loude cride they with murie stevene,
> "God save swich a lord, that is so good,
> He wilneth no destruccion of blood!"
>
> [2561–64]

Then the retinue rides grandly off. Throughout, the play upon the will of Theseus is insistent (see the phrases I have italicized). Sometimes the vocabulary borrows from that associated with divinity. Scattered before and in proximate following lines come other affirmations of the virtue or might of Theseus.

Proving delicate irony is difficult. One can only appeal to other readers to compare another description:

> Whan they were set, and hust was al the place,
> And Theseus abiden hadde a space
> Er any word cam fram his wise brest,
> His eyen sette he ther as was his lest,
> And with a sad visage he siked stille,
> And after that right thus he seyde his wille.
>
> [2981–86]

The total respect of the narrator is now with Theseus, and there is scant reference, serious or inflected, to his power, as the duke hesitates before his final exercise of it in the poem.

The hesitation is an acute contrast to his impetuosity in the case of the suppliant widows. One had known a Theseus whose aplomb seemed capable of surviving any strain. And this pause before disposition of his dependents comes "certeyn yeres" after the tournament. The interval is not in Boccaccio, where wedding follows hard upon funeral, Teseo even specifying that he wishes the ceremonies to be held before tournament guests depart. For Boccaccio wants to stress how quickly man rejoices after sorrow, how easily he puts it away. Boccaccio's people are not indifferent. Teseo mourns, but more quickly than his English epigon he can say,

> E però far della necessitate
> virtù, quando bisogna, è sapienza,
> e il contraro è chiara vanitate.

[12. 11]

[But to make a virtue of necessity when one must is wisdom, and the opposite plain vanity.]

And so this wisdom seems less hard-won, more simply pragmatic. It is not so clearly the product of the precise, personal experiences of this duke in this poem. The people rejoice at the wedding, and Boccaccio remarks that already Arcita is obliterated from every mind. Everyone waits only for, thinks only of the coming wedding day (12. 48).

But in the English story everyone is heavily conscious of Arcite, and sorrow stains and mutes the sobered regathering that hears Theseus' final speech with its cosmic commitment to love and resignation. Chaucer gives short measure to the wedding (elaborate in Boccaccio, and preceded by an expansive catalogue of Emilia's revived charms).[10] The comparison is not intended to belittle Boccaccio but to point to the different direction of Chaucer's significant shaping. This difference is well symbolized by Palamon's omitting, in Boccaccio, from the temple friezes commemorating Arcita, a scene of the accident:

> Solo la sua caduta da cavallo
> gli uscì di mente né vi fu segnata:
> credo che' fati voller senza fallo,
> acciò che mai non fosse ricordata;
> ma non poté la gente amenticallo,
> sì nel cor era di ciascuno entrata
> con greve doglia, sì era in amore
> di ciascheduno il giovane amadore.

[11. 88]

[The fall from the horse alone he put out of his mind, nor did he record it there. I think that fate prompted this so that

10. Even in Boccaccio the wedding does not *seem* hasty, for the account of Arcita's death is leisured; his funeral is handled alike spaciously, and his commemoration includes Palamon's building a temple and adorning it with Arcita's history, so between funeral and feast the poet reviews almost the whole of his lengthy poem.

it should never be remembered. But the people could not forget because it had entered everybody's mind so grievously and sadly and because everybody loved the young lover so much.]

This is one way of survival—to amputate from memory those memories at the heart of the loss. Folk consolation offers a home remedy: you must not dwell on this. Surgery offers lobotomy. By the omission, Boccaccio's Palamon also settles on the most troubling part of the experience, the inexplicable accident.

But Chaucer through Theseus offers a different therapy, one that includes and fully acknowledges the crisis, the numbing defeat, and then goes on without being numbed, without pretending nothing has been lost. I would like to suggest that Theseus needs to take more time in ordering the wedding than does Teseo. It is not merely precise observance of courtly decencies. The death of Arcite has followed the well-meant decree with what must seem to Theseus a preposterous irrelevance. He is thwarted, and not in his career of taking life, but in his precautions to spare it. He is brought to consider the worth of action in a world over which Fortune presides, the worth of power and the power of good will in it. "We witen nat what thing we preyen heere," Arcite has mournfully observed. The duke's case is parallel, but the more poignant and pressing because of his responsibility for action.

When the tournament's winner loses, the reversal presents Theseus with a radical decision. He must decide whether to live in the way he is used to doing or change his life. A ruler, this means that he must continue to act or must abdicate. Theseus does not abdicate—one motive for calling the final parliament is to "have fully of Thebans obeisaunce"—but now he must act without confidence that actions will bring appropriate results, without the illusions which give action savor. When things go awry, he goes on. Heavily he had arranged the ceremonial funeral of "goode Arcite"; after an interval of years and in a mood severely remote from that appropriate to a romance's happy ending, he nonetheless provides that ending, calls a silent Palamon to court, and arranges the wedding with Emily.[11] Theseus makes the best arrangement with what is left, with those who are left. Saturn's frivolity and partiality have countered his impartial and serious good will, and Saturn is stronger. Not so much whirl as whim is king and might suitably be inscribed over the gateway lintels of the tournament theater. To be sure, Theseus has not the reader's view into the councils of the gods; if he had, his midnight's and his noon's repose would be the more disturbed.

What of the gods in the tale? Ultimately, there is the "Firste Moevere of the cause above," that "Prince and that Moevere" whom Theseus explains to have made the "faire cheyne of love" that binds the cosmos. Theseus identifies him as "Juppiter, the kyng" (3035) who is to be thanked "of al his grace" (3069). This is most consoling; but if Chaucer wished to equate Jupiter with God and to separate Jupiter's providential dispensation from arrangements worked out by lesser gods, he has not been clear about it. Theseus is not the only character to name Jupiter. Dying, Arcite prays that "Juppiter so wys" (2786) may guide his soul, and he hopes that Jupiter may "have of my soule part" (2792). But the narrator reports another psychopomp at this soul's passover: "Arcite is coold, ther Mars his soule gye" (2815).[12] This evasiveness, the slippery transition from Jupiter to Mars (is it even intentional?) is congruent in this tale, where, in extraordinary degree, incompletions, failures in cogency, discrepancy, mark the encounter of human and divine realms.

Even before the duke's reference to the First Mover, the tale has invited scrutiny of the ways of God to man, and his admired Boethian speech is usually considered an affirmative resolution of the problem as it is embodied in the poem. Dale

11. The fatal accident had arrested Palamon as well as Theseus. The change in Palamon is not one to be positive about. Theseus is articulate. Palamon, suddenly, is not. He does not once speak after Arcite's fall.

12. This remark either reflects back to Arcite's hope in Jupiter and is thus a comment on the uncaring gods, or it is a reflection on Arcite's unfortunate prayer to Mars: "You prayed to him, now see what it does for you." The inherent callousness of either is akin to that of the possibility that the dreamed shape of Mercury was sadistic when it tells Arcite in exile to come to Athens where "is thee shapen of thy wo an ende" (1392).

Underwood (p. 468), using the speech's perspective, writes that the chain of love is restored in the ending, for Arcite renews the bond of human brotherhood with Palamon, and thus, in the divine chain of love, the bond between man and man; Theseus renews the bond between man and God; and Palamon's wedding renews the bond of peace between man and woman and also between Thebes and Athens, between groups of men in society. But Elizabeth Salter (pp. 34–36) questions whether the proposition of Theseus that "nature hath nat taken his bigynnyng / Of no partie or cantel of a thyng, / But of a thyng that parfit is and stable" (3007–09) helps to make acceptable "the sinister dealings of the divine with the human." She traces the movement of the speech from a high, philosophical beginning to its dwindling off in a "list of useful points." In a brisk ending "Theseus bids us to cast-off sorrow and 'thanken Juppiter of al his grace'. If we feel the irony of the phrase as a description of Jupiter's ways, we are quickly led on to other things. The speech, which began in so elevated a manner, passes almost without notice into the narrator's soothing voice as he says goodbye to the story." The eloquence of the duke is clear, but masks confusion: "what is debatable is the wisdom of invoking 'the Firste Moevere of the cause above', with its inevitable Christian associations, to cover the activities of Mars, Venus and Saturn in this particular poem."

For not Jupiter but Saturn is the actual god of the machine —"Eld," old Chaos—dotty and fond, capricious and lethal, not remotely interested in human rescues and ransoms. If the reader were to judge by Saturn's behavior, the answer to Palamon's question would have to be yes, the gods are as indifferent as if men were sheep. The gods' mutterings and incarnate statues in the temples, their council, their efficiency about earthquakes—these do have a vital, local life. Diana seems absurd but still appropriately accomplished in her method of departure: "And forth she wente, and made a vanysshynge" (2360). Saturn's pliancy and the chagrin of Venus have found a colloquial language: "She seyde, 'I am ashamed, doutelees.' / Saturnus seyde, 'Doghter, hoold thy pees!'" (2667–68). But when the gods get down to work they are shown up.

Morally, what is owed *these* gods? How seriously are we to take them? Only Diana, who straightforwardly cuts off Emily's hope to remain single, seems to be minding the store like a responsible merchant of destiny (2348–51). To the reader who is privy to their councils, it looks not as if the fates are immutable because of divine foresight but as if they are hastily improvised to compensate for divine oversights. The gods are not ashamed to act out one of those riddles that depend upon the winner's wary scrutiny of its language (Inchme and Pinchme went down to the river. Inchme fell in. Who is left?). Having by the game's rules been led to suppose the tournament victor will possess Emily, Arcite makes the mistake of praying for victory. He prays to Mars not so much as the god of war but as the lover of Venus; this seems to preclude the common argument that Arcite values war over love.[13] The gods take advantage of this verbal slip, keeping their promises by a shabby technicality. Arcite's mistake is to assume that the world is rational, that means lead to ends.

The gods will not do. Though terribly dangerous, they are not serious. Saturn, a grim comedian, all too flexible, has tawdry views of his role that if they were those of merely an old man would count as petty delusions of grandeur. The temples are another matter. These can be taken seriously. The paintings commemorate the power of the passions of love and anger, either of which can wreck civilized life; and in Diana's temple, the rigors, denials, and blastings which wither

13. To make Arcite more fully the lovesick swain, Chaucer cuts Arcite's career as a soldier after leaving prison. Although Martian references cluster around Arcite, Palamon is more anxious for the duel and is more given to martial schemes. Throughout he takes the initiative; to use the terms *agere et pati*, he is more naturally an agent, Arcite more a patient. Whereas Arcite is delivered from prison, Palamon breaks out; whereas Arcite goes home and mopes, Palamon is on his way to raise an army when he accidentally meets Arcite; Palamon proposes the duel; Palamon, not Arcite, is spokesman when Theseus interrupts the duel. The narrator makes clear that Palamon fought as furiously in the tournament as Arcite did. But all of this is irrelevant to his gaining of Emily. She comes to him when he has stopped acting, when he has not spoken a reported word for 846 lines. He is recalled to Athens for another purpose and *given* Emily. The initiative of Theseus, not the dying wish of Arcite, is effectual.

and deny all life. We recognize the perils in pursuing with a single exclusiveness values whose radical inadequacies are so handsomely and ominously enshrined. But when the gods manifest themselves, the theophany is almost flippant.

May not the conduct of the gods be an objective correlative for a real, a fairly frequent human event, one not particularly amenable to aesthetic ordering? The Knight's Tale annotates that some of life's disasters and defeats may be incommensurate, essentially so. Such events are not tragedies, for it is a part of tragedy that the downfall, though hugely disproportionate, is felt in some way to be "earned," if not deserved, to be linked with the hero vitally and intimately. What happens to Arcite is more deeply troubling philosophically (not emotionally) than what happens to Troilus, for Troilus' fate is partly the result of his choices. But Arcite is no geologist. The earthquake that startles his horse is simply senseless. We know, although the human characters do not, that behind this event stand the immediate dexterities and ingenuities of the gods; but the palace insiders are fundamentally right when they say that "fallyng nys nat but an aventure" (2722). This falling is only an accident, for this is what the gods amount to: the gods are a correlative for arbitrary accident. Some events can be explained only if one imagines gods like Venus, Mars, and Saturn in this tale in charge—accident, an antonym of art, is what the luxuriously intricate art of the Knight's Tale centers upon.

The gods suggest that the universe may be irrational.[14] If the result is not tragic but comic or disquieting, this may be because potentially tragic material is denied tragic treatment. No hero challenges the order of necessity. And because the gods are so frivolous there is no tragic frame for the human events. Chaucer's occasionally comic, even tough tone, his refusal to linger on pathos, eases the urgency with which the possibility of an absurd universe is presented. And the last

14. This does sound like an unmedieval reading; I can only point to the text. I do not suggest that Chaucer believed the world was irrational or that he was agnostic in a modern sense. I would guess that he believed the world was ordered but noticed that it nonetheless harbored irrationality, and the Knight's Tale reflects that observation.

speech of Theseus, what it omits, what it contains, implies the fruitlessness of dwelling upon such possibilities.

Though it does not solve the issues the tale raises, one need not conclude that the ending is slick or evasive. Suppose the speech is not considered an attempt at a resolving chord. Suppose it is looked at dramatically, as the speech of *Theseus*. Immediately then we hear its minor key. At once the first words, setting forth the largest philosophic claims, become tentative. The narrator specifies the duke's attitude, his silence, his sad face, his continued sighing. The metaphor of the chains of love binding the universe is a voicing of faith, of hope, not an assurance. What is striking is the elegiac tone, that Theseus speaks with such grave love for a world he has not known. (The last stanzas of Spenser's Mutability Cantos are explicitly Christian, and their mood is like this.) The narrative has indicated no morally plausible relation between the sides of human aspiration and action and that of human disappointment and endurance. The duke's attempt to forge one is modestly offered. Theseus does not put his expression of faith into too glaring a contiguity to Arcite's death. His Boethian words make an affirmation beyond resignation. Nonetheless they scarcely give grounds for euphoria. They include bleak sayings—consciousness of mortality ("He moot be deed, the kyng as shal a page" [3030]); consciousness of change (the oak has a long nourishing, "Yet at the laste wasted is the tree" [3020]); consciousness of impending defeats (it is lucky to leave "this foule prisoun of this lyf" [3061] young and in honor as Arcite did). This last redisposal from Boccaccio is telling: there not this life but the dark regions of death are called the prison, this not by Teseo but by an attending physician. The bitterness lingers, for although the poem has prepared for so dark a view of life, the immediate context of Theseus' resignation has not. His voice gains cheerfulness only with the practical advice. The counsel to marry and be merry is not logical. Palamon and Emily could easily have expected the account of transience to issue in the advice not to trouble to marry, not to contribute to a cycle so futile. But the pragmatic counsel is harmonious with the way things

have happened in this poem. Festival has been an ever-return-
ing possibility. Perhaps the most valid religious feeling in the
poem, beyond a healthy and tutored respect for the capacities
of Fortune to wreak inexplicable disasters, is a reverential
attitude toward vernal renewals, a piety toward natural and
social cycles of festival and mourning. The speech adverts to
this cycle (3068) and to imprisonment (3061), chief among the
poem's dominant motifs. Not philosophically fully satisfactory,
aesthetically the speech does afford a resolution, a closure of
design as the structures and images of the poem meet. To
these images we shall shortly turn.

Discussion of the Knight's Tale from the viewpoint of action and suffering keeps referring to three scenes: the intercession of the Theban suppliants, the fatal accident, and the
closing Boethian speech of Theseus. Almost any account of
the tale would count these the beginning, climax, and de-
nouement, though some might want to treat the first hundred
lines as prologue. Stepping back from the tale, one recognizes
the formal concinnity of the enveloping action which moves
from a mythic, epic wedding through a war and its aftermath
to a romantic and domestic wedding. The stately, balanced
conduct of the foreground action, that romance inset into the
war's aftermath, has been recognized. But if we look closely
at beginning, middle, and end, it will appear that the harmony hides a more jagged plot line. Links are problematic,
even disrupted.

Important movement does begin in the first developed scene
when the suppliants interrupt the triumphant "feste" of
Theseus. Much that is to take on fuller life finds significant
place here. The scene initiates the events of the plot which
are to make the heroes, still offstage, patients. The feast perturbed with crying, the icon of Fortune's wheel, an intercession—all to figure throughout the economy of the poem—are
here. It introduces Theseus in vital, characteristic functioning
pointing toward another day long in the future; this duke
with his sudden and arbitrary mercy, his impulsive display of
power, is recognizably the duke who on another fetsival will

decree a safe tournament. Thus this scene, dramatically real-
ized, begins the action and is largely exemplary of interests
lying ahead.

Remotely the scene also leads to the enamorment, for it
initiates the events that bring the heroes to Athens where they
see Emily. The love story, of course, is the main thread accounting for the poem's narrative interest. Management of
this middle centers conventional anticipation upon the tournament which will presumably settle the love question. But
this resolution is shunted aside by the profoundly disconcerting
climax, Arcite's accident, which follows, but does not follow
from, the tournament, but from the colloquy of the gods. This
accident brings about one hero's death and so clears the way
for the marriage feast of the other. It also brings Theseus,
who in the interests of life had decreed a safe tournament, to
confront the power of Saturn who specializes in death.

Up till this point, Theseus had comprehended the interests
of the poem's gods. Once a servant of Venus (1814), he is beyond this now. He figured gloriously as a captain of Mars
(975 ff.), and latterly he has served Diana (1673–82). He represents therefore the possibilities for high personal amity,
successful public exertion, and aloof detachment which it is
one function of the friezes devoted to love, war, and chastity
to figure forth. He built no temple to Saturn. What that god
represents the duke does not, in either sense of the word,
comprehend. The duke's awareness of the confrontation with
Saturn must remain dim; he does not see the god, he does
perceive chaos and check. The final point of the tale for Arcite, the climax of the tale for everyone, is a turning point for
Theseus when he must touch the ultimate limit where the
human actor resigns to be a patient, where he must realize
that of no human, not even the duke of Athens, can it be said
that what he wills he does. The most interesting development
in character is therefore one that *agere et pati* brings into
salience. What Theseus learns, to make a virtue of necessity, is
a formula that takes on significance and poignance from the
entire poem.

Looking back, it appears that the major scenes of Theseus

are arranged in a progression, a kind of growth from warrior to philosophizing king. With the Theban suppliants, he reacts in instant, thoughtless pity followed by a ruthless campaign. When he stops the knights' fighting, a domestic prince voices worldly reflections upon the blindness of others and conscientious reflections upon ruling. Finally his considerations embrace universal themes, and he counsels the ignorant—a category in which perhaps he would now include himself—to be resigned: "take it weel that we may nat eschue" (3043). (This is, of course, a variation on one of the most common of statements based on *agere et pati*—what men cannot change, they then must bear.) This development is not a simple ascent from pure emotion to reason. The composition of the prayers of Arcite and Palamon is strictly rational—in fact, very clever— but it does not win for the gods the approval that the duke's final humane statement, deeply tinged with emotion, more perplexed than his other pronouncements, gets from the narrator. His reason and good will bring him to know the world as a place where the man-made structures, tournament theater and tourney, a law indifferent to praise or blame, are fragile, asserted only to be made vain, lost on a darkling plain where ignorant armies clash. The least hollow victory of Theseus is facing without paralysis or cynicism this ultimate powerlessness, knowledge that "Ther helpeth noght, al goth that ilke weye."

3

Feasts Perturbed and Prisons:
Image in the Knight's Tale

Any fair account would have to say that the first impression in most readers' experience of the Knight's Tale has not to do with the actions and passions of characters but with the tale's own artifice. Critics agree that it constitutes a conspicuous display of artistic resources; of something so well wrought it may not seem pressing to inquire whether what is wrought is a burial urn or a bridal cup. Initially one notices symmetry, color, processional effects, small mockeries—a levity now uneasy, now piquant. Yet consideration from the perspective of action and suffering discloses the poem's severe pessimism about human possibilities for action. This seeming contradiction should not surprise: the élan of form in presenting discouraging views is a grace well within the reach of art.

Though one may enjoy a number of things about the tale, what returns to challenge our dealings with it is Palamon's troubled meditation—are human beings no more than sheep to the gods? Such questions about the nature of the universe, raised, dropped, shrugged aside, are returned to naggingly, repetitiously. Plot and characters, particularly the contrast of Theseus to everyone else, express a vision of a receptive, suffering universe; this vision is hauntingly reaffirmed in the poem's texture, in such patterns as the festal-mourning cycles, prison and entrapment images and metaphors, and animal references. These three groups constitute the poem's chief figures; each supports the others even as it makes its own discriminations.

Cycles and Seasons

The Boethian speech of Theseus at the close refers to the great cycle of the cosmos from life to death, from death to life, and to its human counterpart, the alternation within a life of festival and mourning.[1] "But after wo I rede us to be merye," Theseus says, for it is written in the order of the Prince and Mover "That speces of thynges and progressiouns / Shullen enduren by successiouns" (3013-14). Theseus finds the principle of cyclic renewal large in every constituent part of the universal order—in the animal, vegetable, mineral, and social, civilized worlds as well as in the individual lives of men and women. His statement particularizes:

[*Vegetable*]
Loo the ook, that hath so long a norisshynge
From tyme that it first bigynneth to sprynge,
And hath so long a lif, as we may see,
Yet at the laste wasted is the tree.

[*Mineral*]
Considereth eek how that the harde stoon
Under oure feet, on which we trede and goon,
Yet wasteth it as it lyth by the weye.
The brode ryver somtyme wexeth dreye;

[*Human: community*]
The grete tounes se we wane and wende.
Thanne may ye se that al this thyng hath ende.

1. Pratt, in *JEGP* 57 : 416–23, has traced this theme. The theme in the Man of Law's Tale and in Chaucer in general is reviewed by Robert Enzer Lewis, "Chaucer's Artistic Use of Pope Innocent III's *De Miseria Humane Conditionis* in the Man of Law's Prologue and Tale," *PMLA* 81 (1966) : 485–92.

[*Human: individual*]
Of man and womman seen we wel also
That nedes, in oon of thise termes two,
This is to seyn, in youthe or elles age,
He moot be deed, the kyng as shal a page;
Som in his bed, som in the depe see,
Some in the large feeld, as men may see;
Ther helpeth noght, al goth that ilke weye.
Thanne may I seyn that al this thyng moot deye.
    What maketh this but Juppiter, the kyng,
That is prince and cause of alle thyng,
Convertynge al unto his propre welle
From which it is dirryved, sooth to telle?

[3017–38]

Of course this is one of those comprehensive readings of their circumambient world that medieval people were so free about making (again and again the consoling discovery of principle behind proliferation, Kind behind kinds). But it is more than a comfortable set piece, a bit of prefabricated wisdom casually placed. As we have seen, long months of reflection prepare this conclusion within Theseus. Further, it is one toward which images and tone have simultaneously led the reader (if not without distraction). Whether in the dread round of the wheel of Fortuna, or in an individual homely stroke, or in the very return of May after May, the image of the wheel, the cycle, alternations from weal to woe, from feasting to weeping and from weeping to feast, builds insistently until Theseus gathers up these strands.

The effect of the image is not always so harmoniously rich as in Theseus' litany of relinquishment that seems to gain in poetry all that it names as lost in life. The circle figures in sick jokes adorning the temple of Mars, where reversals imply the President of the Universe to be somewhat more blunt a humorist than even Hardy's prankster: the huntsman strangled by the wild bears he hunted; the cook, "for al his longe ladel," scalded; the carter overridden by his cart ("Under the wheel ful lowe he lay adoun" [2023])—all actors transformed into poetically just sufferers. There too Conquest sits with the sword of Damocles above him; and there, in what may be the most condensed image of the festival-mourning cycle, the "shippes hoppesteres" burn.[2] In the temple of Venus, paintings depict both mournings—"The broken slepes, and the sikes colde, / The sacred teeris, and the waymentynge"—and "Festes," with "instrumentz, caroles, daunces."

By turns woe and mirth are states of being and of mind in the heroes. "Who sorweth now but woful Palamoun / That noot namoore goon agayn to fight?" But at the poem's end Palamon is "in alle wele, / Lyvynge in blisse, in richesse, and in heele" (3101–02). The sorrows of love turn Arcite's habit and disposition "al up so doun," but in his greatest dolor in exile, the winged god Mercury visits him and in terms anticipating the diction of Theseus, "bad hym to be murie." Mercury instructs him to go back to Athens, for "Ther is thee shapen of thy wo an ende" (1392). (The ambiguity in the lines, the possible duplicity of Mercury, need not detain us just now.) At Athens, Arcite is indeed occasionally "lusty," but the melancholy fit falls upon him almost in the middle of a rondel to May. His depression chronicles an annoying human unreliability about meeting scheduled public occasions with the requisite personal inclinations. But Arcite's temper is typical of lovers, Chaucer's knight remarks; they are always changeable,

> Now in the crope, now doun in the breres,
> Now up, now doun, as boket in a welle.
> Right as the Friday, soothly for to telle,
> Now it shyneth, now it reyneth faste.

[1532–35]

Cyclic images thus permeate the knight's story, governing the calendar of crucial events, looming awesomely in the icon of Fortune's wheel, compressed into savage proximities in the Martian temple's friezes, present in the moods and fortunes of the heroes, insistent in verbal reminders and in the resolving chords of Theseus' speech at the poem's close. We shall here be concerned particularly with the poem's cyclic imagery

2. The dancing girls, festive by profession, are named only at the moment of their death. However, this may be simply a metaphor for the way burning ships look; see Robinson, p. 677, note on line 2017.

as focused in the movement from festivity to mourning and
from mourning back to festivity. Of course, not all alternations from feast to woe are equivalent; the inevitable evolution that Theseus describes is different from the sharp
disruption of the interrupted feast, the feast perturbed with
crying.

The poem's first dramatized scene embodies the festival-
mourning motif in this dissonant shape. Coming home in
triumph, Theseus finds it necessary to inquire, "What folk
been ye, that at myn homcomynge / Perturben so my feste
with criynge" (905–06)? The "eldeste lady," spokesman for
these undifferentiated, fierce, regal griefs, invokes for the first
time the name and character of Fortuna and her wheel:

> . . . ther is noon of us alle,
> That she ne hath been a duchesse or a queene.
> Now be we caytyves, as it is wel seene,
> Thanked be Fortune and hire false wheel,
> That noon estaat assureth to be weel.
>
> [922–26]

But even earlier, before he is thirty lines into his narrative,
Chaucer foreshadowed the festival-mourning cycle. This comes
before the reference to the supper that someone will win,
that is, before the world of the Knight's Tale replaces the
world of the pilgrims. Among those things the knight says
he will omit because "wayke been the oxen in my plough" is
the wedding feast of Theseus and Ypolita "And of the tempest at hir hoom-comynge" (884). This reference to festival
and peril, missing in Boccaccio, has been attributed to contemporary events, most often to the sea storm that destroyed a
vessel in which Queen Anne was to have come to England.[3]
There can be no objection to such likely, interesting conjec-
tures. But the reference also is a motif that is at once expanded in another context and in dramatic form (the scene

---

3. Robinson, p. 670, note on line 884. It has also been argued that
tempest may mean merely an excitement or commotion. If Chaucer used
the word in that sense, it may have been a reference to Queen Isabella of
Bavaria's entry into Paris in June of 1389 and the celebrations of her
coronation. See Parr, in *PMLA* 60 : 315. This would prevent my reading.

of the suppliant women); that comes to fullest development in the climactic tournament feasting which turns into all the train of elaborate woe which is Arcite's funeral; and that is stated at the poem's close when funeral pomp is relinquished for the rather chastened jubilation of the surviving lovers' wedding.

The feasts and mournings of the poem's last third reward attention. The feasting scenes do not report imbibings or supply the notes on comestibles that often furnish forth medieval hall scenes with their vision of wealth, plenitude, and joy. Nothing in the Knight's Tale compares with the Christmas feasting in *Sir Gawain*, let alone the good living in "The Land of Cockayne." But although food and drink do not occupy the forefront of the author's attention to festal matters, the reader is assured that there are great feasts, strictly speaking, before and after the tournament. It is May, that poignant season of festive renewal when other major events of the story also occur; and in other Mays we have seen Emily and Arcite honoring the vernal season. Then the duke, too, turning from the perturbation of war to sport, hunts the hart. The earth in her ancient renewals of youth prompts human beings to corresponding celebration; this is the feasting spirit as a natural expression. What the specific feasts frame—the tournament— is not a natural festival but a manifestation of an epoch, a special civilization. It has been said that the formal hunt is one means by which an aristocratic medieval society celebrated its existence; the same is even more true of the tournament. And the tournament of Theseus is a consummate expression of this society's assurance and reassurance of its being and ethos. It is not only a formal ceremony; it is, further, an occasion of peril rather like an automobile race or steeplechase. It must have held the same ambiguous fascination for a medieval audience as these do for a modern one.[4] A nar-

4. Brief accounts of the tournament as an institution are found in Sidney Painter, *French Chivalry* (Ithaca, N.Y.: Cornell, ca. 1940; reprinted 1957), pp. 45–54, 154–56; and Léon Gautier, *La Chevalerie* (Paris: Sanard et Derangeon, 1883), chap. 17, pp. 673–704, who writes that chroniclers of one 1240 tourney report variously from sixty to eighty-four deaths. A longer account is that of F. H. Cripps-Day, *The History of the Tourna-*

cissistic recreation for a society of which knighthood was still
a vital constituent, a busman's holiday, the tournament was
also an agon. With ruthless clarity, as in all team athletic
events, its decisions divided titular agents from titular patients.
While it kept the community in practice for war, it had the
further refinement that it might offer a scapegoat or two to the
god. On this occasion Theseus tries vainly to strip the tournament of its intrinsic peril so as to transform it wholly into a
festivity. But the design of the institution resists individual hu-
manitarian shaping. If the reader were not advised that Saturn
arranged the earthquake, he might say that the impetus of
the very institution was asserting its identity and virility.[5]

---

ment in England and in France (London: Bernard Quaritch, 1918).
Froissart's Chronicles gives contemporary and sometimes detailed accounts
of some nine tournaments, in two of which fatalities are recorded.

5. Though I am uneasy about historical-genetic arguments, there is an
account of a 1389 jousting accident in Ranulf Higden's Polychronicon
which I submit here not only because Chaucer would have known about
it but also because of likenesses to the Knight's Tale, and because of its
phrase "Thereupon laughter was turned into tears." Here is Higden's
account:

"The King kept Christmas at Woodstock. There, on the last day of
December, the Earl of Pembroke, a young man not quite seventeen years
old, insisted upon trying out his horse with another knight, Sir John
Saint John, in preparation for the next tournament. When the two
met, the knight, at the earl's bidding, flung his lance from one side.
The part which he gripped hit the ground and stuck, while the other
end flew up in the air. At this the earl's horse took fright and flung him
with great force, so that the spear entered his body near the groin and
inflicted a mortal wound. His helmet being knocked off at the same
time, he was knocked senseless and died about noon.

"Thereupon laughter was turned into tears ["Confestim lacrimae suc-
cedunt ridentibus"], and there was universal mourning. The King was
overcome with grief, and the Queen and her women shut themselves in
her chamber and gave themselves up to their sorrow. The earl's servants
could not think what would become of them and wondered whether life
was better than death. The funeral was held at Hereford with great
ceremony, and the earl was buried by the side of his father. The knight
who had wounded him took to flight."

Source: Polychronicon Ranulphi Higden, Monachi Cestrensis, ed. Rev.
Joseph Rawson Lumby, Rerum Britannicarum Medii Aevi Scriptores, no.
41, pt. 9 [London: Longman & Co., 1886], 9. 219–20. The compilation of
Edith Rickert, Chaucer's World (New York: Columbia, 1948; paperback
ed., 1962), p. 216, called my attention to this. The translation is hers.
Had the Teseida been lost, this might have been advanced as a topical
inspiration for Chaucer's story.

The tournament also offers the occasion for other parties, these with less potential for disaster. Chaucer denies any intention of going into the preliminary formal gathering. "What haukes sitten on the perche above, / What houndes liggen on the floor adoun" (2204–05), he will skip over. The *occupatio* is real enough compared with Boccaccio, who goes into the feasting accoutrements at length and has much reason to do so; for rather than going back to Thebes to line up their adherents, Palamon and Arcita stay in Athens, setting up establishments that evidently rival the duke's in sumptuous housekeeping, entertaining, and cultivating the arts of *amour courtois* through a full year before the tournament. But even in Chaucer the ducal scale of the pre-tourney affair may be sensed. The splendid passages on each major adherent represent the magnificence of the company gathered at Athens.[6] (These replace the book-long catalogue in the *Teseida,* a listing which reminds the audience that Thebes fell before Troy —for not only are Agamemnon and Menelaus there, but so is a *young* Nestor.) [7] With Emetreus and Lygurge, Chaucer does in effect tell us what hawks fly above, what hounds lie below, and this leisurely heraldic piece immediately precedes the more perfunctory account of the duke's meticulous hospitality which at a Sunday evening dinner includes "mynstralcye," "yiftes to the meeste and leeste," dancing, singing, and conversation about love. A whole day of celebration honoring Venus and May follows: "al that Monday justen they and daunce, / And spenden it in Venus heigh servyse" (2486–87). Consciousness of the next day's test cuts short the feasting that night,

6. The exotic appeal of these portraits is often noted. For an appreciation of their contribution to the poem's texture, see Muscatine, *Chaucer and the French Tradition,* p. 182. Walter Clyde Curry, *Chaucer and the Mediaeval Sciences,* rev. and enlarged 2d ed. (New York: Barnes & Noble, 1960), discusses the portraits, pp. 130–37, as a part of his thesis that the real conflict of the tale is between the planets Saturn and Mars, Lycurgus being a Saturnalian figure and Emetreus a Martian one.

7. Although medieval people were supposed to be careless of chronology, Nestor is so famously old that this argues Boccaccio's interest in it. Morton W. Bloomfield writes that Chaucer grew increasingly preoccupied with accurate chronology, and that his work was innovative in its awareness of history, an interest he may have got from Boccaccio. See "Chaucer's Sense of History," *JEGP* 51 (1952) : 301–13.

but the bruit of preparations for the tourney resumes the celebratory note in the morning. The excitement and clatter, the betting of soi-disant experts, the gear of the fighters, are matters the specifics of which interest the narrator more than do those of the formal Sunday evening feast. He gives one of the brightest Chaucerian social scenes, sights and sounds mingling to convey bustle and suspense, an atmosphere which the common people share with the aristocrats who will fight (see lines 2491–2522). This informal scene, rendered in verse attentive and loving of things and sounds, dissolves into the decree of Theseus and the processional of duke, ladies, and champions to the theater.

A sizeable portion of the poem's central span is thus devoted to festal preliminaries of the tournament, a span broken into two portions by the prayers in the temples. The festal sequence in itself is richly varied, even apart from this central interruption in another tone. It includes an evening party, Maying, and the morning preparations, and it is symmetrically mounted between processions of pageant-like formality and color, that of Lygurge and Emetreus into Athens at the beginning and of Theseus to the theater at the end.

The feast after the tournament is yet another development of the motif. Chaucer once more retards Boccaccio's straightforward contrasts and sharper ironies. In Boccaccio, gloom is immediate. The accident overwhelms Arcita's compeers. They seem not to have won, Boccaccio says, a plain note on the collapse of elation, on a winning that has no feel of victory. But everyone carries on. Arcita rides back to the palace in a triumphal car with Emilia at his side, and the populace runs out to see the triumph and marriage which is also a profound defeat:

> Nulla persona in Attene rimase,
> giovane, vecchio, zita overo sposa,
> che non corresse là con l'ale spase
> onde venia la coppia gloriosa.
> Le vie e' campi e i tetti e le case
> tutt'eran pien di gente letiziosa;
> e in gloria d'Arcita ognun cantava
> e della nuova sposa che menava.   [9. 41]

[No one was left in Athens, young man, old man, maiden, or wife who did not run to the place where the glorious couple came. The streets, the ground, roofs, and buildings were full of glad people; and everyone sang of the glory of Arcita and of the new wife he brought.]

Teseo invites combatants to change their garments and feast with him since

> Questo ch'è stato, non tornerà mai
> per alcun tempe che stato non sia.
>
> [9. 59]

[What has been will never again return, for time passed is not to be.]

The changing of the garments is not only realistic; it is also the presentation of a calculated guise suitable to festival, as throwing dirt on the face is the classical stance, as well as the primitive impulse, of mourning. Here, the gesture is hollow. Later when Palamon and Emilia are to be married, there is another change from mourning garb to new garments. And so Arcita's wedding (in Boccaccio the ritual is performed) is celebrated with all deliberation as a feast. But Arcita is not the only fatality. In the field, workers quietly gather up the slain champions' bodies and burn them late at night, so as not to disturb the wedding revelers (10. 2–3). The juxtaposition is more sharp than anything in Chaucer, who is painterly where Boccaccio is clear-cut, hard-edged.

In Chaucer, there is no triumph, and that classic piece, the folk marveling as someone touched with glory passes by, is sacrificed. Arcite is treated as most would wish to be, were their breasts "tobroken": he is carried to the palace, cut out of his harness, and put to bed. In another part of the palace, the post-tournament festivities are under way. They proceed as if the only mishaps were minor ones, for the company is slow to realize that Arcite's injuries are critical. These are the lines on the post-tournament feast; to be remarked of them, their faintly anxious optimism:

Duc Theseus, with al his compaignye,
Is comen hoom to Atthenes his citee,
With alle blisse and greet solempnitee.
Al be it that this aventure was falle,
He nolde noght disconforten hem alle.
Men seyde eek that Arcite shal nat dye;
He shal been heeled of his maladye.
And of another thyng they weren as fayn,
That of hem alle was ther noon yslayn,
Al were they soore yhurt, and namely oon,
That with a spere was thirled his brest boon.
To othere woundes and to broken armes
Somme hadden salves, and somme hadden charmes;
Fermacies of herbes, and eek save
They dronken, for they wolde hir lymes have.
For which this noble duc, as he wel kan,
Conforteth and honoureth every man,
And made revel al the longe nyght
Unto the straunge lordes, as was right.
Ne ther was holden no disconfitynge
But as a justes, or a tourneiynge;
For soothly ther was no disconfiture.
For fallyng nys nat but an aventure,

.   .   .   .   .   .

For which anon duc Theseus leet crye,
To stynten alle rancour and envye,
The gree as wel of o syde as of oother,
And eyther syde ylik as ootheres brother;
And yaf hem yiftes after hir degree,
And fully heeld a feeste dayes three,
And conveyed the kynges worthily
Out of his toun a journee largely.
And hoom wente every man the righte way.
Ther was namoore but "Fare wel, have good day!"

[2700–22, 2731–40]

Boccaccio's people and Chaucer's are alike in that both put
on their best faces. Theseus is ever a tactful, gracious host.
But at work here is not only the gesture of a homogeneous
community but also something at once more and less. Where
Boccaccio's company acts with knowledge and a deliberate,

almost formal defiance of their knowledge (flaunting their *vertu* in necessity), Chaucer's tends to delude itself. The momentum of celebration survives the reasons for celebration. Where Boccaccio's revelers judge Arcita to be fatally injured but celebrate anyway, partly because of the doctor's advice to make him happy before he dies,[8] Chaucer's feasters suppose, they hope, that everything is all right: people say that Arcite will not die, he will be healed. The element of wishful thinking is strong. The approaching death of Arcite is not the only thing that the party wishes to minimize. Several others are seriously injured. After running through medical treatments, in a bland, grim meiosis the narrator remarks: "they wolde hir lymes have." The tournament feasting tapers off with a critique, as it were, of the feasting mentality, a profile of unwarranted optimism, a festivity that refuses to be perturbed.

Almost at once, a treatment of the mourning mentality follows. If the tournament theater is essentially a place of entertainment which revolves about a death trap, the great funeral is also bi-focused, partly designed to divert all but the dead man back to the ways of life. While some of its usages emphasize the close of one life and its worth—casting of jewels into the fire—others, the funeral games for instance, signalize the return of the energies of the living toward life. Three things about Arcite's funeral are striking. First is the magical, almost eerie passage in which the focus shifts from the human panoply of grief to a totally different point of view which happens to occupy the same space—that of the wood gods, birds, and beasts to whom the funeral means flight from their favorite places when the trees are felled for Arcite's pyre and the sun strikes cleared ground. Second is a cumulative, weighty impression of the funeral as a plushy, elegant social occasion. The elaboration of preparations and of public mourning holds up for display the ceremonies sanctified by time and glamorized in great literatures and insists upon their propriety.

---

8. "Fateli festa e consolazione, / sì che ne vada l'anima contenta, / il più si può, all'etterna prigione" (10. 14)—literally, "make him a feast and console him so that his soul will go happy, insofar as possible, to the eternal prison."

Third is a vaguely discrepant impression that the tears flowing through these channels come in a measure somewhat extreme. If Arcite's funeral is a feast, it is one perturbed with copious crying. Both the conduct expressing grief and that reaffirming vitalities and normalities almost seem to be part of a spectacle indifferently and vastly entertaining to the people of Athens.

The tone is curious. What seems to happen is the same pushing of the obvious and fitting to an extreme as in passages on Theseus discussed above (see pp. 63–65). There is "Cracchynge of chekes, rentynge eek of heer," and this on the part of townspeople—to whom the hero is rather much a stranger, as Chaucer makes us remember by referring to him as "this Theban":

> Infinite been the sorwes and the teeres
> Of olde folk, and folk of tendre yeeres,
> In al the toun for deeth of this Theban.
> For hym ther wepeth bothe child and man;
> So greet wepyng was ther noon, certayn,
> Whan Ector was ybroght, al fressh yslayn,
> To Troye. Allas, the pitee that was ther,
> Cracchynge of chekes, rentynge eek of heer.
> "Why woldestow be deed," thise wommen crye,
> "And haddest gold ynough, and Emelye?"
>
> [2827–36]

When the body is borne into the hall, the place "roreth of the criyng and the soun." All this before the ritual keening around the pyre.

Such exhibitions by what are, strictly speaking, disinterested women, are among the principal functions of all women in the epic and of the supernumerary women characters in romance. If this is, however, the classical opportunity for "Mourning in others, our owne miseries," [9] the comic tinge is unprecedented, for such passages are customarily regarded seriously by their narrators and the reader feels no inclination to take them otherwise. That such opportunities are seized upon usually evokes, if anything, a depression at the sad etcetera of the world's wrongs. One might rationalize that sorrow was

9. Spenser, "Astrophel: Lay of Clorinda," 96.

once expressed more overtly than it is today and that Chaucer merely gives us contemporary mores straight—it is up to us to make the culturally relative allowances. But however different the times, the reader never suspects irony when Homer describes Hector's funeral, to resort to Chaucer's parallel, or when Homer describes the slave women mourning, ostensibly for Patroclus, but each really for her own sorrows. Chaucer is closer to Joyce's suggestion that a funeral may be a funferal. Another possible explanation is that Chaucer's attitude toward the common people gathered in an expression of public feeling ranges elsewhere rather narrowly between condescension and contempt, and that this equivocal effect is another instance.

But it is not certain that the glancing irony is so confined or that the rabble's appetency for grief alone gets suspicious emphasis: "Shrighte Emelye, and howleth Palamon." Chaucer's inversion of sentence order calls attention to the strident verbs. This is the heroine who had no preference as to who won and the alter-hero who a year before, even a few days before, had cheerfully tried to kill Arcite. Nor is Chaucer suggesting that they are insincere. Nor need we credit him with pre-Freudian insights on the guilt residue in grief. But he is calling attention to the repentances (repent means to change), to the inconsistencies, in life.

In contrast, the grief of Theseus ("No man myghte gladen Theseus, / Savynge his olde fader") takes more restrained ways. Much of it finds outlet in service. He carries swooning Emily out of the death chamber. He provides the funeral, giving orders for the cutting of the trees. Apparently he himself dresses the body of Arcite and lays it on the bier. After these offices follows a single line on the duke's overt mourning: "Therwith he weep that pitee was to heere" (2878). For the only time in the account of the funeral, the poetry during these intimate preparations by Theseus hovers near the central subject—Arcite dead—and suggests the finality of his immobility. The white gloves have been drawn onto hands that are strictly idle, the glittering sword dresses a last appearance.

Mainly, however, the narrator's distance from the funeral rites is noticeable. (In contrast, his empathy is clear in the final quiet scene when the death of Arcite, though long past, governs the mood.) The comic tone flickers lightly, discontinuously; it does not interfere with the dominant impression— the funeral worthy of a royal youth prematurely cut down when he stood at the pinnacle of martial triumph and at the verge of his felicity in love. The comedy is a discreet accompaniment. To Chaucer's covert comment and detachment it may be pertinent to contrast John Berryman's lines for Delmore Schwartz where authorial involvement is intense, but the tone overtly derisive, complicating the simple emotional core:

> . . . let no activity
> mar our hurrah of mourning,
> let's all be Jews bereft, for he was one
> He died too soon, he liked "An Ancient to Ancients"
> His death clouded the grove
>
> I need to hurry this out before I forget
> which I will never [10]

Did Chaucer simply stumble into the trap of his own vein, becoming parodic because he could not resist? Some critics have implied this in commenting on his rapid shifts among levels of style.[11] In the funeral scene, however, an analogous effect owes not so much to stylistic shifts in diction as to the hyperbolic propriety.

This odd effect is functional. The detachment, the comic edge, provide balances that the poem perhaps badly needs. Chaucer has kept one of Boccaccio's points of perspective on the funeral, the desertion of the woods. The natural world and its mythic guardians are merely inconvenienced by the fuss human beings are making about a death. But Chaucer excludes the other perspective, the order and high beauty of the eighth sphere with Arcita "suoni ascoltando pien d'ogni dolcezza"

10. John Berryman, *His Toy, His Dream, His Rest: 308 Dream Songs* (New York: Farrar, Straus and Giroux, 1964), no. 151, p. 80.

11. For examples of diverse comment on Chaucer's stylistic shifts see Baum, *Chaucer: A Critical Appreciation*, pp. 88–92; Bertrand H. Bronson, *In Search of Chaucer* (University of Toronto, 1960), pp. 22 ff.; Salter, *Chaucer*, pp. 12–13; Robert M. Jordan, *Chaucer and the Shape of Creation: The Aesthetic Possibilities of Inorganic Structure* (Cambridge, Mass.: Harvard, 1967), pp. 179–84.

("listening to sounds full of every sweetness") and laughing softly at the weeping around his corpse (11. 1, 3). For this cosmic laughter, Chaucer substitutes a quiet worldly cynicism. But Chaucer's mundane substitute is bracing; it also prevents grief from swallowing the poem's world. Moreover, the narrator's immunity, even private gaiety, comes as from one who sees beyond the present of the funeral to exactly those conclusions that Theseus comes to following years of pondering—at the tale's end, after the woe, these same people will again be merry. Along with the flight of the wood gods the narrator's tone is a reminder that there are other perspectives on all events than the merely immediate, the merely personal, the merely lyric, even the merely tragic, while allowing these to remain vital, primary.

The motif of the feast perturbed with crying subsumes several versions of the relationship between suffering and action. The festival may be all on the side of one character, the grieving all on the side of the other, as in the encounter between the duke and the suppliant widows; they may alternate within an individual life, as when Arcite, receiving the plaudits of the tournament audience, riding about the theater without his helmet, and "Lokynge upward upon this Emelye" is thrown. They may be fused, as they are for Arcite when he wins Emily's love on his deathbed. The same event may bring both feast and mourning as the tournament does to Palamon and to Arcite both. They are glad "sufferers" of the tournament, the poem's climactic festival, for it brings an opportunity to win Emily; and Palamon and presumably Emily are also glad sufferers of the final marriage feast. Theseus is the actor, the initiator, of these events, but the tournament itself defeats all and makes them the patients of Fortune—Palamon, who loses the jousting, Arcite, who loses his life, and Theseus, who loses his heroic optimism when he tries vainly to neutralize the institution and do away with its most dire risks.

Festival and mourning make up much of the narrative tissue of the last fourth of the poem, which becomes largely an account of successive social occasions formally observing joy and sorrow. Further, the festal-mourning pattern extends the potential density and coverage of this tragic romance substantially, for it is a domestic version of Fortune's wheel and implies a social extension that the wheel frequently did not. Festival and mourning are applicable not only to the lots of "hem that stoode in heigh degree" but also to those who never climb onto the spokes of fortune's wheel. (True, in the Knight's Tale, the feasts and distresses are of those with "heigh degree.") And unlike the wheel of fortune, the cycle of festival and woe need not have theological or moral implications.

Nor does the social cycle so strictly imply that man is a sufferer, a patient of destiny. Not so strictly. But Theseus at the end "sees" the cycle as a necessary participation in nature, an inevitability which encloses social and natural life, an inevitability which Arcite, who died young in his sad, distinctive glory, has now escaped.

Prisons and Traps

In festival and even in mourning, people have alternatives of behavior, and where alternatives exist, action is possible. A human being may grace and improve upon, absent himself from, or subvert, appointed or inflicted occasions. But the Knight's Tale's other chief collocations of imagery suggest more severe restrictions upon human action. The first of these is the metaphor of prison—a prison preternaturally elastic, now contracting, now expanding, now apparently receding to a background, a past, always, as it turns out, circumscribing the heroes.

Before the prison becomes a symbol of ultimate stultification and limit, it is, like the power of Theseus discussed above, an objective fact in the narrative. The major action up to the death of Arcite covers something like eight years; Arcite spends an unspecified number of these years in prison, Palamon spends seven there. The prison has chains; Palamon's tears wet the "pure fettres on his shynes grete." It has torture instruments—"It nedeth noght to pyne yow with the corde," Theseus observes dryly (1746). Evidently confessions so exacted are known in Chaucer's Athens. The prison's windows have bars "Of iren greet and square as any sparre" (1076). Still this prison is not *symbolically* impressive or horrible—as is the dungeon of Orgoglio. It has not and is not meant to have this psychological dimension or give the reader a comparable frisson. Spenser's prison professes itself to be an allegory for a state of mind. Chaucer's knight professes his prison to be a place, a real prison, the strong tower of Norman England, standard in every respect, evidently located in the same complex as the palace. Palamon and Arcite are allowed freedom within it. By leave of his jailers Palamon is pacing in a high room overlooking both city and garden when he sees Emily. Fetters are in use, one suspects, only when Chaucer needs a hyperbole to stress Palamon's woe. This solid, common structure is the starting place.

But the prison as a metaphor is not limited. It spirals about and through the poem, encompassing more and more aspects of life until it seems to impinge everywhere, to enclose all festivals, all griefs, and define all human actors as pathetic sufferers. The narrator advances this vision of life as imprisonment in several ways—by the reference to so many of the people as captives; by the princes' perception, presented mainly through Arcite, of frustration, loneliness, ultimately of confinement; by the temple paintings with their collection of deluded monomaniac or megalomaniac infatuates enclosed in a passion or a fate; and through entrapment and animal imagery.

References to captivity begin with the suppliants' interruption of the duke's return to Athens. "Now be we caytyves," the widow of King Capaneus says to Theseus before she announces her individual identification. The same order of reference occurs later. "Two woful wrecches been we, two caytyves, / That been encombred of oure owene lyves" (1717–18), Palamon tells Theseus—again, before giving names. As Philostrate, Arcite tells himself he has become "so caytyf and so thral, / That he that is my mortal enemy, / I serve hym as his squier povrely" (1552–54). The narrator applies the words "kaytyf in servage" to the icon of Cresus in the temple of Venus; they might as well fit any other figure there. The word amplifies and varies repeated, monotonous reference to Palamon or Arcite or both as "this prisoner" and "these prisoners," a status further, if perfunctorily, proclaimed to be wretched, woeful, sorrowful or something at least equally unpromising and dreary from a secular point of view, a "martyrdom." These references establish at a basic level a tonic note of the poem.[12]

The heroes then are prisoners; they themselves and the narrator harp on this. But the heroes' awareness of this status does not remain static; it grows and changes through the poem. They come to discover that love, and life itself, are areas of restriction compared with the span of their hopes. In fairness to them, it must be granted that they did not hope extravagantly; idealistically, surely, but not exorbitantly. They wanted to win a certain lady, as many knights must have managed to do. They wanted to dwell in a peaceful, prosperous, proud city such as they remembered Thebes to have been; some people do live in such fortunate cities. They are not after some return to a childhood in the sense that a nineteenth-century romantic might be, are not yearners for a visionary past or a visionary future. They do not wish for infinitudes and impossibilities. Not that the "blisse" possession of Emily implies to each cousin is ordinary or, realistically, attainable, but there is little evidence that Palamon or Arcite basically long for death or seek pleasure in frustration as has been legitimately suspected of some courtly yearners. They want to marry. They wish (if with intent, single-minded passion) for sensible goods that all men would have, that many men possess.

Palamon's and Arcite's experience in the literal prison, their sufferance within it, lends a limited credibility, at least, when they say that this or that is worse than being in prison, for they know what being in prison is. Both find life there oner-

12. According to the Chaucer concordance, the words *prison, prisoner,* and *prisoners* are used thirty-five times in the Knight's Tale, overwhelmingly more than elsewhere in Chaucer. *Caitif* might also mean simply *wretch.* The more general meaning seems to have come from the specific one—to be a captive was to be wretched. The occurrence of *caitif* is rather narrowly distributed in Chaucer's poetry, the Knight's Tale with four, and the Parson's Tale, the Boethius, and the *Romance of the Rose,* all with five each, accounting for almost all entries in the concordance.

ous and bemoan it. Palamon is up early complaining his lot on that May morning when first he sees Emily. When he thinks perhaps she is a goddess, immediately he prays to her; and he prays for deliverance from prison. (*That* he prays has so bemused readers that the content of the petition tends to be overlooked.) Arcite counsels resignation, trying to comfort his cousin with Christian or Stoic nostrums: "For Goddes love, taak al in pacience / Oure prisoun, for it may noon oother be" (1084–85). And again, "We moste endure it; this is the short and playn" (1091). The double enamorment with Emily and the quarrels over her, one surmises, enliven the monotony of dungeon life a good deal.

Then Arcite is released, and learns that the prison walls have only expanded:

> Now is my prisoun worse than biforn;
> Now is me shape eternally to dwelle
> Noght in purgatorie, but in helle.
>
> [1224–26]

He notes that Palamon lives where he can see Emily: "In prison? certes nay, but in paradys!" (1237). For his part, Palamon disagrees:

> Sith thou art at thy large, of prisoun free,
> And art a lord, greet is thyn avauntage
> Moore than is myn, that sterve here in a cage.
> For I moot wepe and wayle, whil I lyve,
> With al the wo that prison may me yive,
> And eek with peyne that love me yeveth also,
> That doubleth al my torment and my wo.
>
> [1292–98]

The question—"Who hath the worse, Arcite or Palamoun?"— would obviously find Palamon and Arcite answering differently. But they are alike in that change brings them to broaden their views, to consider the lot of other men; and their conclusions here are alike. Some men wish for riches, Arcite thinks, and riches bring about murder or illness, and "som man wolde out of his prisoun fayn, / That in his hous is of

his meynee slayn" (1257–58). Palamon, after a long invocation
to the goddess Fortuna, puzzling why men so suffer "And
dwelleth eek in prison and arreest" (1310), concludes that he
does not know why, "But wel I woot that in this world greet
pyne ys" (1324). The hypermetric line—with the single-syllable
words that tend to equalize the stressed and unstressed accents
of its iambs—solemnizes this desolate conclusion.

At home in Thebes, Arcite does live like a prisoner. Chaucer
omits the tour of adventures that Boccaccio arranges for the
freed prince. Rather, "solitarie he was and evere allone, / And
waillynge al the nyght, makynge his mone" (1365–66). It is
often stressed of Arcite that he is alone; a motif not invariably
mixed with the web of prison imagery, it casts a kindred
shadow over the same experience. Partly this is a foreshadowing of Arcite's fate. Also, as the only living royal Thebans,
both heroes have something of the elegiac quality of last
survivors. Preparing secretly for the fight in the grove, Arcite
is "allone as he was born." The verse is close to the quiet,
hasty, solitary action that it narrates:

> Arcite is riden anon unto the toun,
> And on the morwe, er it were dayes light,
> Ful prively two harneys hath he dight,
> Bothe suffiisaunt and mete to darreyne
> The bataille in the feeld bitwix hem tweyne;
> And on his hors, allone as he was born,
> He carieth al the harneys hym biforn.
>
> [1628–34]

Anapestic substitution hurries the first line, and in line 1633
the caesura's placement before "allone as he was born" helps,
with parenthetical location of the phrase, to create space
around it, enhancing its evocative power. (In the large economy of the narration, this is a part of a suspenseful quickening
just before the battle.) It is one spot in the leisurely paced
poem where a series of sharp single actions and scenes flash
by—Arcite's ride to the town, the two facing one another,
their excitement reflected in changing color, their helping one
another to arm. (Palamon, of course, waiting in the grove, is

just as alone as Arcite; we might even imagine him to be more so, but the imagination of the narrator goes with Arcite, who is to be alone in his grave at the poem's end.)

Isolation is of many kinds. Arcite's is not an isolated imprisonment in a malformed self. Compare again Spenser's Red Cross Knight in Orgoglio's stronghold or Eliot's protagonist hearing the key

> Turn in the door once and turn once only
> We think of the key, each in his prison
> Thinking of the key, each confirms a prison.[13]

Arcite's case is less morally complex than the one, less psychologically complex than either. The same factors that make him a prisoner isolate him. Once free, he is imprisoned in the one wish that precludes all other choices and ways of being open to him; in a historic situation, the decline of Thebes, which strips him of his normal community; and in an exile depriving him of the only "companye" he would choose. Encouraged by the dream of Mercury, he does get around this last, although in a manner he feels to be shabby and Palamon (not the most disinterested commentator) feels to be contemptible (see lines 1552–54, 1580–86).

But reasonable historical and biographical causes of Arcite's isolation seem not to answer for the effect of the poetry, not here and especially not later when on his deathbed Arcite does not protest, does not express fear, but sadly wonders about the grave's utter loneliness in words so famous that there is no need to quote them. Chaucer conveys through Arcite something simple and stark, irreducible, mournful—every human being's isolated vulnerability at birth and death. Arcite's solitude is that of the human situation, the effect like that of the words in Job: "Naked came I out of my mother's womb and naked shall return thither" with the plangent substitution of Arcite's "allone" for "naked." [14]

13. T. S. Eliot, "The Waste Land," *The Complete Poems and Plays* (New York: Harcourt, Brace, 1952), ll. 412–14.

14. Chaucer's use of solitude and nakedness to evoke generic human vulnerability would perhaps bear investigation throughout all of his poetry. The naked Noah as a type of the Passion does not seem to inform

However, the poem does move once to a contrary real, if brief, expansiveness when both prisoners are free and have what seems to them their first fair chance to act so as to attain Emily and "blisse." At the end of book 2 when Theseus arranges for a tournament and the knights go off to recruit their champions, there is a pronounced upbeat. The heroes ride back to a more spacious place with a chance to start out again from home in their own character as royal princes, to perform, as the chivalric phrase has it, *deeds* of arms, a chance to unite their free past in Thebes with a fitting, free future, as if the costly rupture of the Thebaid had not been nor they been casualties of it. The reader, after following so much dreary incarceration and servitude (reading lightened, perhaps, for the unkind or the cynical by Arcite's severe case of "the loveris maladye / Of Hereos"), experiences this sense of release too:

> Who looketh lightly now but Palamoun?
> Who spryngeth up for joye but Arcite?
> Who kouthe telle, or who kouthe it endite,
> The joye that is maked in the place
> Whan Theseus hath doon so fair a grace?
> But doun on knees wente every maner wight,
> And thonked hym with al hir herte and myght,
> And namely the Thebans often sithe.
> And thus with good hope and with herte blithe
> They taken hir leve, and homward gonne they ride
> To Thebes, with his olde walles wyde.

[1870–80]

The upbeat comes in part from metrical management, from tonic sound. After an earlier restlessness, the secure closing rhythms, a beat of closely equal iambs in the last line and a half, emphasize the plosives, bringing to the verse the thud of hoof beats: "homward gonne they ride, / To Thebes, with his olde walles wyde" (emphases mine). Diction helps: "looketh lightly," "spryngeth up for joye," "joye that is maked," "so

---

this motif in Chaucer; rather, there is a heightening of the human, nontropological significance. For a note on Noah as a figure of the Passion see Helen Gardner, *The Business of Criticism* (London: Oxford, 1959; Oxford Paperbacks, 1963), pp. 90–96.

fair a grace," "herte and myght," "with good hope and with herte blithe"—vital optimism rare in this tale. But the new atmosphere comes most from the narrative movement opening a hazard of new fortunes, a chance for these sufferers to act.[15]

The perception of the knights alters with experience, but they do not take full account of what they see; like Troilus, hope "alwey" them "blente" (*T&C*, 5. 1195). They learn nothing from the paintings in the oratories, our next concern.

If Chaucer is perfunctory about the prison tower, he gives full measure to the "noble theatre" of the lists, construction of which absorbs the skilled craftsmen of the whole land. It is round as the wheel of Fortune itself, with marble gates and flawless sight lines ("whan a man was set on o degree, / He letted nat his felawe for to see" [1891–92]). The temples to Venus, Mars, and Diana are its glory. Deservedly much has been written about these temples and their friezes. Quite generally they are held to add to the poem's tragic dimension. They have further been read as aspects of the psychology, as projections of the desires, of the three principals; as a contribution to a subsurface motive of disorder which runs under the ordered surface of the poem; and as an example of an aesthetic interest in excess of thematic requirements.[16] Although even those who read the poem as a comic tale of love and languishment grant the pessimism of the friezes, it has not been sufficiently noticed that each displays on its walls a kind of prison.

On the wall of the temple of Venus the prison assumes the

15. The doublet "with good hope and with herte blithe" (1878) contrasts with the "wanhope and distresse" (1249) with which Arcite left Athens the first time.

16. Muscatine, p. 189, finds the decor of the temples a part of a subsurface insistence on disorder in the poem which is its most compelling claim to maturity; Frost, in *RES* 25 : 300–01, finds that the images in the temples contribute tragic effect and notes that the temple of Mars is built like a dungeon; Jordan, pp. 173–78, argues that the temple passage outgrows the requirements of theme and so thrusts its structural and aesthetic values into the center of the reader's consciousness; Neuse, in *UTQ* 31 : 299–315, in a basically optimistic reading of the poem still observes the pessimism of the temples and suggests that the gods ultimately function as metaphors of man's will and appetite.

guise of a garden, but the people pictured in it and the label
"las" (snare) identify its true nature:

> Nat was foryeten the porter, Ydelnesse,
> Ne Narcisus the faire of yore agon,
> Ne yet the folye of kyng Salomon,
> Ne yet the grete strengthe of Ercules—
> Th' enchauntementz of Medea and Circes—
> Ne of Turnus, with the hardy fiers corage,
> The riche Cresus, kaytyf in servage.
> Thus may ye seen that wysdom ne richesse,
> Beautee ne sleighte, strengthe ne hardynesse,
> Ne may with Venus holde champartie,
> For as hir list the world than may she gye.
> Lo, alle thise folk so caught were in hir las,
> Til they for wo ful ofte seyde "allas!"
>
> [1940–52]

Several tales behind these icons involve a "las" more concrete.
Hercules in the deathly garment, Jason's bride similarly confined in pain by the "enchauntementz of Medea," and Cresus,
the net in his case a noose—the legends emphasize the cruel
ingenuities of the "las" of Venus. The fatal baldric Turnus
wears which reminds Aeneas, when he is inclined toward
mercy, of the death of young Pallas is a related "las." The
narrator does not leave the moral of his description of the
frieze to be inferred: he states that beauty, strength, wisdom,
courage, wealth, and even magic—stunning excellences, useful
and awesome in life, potent in legend, are as nothing compared with the power of erotic passion. Narcissus, Hercules,
Solomon, Turnus, Jason, Cresus, all endowed in exemplary
ways and in startling degree, dwindle into a gaggle of helpless
things in a net.

The temple of Mars *displays* its prison. The oratory is one
of those self-centered artifacts which is about itself, like the
pictures of painters painting a picture of a painter painting.
On the wall is a portrait of the senior temple of the god in
Thrace. Clearly, this is a prison. It stands in a barren landscape, an uninhabited forest waste that ensures no fugitive
will escape to a human community:

> . . . a forest,
> In which ther dwelleth neither man ne best,
> With knotty, knarry, bareyne trees olde,
> Of stubbes sharpe and hidouse to biholde,
> In which ther ran a rumbel in a swough,
> As though a storm sholde bresten every bough.
>
> [1975-80]

Steel, windowless, with a door of adamant—details not only identify the oratory as a prison, but charge it, heighten it fearfully:

> Wroght al of burned steel, of which the entree
> Was long and streit, and gastly for to see.
> And therout came a rage and swich a veze
> That it made al the gate for to rese.
> The northren lyght in at the dores shoon,
> For wyndowe on the wal ne was ther noon,
> Thurgh which men myghten any light discerne.
> The dore was al of adamant eterne,
> Yclenched overthwart and endelong
> With iren tough; and for to make it strong,
> Every pyler, the temple to sustene,
> Was tonne-greet, of iren bright and shene.
>
> [1983-94]

This cold and iron place projects the evil and horror that the strong tower of Theseus lacks, for it is dedicated to the murderous passion, anger, in many forms:

> Ther saugh I first the derke ymaginyng
> Of Felonye, and al the compassyng;
> The crueel Ire, reed as any gleede;
> And pykepurs, and eek the pale Drede;
> The smylere with the knyf under the cloke;
> The shepne brennynge with the blake smoke;
> The tresoun of the mordrynge in the bedde;
> The open werre, with woundes al bibledde;
> Contek, with blody knyf and sharp manace.
>
> [1995-2003]

Some of the figures suit an asylum for the criminally mad: "Meschaunce, / With disconfort and sory contenaunce . . .

Woodnesse, laughynge in his rage . . ." (2009 ff.). There is a suicide, with a nail driven into his temple. The place is full of dissonant noise ("chirkyng"—how one paints noise Chaucer does not say).

Whereas in the temple of Venus personifications are mingled with legendary figures, the Martian temple joins personifications with notables of history and nameless, ordinary figures. Julius, Nero, and Antonius, who acted famously, only suffer here. So do the mere journeymen of destiny; here is the carter overridden, the cook scalded, the hunter hunted down. Various modest modes of action and achievement, of prudence and craftsmanship are made icons of futility. That quondam devotee of Mars, Theseus, is the patron who ordered the building. If he also saw to its decoration, he was without radical professional illusions.

Diana's temple, too, is a rendering, a free one, of the prison motive. It is a place of penalties, of unsought fixities. There Chaucer moves far back into remote legend and chooses principally from tales of one kind, metamorphoses. Transformation to animal might mean release, a freeing from the ego's prison—letting go. However, Ovid often develops the theme in an opposite direction: metamorphosis brings not a new freedom but drastic repression, limitation, captivity, in fact. So it is in the stories of Daphne, Callisto, Meleager, and Actaeon, displayed on the temple frieze of Diana.

Certain common patterns beyond metamorphoses inhere in the legends wrought on the goddess's walls: the transformation is usually punitive, the legends all involve ignorance, and they all involve an ironic violation of a normal intimate bond. Punishment is of course the prison's primitive function, and every story except Daphne's is of punishment. Juno and Diana punish Callisto without much marking whether she is to blame; Diana's vengeance upon Actaeon is swift and thorough. Meleager's mother avenges her brother upon her own son. In every story except possibly Actaeon's, the erotic passion is—as much as with the figures on the wall of Venus—a primary cause of the suffering. Most curiously each story involves suffering through someone who should normally cherish the victim, and in all except that of Daphne this element is coupled with ignorance. This aspect, explicit only with Actaeon in Chaucer, is clear in all the Ovidian episodes. As Meleager's mother burns the log that is coterminous with his life, Ovid writes that

> Meleager, though he knew nothing of what was happening, and was not even present, was scorched by that flame. . . . He endured his agony with indomitable courage; but still, he grieved that he should meet so inglorious an end.[17]

When Callisto tries to approach her son, the ursine shape terrifies him and he almost kills her. Ovid's are all nonrecognition scenes.

Still another common pattern is that the victim remains himself under the metamorphosis and so suffers in his old mind as well as under his new guise. Even as a tree, Ovid writes, Daphne shrinks from Phoebus:

> He placed his hand against the trunk, and felt her heart still beating under the new bark. Embracing the branches as if they were limbs he kissed the wood: but, even as a tree, she shrank from his kisses. [*Met.* 1. 553–56; Innes, p. 47]

When Diana transforms Actaeon she puts "panic fear in his heart" and as he runs he marvels to find himself so swift, but

> When he glimpsed his face and his horns, reflected in the water, he tried to say "Alas!" but no words came. He groaned —that was all the voice he had—and tears ran down his changed cheeks. Only his mind remained the same as before. [*Met.* 3. 200–03; Innes, pp. 85–86]

Like the sufferers under Venus, these under Diana are legendary. However, the passage closes with a homely icon like those of the nameless sufferers under Mars. It is on this that the eyes of the goddess's statue are fixed—with what limitations upon her compassion may be imagined from the metamorphoses above:

17. Ovid, *Metamorphoses*, 8. 515–19, trans. Mary M. Innes (London: Penguin, 1955), p. 209. All quotations from the *Metamorphoses* are from this translation. Hoffman, *Ovid and the Canterbury Tales*, pp. 71–89, discusses the Ovidian origin of details in the temples.

> Hir eyen caste she ful lowe adoun,
> Ther Pluto hath his derke regioun.
> A womman travaillynge was hire biforn;
> But for hir child so longe was unborn,
> Ful pitously Lucyna gan she calle,
> And seyde, "Help, for thou mayst best of alle!"
>
> [2081–86]

Since many friezes operate through time as a cartoon strip does, Chaucer might easily have told how the prayer is answered, but he does not. Rather he breaks off to comment on workmanship: "Wel koude he peynten lifly that it wroghte" (2087); the artist spared no expense. The nameless woman is fixed in pain as Keats's figures on the urn are fixed in expectancy. This long travail is to be remembered, I think, when Emily confides to the goddess that she loves hunting and walking in the woods "And noght to ben a wyf and be with childe" (2310). Pluto's "derke regioun," it need scarcely be said, is an efficient, an ultimate prison.

The prison images in the friezes thus move from the snares of Venus, through the artifact of iron in the temple of Mars, to the prison of the other life, the region of Pluto. The series that begins in Venus' temple with insomnia and sighs and ends with the cries of an anonymous woman in labor make it seem fitting that the deity who successfully composes the dispute among the gods and the president divinity of the tournament should be, not Jupiter, but Saturn whose wide and cheerless realm includes "the prison in the derke cote" (2457)—and whose office is in part the warden's one of "vengeance and pleyn correccioun" (2461).

Animal motifs

The shrines embody a mythic extension of the prison. The tale keeps the prison motif present at the subhuman level through references to traps and cages. Possibly Saturn's words quoted above play upon "dovecote" as well as referring to a dungeon room; if so the "derke cote" takes place alongside the "las" of Venus (1951), Love's "laas" (1817), and such conventional figures as Fortune's snare (1490)—all so threadbare they hardly operate with metaphorical charge. It takes place, too, beside Palamon's vivid sense that he is left to "sterve here in a cage" (1294).

And this is more important. We need to reckon with these snares that extend the imprisonment imagery and join it to animal motifs, which Chaucer, uninhibitedly eclectic, takes from many sources. From archetypal myth via the redactions of Ovid the metamorphosed beasts emerge, combining the most primitive psychological appeal with the most sophisticated literary one. Akin to these is the beast-man, the Minotaur, embroidered on the banner of Theseus. From the heraldic world come the creatures named in the account of Lygurge of Thrace and Emetreus of Inde: the great wolf-hounds, large as deer, the lily-white eagle that Emetreus carries for "deduyt." Four white bulls draw Lygurge, who wears a bearskin. His glance is like a gryphon's, and Emetreus is like a lion.

Literary genre accounts for some of the animals in epic or simple similes, for the most part stock. (Significantly for the place of Theseus as an exemplar of human reason, he is never compared with an animal; he *conquers* the Minotaur, he resolves *not* to be like a lion.) But Palamon *is* like a lion, and he and Arcite fight "as it were bores two" (1699), Arcite is as cruel as a tiger whose whelp is stolen, etc. The only time this sort of simile is handled with much distinction is when the heroes are compared to hunters, not animals, but at the touchy moment that brings animals and men to something like par, when the hunt might go either way, the soi-disant doer might become the creature to whom something is done (see 1637-47).

Iconographic tradition furnishes or enhances some of the animal images. The temples display the graven creatures sacred to the gods: the doves of Venus, a wolf devouring a man near the statue of Mars, the hart on which Diana sits with her hounds about her. Jealousy has a "cokkow." Some animals are from woods and stables: the lark that awakens Palamon, letting him know that it is time for prayers to Citherea; the great hart that Theseus hunts; the riding horses; the steeds that bear the funeral achievements of Arcite; those hawks and hounds which Chaucer refuses to bother about at the banquet. The birds and beasts disinherited when the grove is burnt are unclassifiable because included in the context and fate of the "Nymphes, fawnes and amadrides," and so making a rare poetic hybrid, the nymphs taking on some actuality from the wild creatures and these taking on a charm from the fairy creatures. From folktales and fears, perhaps justified, comes the sow that in the temple murals worries a child in its cradle.[18] Arcite's homily on the dogs who fight for a bone to be defrauded by a kite is a curt beast fable. One realistic animal—the horse that throws Arcite—is a convenience of plot. The Knight's Tale is like a tapestry, as is often said; it is one crowded with animal life, as busy as a Brueghel painting.

Another group of animal references vividly corroborates the prison imagery, putting down as sufferers Palamon, Arcite, and sometimes the whole human race, generically. The metamorphoses of Diana's temple might do this, might rouse the powerful responses evoked by atavistic myth or surreal dream, for these are their primitive sources, their mode before they are shaped, fixed in any one treatment, and certainly before they become illustrations of Ovid on the walls of a temple existing in a medieval tale. But in Chaucer they do stay up on the wall, faint in outline, names suggestive of strange privations and disaster on a scale grand but remote. The stories become reverberant in the poem only upon consideration. Chaucer possibly expected his audience only to feel that the temple of Diana is, like the other oratories, wonderful, but that there is something strangely wrong going on in the decor and that this dissonance has something to do with the wonder.

The thematically urgent similies compare men to animals in distinctly nonheroic ways, in denigratory figures of speech usually voiced dramatically. Lions, tigers, and boars are not so much in it as hares and sheep and whelps and fowl.

Early in the story Palamon and Arcite try to puzzle out the

18. Beatrice White, "Medieval Beasts," *Essays and Studies* 18 (1965): 37.

matter of their imprisonment and Arcite's release, to general-
ize from events; in short, they try to "think." Both turn to
animal analogies to express their sense of man as radically
ignorant of his good, as helpless. "We witen nat what thing
we preyen heere," Arcite says in words that are to become as
applicable to his future prayer to Mars as to his past wish to
get out of prison. He continues:

> We faren as he that dronke is as a mous.
> A dronke man woot wel he hath an hous,
> But he noot which the righte wey is thider,
> And to a dronke man the wey is slider.
> And certes, in this world so faren we;
> We seken faste after felicitee,
> But we goon wrong ful often, trewely.
>
> [1261–67]

Arcite's inelegance might account for his language—he is the
one who has compared himself and Palamon to two hounds
fighting for a bone. This diction has been written off as a
Chaucerian lapse in taste. But is the comparison not meant
to be exactly offensive? Palamon speaks less proverbially, but
he, too, in a plaint to Fortune, expresses the helplessness of
men in terms of an animal, one less liable than a drunken
mouse to be a target of comic disdain but also weak, unimpres-
sive. Palamon begins by wondering precisely whether God
does temper the wind to the shorn lamb, and then moves to
a more general comparison:

> . . . O crueel goddes . . .
> What is mankynde moore unto you holde
> Than is the sheep that rouketh in the folde?
> For slayn is man right as another beest,
> And dwelleth eek in prison and arreest,
> And hath siknesse and greet adversitee,
> And ofte tymes giltelees, pardee.
>   What governance is in this prescience,
> That giltelees tormenteth innocence?
> And yet encresseth this al my penaunce,
> That man is bounden to his observaunce,
> For Goddes sake, to letten of his wille,

> Ther as a beest may al his lust fulfille.
> And whan a beest is deed he hath no peyne;
> But man after his deeth moot wepe and pleyne,
> Though in this world he have care and wo.
> Withouten doute it may stonden so.
>
> [1303–22]

Drunken mouse and cowering sheep poignantly fix man's powerlessness, a powerlessness partly owing to ignorance. Arcite's point has not been that a drunken mouse or a drunken man is ludicrous (this second point is only Chaucer's) but that he must be shown the way to go home. Arcite applies the figure to himself:

> Thus may we seyen alle, and namely I,
> That wende and hadde a greet opinioun
> That if I myghte escapen from prisoun,
> Thanne hadde I been in joye and perfit heele,
> Ther now I am exiled fro my wele.
>
> [1268–72]

Neither knight presumes to have insight. Palamon raises the question of how man, when he is so helpless, can be held responsible, but he defers to authority: he does not know, he will leave that to divines (1323). Again in their prayers the two knights, least of all *alazons,* confide their ignorance to the gods. "I recche nat but it may bettre be / To have victorie of hem, or they of me" (2245–46), Palamon says to Venus as he throws himself on her mercy (which turns out to be exactly the right thing to do). Arcite, whose prayer events prove to be less astute, reminds Mars, "I am yong and unkonnynge, as thow woost" (2393). And the reader sees that Arcite is terribly right, especially as he comes up against the resourceful, legalistic smartness of Saturn. The only time his mind works nearly so swiftly and exactly as the situation seems to require is when he tells Palamon that it was he, Arcite, who first loved Emily as a woman. His reputation among critics more or less the product of this one apt rejoinder, he is rather like some Restoration dullard enjoying a wit's reclame in virtue of a single bon mot. One of the ironic aspects of Arcite's experience is that even such numb and modest wisdom as he has is not available to him for relevant use. Quite early he says the things Theseus says later: "We moste endure it; this is the short and playn" (1091). He subscribes to the predestined order of life under fortune: "shapen was my deeth erst than my sherte" (1566); but this is no help in immediate ways. Still must "everich of us take his aventure" (1186).

The mouse and sheep speeches of Arcite and Palamon follow decorously as each reckons with an immediate disappointment, Arcite's that he is released from prison, Palamon's that he is not. As dramatic plaints they should not be too hastily set down as authoritative pronunciamentos on the indignities of being a man. But the young men are not the only ones to speak so. Theseus marvels that all the hot troubles of the knights are for Emily who "woot namoore of al this hoote fare, / By God, than woot a cokkow or an hare!" (1809–10). Such figures frequently express the characters' sense that they are, that someone else is, limited, foolish, ignorant, or powerless. And in the action, so it goes: Arcite fails ignorantly, ignorantly Palamon succeeds. The tale seems to say not that these two young men are particularly befuddled but that all human beings are limited and ignorant, and that ignorance works devastation when coupled with eristic or careless gods. Unwittingly Actaeon stumbles upon Diana bathing; his hounds worry him to death, unwittingly. As in the myth, so in the frieze, in the tale. Human beings do not see ahead; some are stupid, some unlucky, all lack prescience. Arcite clings, while he lives, to the loyalties that claimed his life and dies with the large question on his lips: what is this world? Darkness surrounds all, as the darkness of the grave will enclose first Arcite and eventually everyone, prince and page. From somewhere outside human experience, Boccaccio asserts that Arcita is in the eighth sphere, laughing at the weeping below; in place of this celestial reassurance, Chaucer gives us Arcite's low-pitched dying questions about human meaning and the narrator's flat declaration that he is ignorant as to life hereafter, that Arcite's "spirit chaunged hous and wente ther, / As I cam nevere, I kan nat tellen wher" (2809–10). Informed on the medicine of the case, the teller reports his lack of information on the spirit.[19]

When the narrator uses animal images, they result in a pathos without much dignity about it, and the reader feels an uneasy embarrassment somewhat like that which the antithesis, an anthropomorphic treatment of animals, may elicit (in Disney, for instance). Arcite dismounted is no heroic sight: "As blak he lay as any cole or crowe, / So was the blood yronnen in his face" (2692–93). This is the young prince who, when the statue of Mars mutters "Victorie," leaves the temple "As fayn as fowel is of the brighte sonne" (2337). No one in the Knight's Tale is solicitous of the feathers of sparrows. In the jumble of horrors in the temple is the disregarded "careyne in the busk"; is it human? is it animal? Nothing is said. The cowering sheep, drunken mouse, blackened crow, the foolish, regardless hare, the abandoned carrion express man as a would-be actor and actual sufferer, "allone as he was born" against his fate. Although Chaucer borrowed from Boccaccio to furnish his "nature" and some things which read most freshly come from him, this ensemble of images owes little to

19. Although more equivocal because of context, the beginning of the *Legend of Good Women,* glosses this disclaimer:

> A thousand sythes have I herd men telle
> That there is joye in hevene and peyne in helle,
> And I acorde wel that it be so;
> But natheles, this wot I wel also,
> That there ne is non that dwelleth in this contre,
> That eyther hath in helle or hevene ybe,
> Ne may of it non other weyes witen,
> But as he hath herd seyd or founde it writen;
> For by assay there may no man it preve.
>
> [Text G. 1–9]

Chaucer here is more concerned perhaps with establishing the credit to be accorded old books than with issues of proof and faith. However, of the consolations presented in the *Book of the Duchess* the possibility that Good Fair White still lives in heaven is not proffered, a singular omission in a poem by a Catholic poet presented to a Catholic prince upon the loss of his Catholic lady. This is curious for Chaucer, and such disclaimers as that of the Knight's Tale are even more curious for the parfit, gentil knight, the wayfarer who fought so long for Christendom. They have not a jot of appropriateness to him, but they are immensely appropriate to his tale, to the design of images and events that form its complex structure.

him. The finest nature bits in the *Teseida* are not tied to
commonplace wildlife. What was, for Chaucer, just one possible vein is the *Teseida*'s usual one: the geese are swans and
frequently Ledaean, the songbirds, nightingales, and usually
Philomelas.[20]

In fact, in English poetry the effect nearest to the Knight's
Tale may be Chaucer's *Troilus and Criseyde*, which has several
similar motives informing its symbols and shaping its structures. This tale too provides occasions to ponder free will and
destiny and the people who do ponder them. Boethius is
again under tribute; the icon of fortune turning her wheel
again presides over the worlds of love and war, both, however, presented with a thicker density. The festival and mourning cycle, too, is in effect observed in the story of King Priam's
son of Troy, "In lovynge, how his aventures fellen / Fro wo to
wele, and after out of joie" (1. 3–4). And the same imagery of
birds and hunted animals gathers, beginning in a metaphor
pinpointing the poem's foreground interest, love, as Cupid
draws upon Troilus:

> For sodeynly he hitte hym atte fulle;
> And yet as proud a pekok kan he pulle;
>
> [1. 209–10]

and culminating with a striking metaphor of the background
of war with great walled Troy and the whole world of the
poem seen as a pinioned bird at the mercy of Fortune which

> Gan pulle awey the fetheres brighte of Troie
> Fro day to day, til they ben bare of joie.
>
> [5. 1546–47]

In the Knight's Tale the traps, the small animals, strongly
insist that man is a patient because of a fundamental aptness.
Small beasts exposed to man and weather are powerless; they
can be chased, trapped, killed with impunity. This is to the

---

20. However, Boccaccio also uses his well-tended nature for thematic
effects. He insists on the verdant beauty of the setting of the battle between the knights, and Arcita feels that the fight will be a disruption
there, bloodying the meadows proper to the dryads, fauns, Priapus, and
Apollo (5. 62).

hunter a submoral action, a livelihood or merely a sport. The description of Arcite's blood-blackened face carries a sting because of the blow to a human dignity that the reader feels he shares with Arcite and not with a crow. This is what human victory and noble simplicity come to, something to turn the eyes away from. But Chaucer does not turn decently away, but looks at the scene, holds it coolly before us.

4

Some Acts, Some Passions:

The Faerie Queene, Books 1 and 2

Let us begin at an ending. St. George has slain the dragon, humanity is enfranchised, and Una, having praised God, thanks "her faithfull knight, / That had atchiev'd so great a conquest by his might" (1. 11. 55). He has released the sufferers who dwelt under the affliction of the dragon. He finishes his quest as an actor, as a victor. The people of the land, the "raskall many," run out "To see the face of that victorious man" (1. 12. 9); and also to admire the body of the great dead dragon. The atmosphere of holiday pervades this rarely sympathetic and concrete picture of the "rude rablement." A mother cautions her child, and explains to "her gossips" that the creature might even now "scratch my sonne, or rend his tender hand." Others, more bold, "to measure him nigh stand, / To prove how many acres he did spread of land" (1. 12. 11). Anachronistically, this detail evokes a souvenir snapshot.

There is a feast. The grateful king gives the knight "princely gifts of yvorie and gold"; players of shaumes, trumpets, and clarions precede him up thronged, celebrating streets to the court, where scarlet lines the floor. St. George has acted his destiny, has enacted his legend. Now the king turns to his liberator and asks for his story.

The mood of triumph dissolves, for the old, regal sufferer asks in terms not of action but of suffering, inquires not of deeds performed but of trials endured, and the telling becomes the occasion of sympathy. The king would hear "Of straunge adventures, and of perils sad, / Which in his travell him befallen had." And the knight tells them "with utt'rance grave, and count'nance sad." Spenser does not recapitulate events of the previous eleven cantos, but the response of the audience is revealing:

> Great pleasure mixt with *pittifull regard,*
> That godly King and Queene did *passionate,*
> Whiles they his *pittifull adventures* heard,
> That oft they did lament his *lucklesse state,*
> And often blame the *too importune fate,*
> *That heapd on him so many wrathfull wreakes:*
> For never gentle knight, as he of late,
> *So tossed was* in fortunes cruell freakes;
> And all the while *salt teares bedeawd the hearers cheaks.*

> Then said the royall Pere in sober wise;
> Deare Sonne, great beene the evils, which *ye bore*
> From first to last in your late enterprise,
> That *I note, whether prayse, or pitty more:*
> For never living man, I weene, so sore
> In sea of deadly daungers *was distrest;*
> But since now safe ye seised have the shore,
> And well arrived are, (high God be blest)
> Let us devize of ease and everlasting rest.
>
> [1. 12. 16–17; my italics]

The very grammar and syntax accentuate the knight as the sufferer, one who is acted upon, the fate-harassed hero, *fato profugus.* The words *sad* and *pitiful* echo through the stanzas, and all see the knight not as the challenger and doer he in fact has proved himself, the dragon slayer who is the very type of Virtuous Action, but as the one to whom things have been done. The knight is the passive subject in the authorial comment in lines 7–8 of stanza 16. And only in the line, "ye seised have the shore," does the king's grammar put the knight as subject actor, not the object acted upon or passive subject of modifying clauses. Surely the invitation to rest should arrive on ears ready to hear; but the Red Cross Knight responds that "streight after this emprize" he will return to the Faerie Queene and serve "six yeares in warlike wize." The closing of book 1 therefore presents the hero as one pledged to action in the service of glory, and this in spite of sufferings.

Now let us turn to the beginning. When in the famous opening the Red Cross Knight rides across the plain, his arms are mighty, his steed mettlesome, his persona promising. A line that owes something to *agere et pati* sums up his effect on others: "Yet nothing did he dread, but ever was ydrad." But there are contradictions. The poise of the description is careful; everywhere the poet hints reservations. The mighty arms are those of a veteran, but this knight is inexperienced. He is the heir of a tradition imposing, but not invulnerable—the shield is hacked. He manages his "angry steede" for the moment, but the restive animal may yet give trouble. A "bloudie Crosse," that oxymoronic icon of the most intense possibilities of action and suffering, adorns shield and habergeon, and in it the knight has "soveraine hope," but his "cheere did seeme too solemne sad" (1. 1. 2). His friend is beautiful, but perhaps in mourning. These shadings would make it easy for a hypothetical bystander to believe that this couple had either come from trouble or was going toward it.

The opening scene indicates the balance of the ending; the affirmation of action, the fact, experienced or foreshadowed, of suffering. When Spenser opens the scene on the plain, he is not far into *medias res;* the Red Cross Knight has as yet neither acted nor suffered in the adult world. Etymologically and legendarily a rustic, he is anxious to begin the new chivalric life of quest, "To prove his puissance in battell brave / Upon his foe, and his new force to learne" (1. 1. 3); explicitly his quest is to be a self-discovery or self-creation.[1] As he dis-

1. Critics differ on the degree to which the knight's quest may be seen as a progress. John Arthos, *On the Poetry of Spenser and the Form of Romances* (London: George Allen & Unwin, 1956), p. 42, thinks the story's

covers himself, earns his name, creates his legend, the reader discovers from that process the ambiguous pilgrimage—is it an ordeal? an adventure?—of the Christian soul now in action, now in suffering.[2]

Our discussion centers on the hero as affronted, deluded, tempted, and helped, not as the challenger, adventurer, warrior-saint, and protector. Therefore it is just to remember that the book begins with his success in action. Significantly both initial and final enemy present shapes of evil, serpent and

---

form is *"le roman éducatif."* For H. S. V. Jones, *A Spenser Handbook* (New York: F. S. Crofts, 1930), pp. 156–57, the Red Cross Knight is also a learner. Nelson, *The Poetry of Edmund Spenser,* p. 174, finds it difficult to accept the legend as a *bildungsroman* because the "whole tenor of the Knight's adventures insists upon the point that man is incapable of achieving his own salvation."

2. Robert Salter, a contemporary of Spenser, discussed book 1 in terms of action and passivity. He descried in book 1 a working out of the fourfold life of man in Christ. The first stage is that of nature in original sin, which Salter says applies to the Red Cross Knight before he accepts the quest. Passivity and activity respectively define the second and third stages: "But when hee [the knight] had arrayed himselfe in the *Armor* of his Dying Lord, his presence is then become *Gracious,* and his Person promising great things. . . . Which hee first *Passively* (as in our second *Period*), and after *Actively* (as in our third *Period*) doth so victoriously passe through and finish; that at the length (as in our fourth *Period,*) hee is become altogether *Impassible,* whether of *Assalts* of the frayelty of *Nature* within, or *Affronts* of *Adversaries* without, as being fully possessed of that Kingdome, against which there is none to stand up." R[obert] S[alter], *Vindiciae Danielis, Strange Prophecies from the Monachie of This Land, or An Essay of the Presages of the late prodigious comet pertaining to these our times: in Parables* (n.p.: 1629), p. 43. William Nelson's study of Spenser led me to Salter. Nelson comments, p. 173, that where one should draw the line between the passivity of the knight's second period and the activity of the third he does not know but suggests that perhaps the battle with the dragon represents the latter and everything else the former. As I do not see the development of the hero as a simple progress but rather as a more jagged pattern of fall and recovery, I would include the early battle with Error as in a period of activity. A. C. Hamilton, *The Structure of Allegory in The Faerie Queene* (Oxford: Clarendon, 1961), pp. 58–88, traces the fall and retrieval pattern in book 1.

Throughout book 1, Spenser uses locutions based upon *agere-et-pati* relationships; not until book 6 are there again so many. See 1.1.2, 1.1.19, 1.5.7, 1.8.44, and 1.11.1. There is also a liberal sprinkling of expressions that may less certainly be assigned an *agere-et-pati* significance, such as the "labour, and long tyne" of 1.9.15, the odds-on favorite being combinations of *labours* with either *pains* or *perils*.

dragon. This means that the hero readily discerns them as threats. He emerges with distinction against the serpent Error. Una congratulates him and wishes "that like succeed it may" (1. 1. 27). But like succeeds seldom, for the knight is soon to meet Archimago, whose talents are protean and who respects his enemy sufficiently not to appear as a serpent. Archimago attacks where the inexperienced hero is vulnerable: his perception and his passion. For like Chaucer Spenser also decries scanty knowledge and lavish passions large among the forces that make human beings patients. When Duessa is beautiful and calls herself Fidessa, the observer and listener, uninitiated in duplicity, finds himself victimized at the cognitive root. Archimago attacks in sleep, when the ego is inadvertent. He awakens the knight from an "ydle dreame" into an even more spurious experience, the vision of the sprite-Una with the sprite-squire. "The eye of reason . . . with rage yblent," the knight dashes off. His mount, the angry steed with foaming bit, has soone borne the knight so far from Truth that she cannot catch up with him. Significantly Una rides an ass, an "unhastie beast." The volatile horse, of course, is the emblem of its rider's failure to control his passion.[3]

From the moment Red Cross rides furiously off he is, in Spenser's word and framework, "astray." In Faerie Land one *runs* races rather than sitting down feckless in the middle of them, one *goes* or *journeys forward,* seeks adventures or missing persons; to be *astray* indicates these actions are thwarted or have been weakly abandoned, the actor lapsed to patient. One may sometimes *wander* in Faerie Land without implied reproof; to be a *stray* is frequently, if not always, suspect. We shall shortly see how Despair uses go–stray connotations against the knight. Because of Archimago even though the Red Cross continues for a time to win, he does not act, he reacts. Though he may impose his will in the immediate situation, in relation to his deepest goals he is a sufferer. The

3. Spenser frequently uses the emblematic equation of horse with passions, rider with reason, indicating the moral poise of his knights by their control over their mounts. In book 1 see 2.14, 3.33, and 7.37. See also Guyon (2.1.7). The loss of his horse (2.3.3) does not much handicap rational Guyon; in Spenser there are worse things than being pedestrian.

encounter with Orgoglio begins a period when the knight is
also overtly the patient. Here he is nearly "to dust . . . battred
quight" (1. 7. 14), nearly "pouldred all, as thin as flowre" (1.
7. 12)—that is, nearly returned to join the "monstrous masse
of earthly slime"—the prime matter of the world—that is
Orgoglio himself. And if the hero evades this ultimate unmak-
ing, he is at least "Disarmd [without arms], disgrast [without
spiritual grace], and inwardly dismayde [un-made]" (1. 7. 11).
The alliterative privatives are radical etymological puns. Orgoglio takes up a "slombred sencelesse corse" (1. 7. 15) and
throws it in his dungeon. The unconscious knight, his soul
(form, act) absent, *is* purely his passivity—a body, inert matter, potentiality.[4] With one brief exception, the prelude to
the encounter with Despair, he remains the sufferer until his
battle with the dragon.

Red Cross: Volatile Patient

This selective look at the design of events in book 1 indicates that to a high degree the Red Cross Knight is, although

4. It seems to me that Spenser may be extending the episode in the
glade with the philosophical distinction between form and matter, discussed in chapter 1 above. With a masculine *parti pris, agere et pati* from
medieval times forward was used to discriminate sex roles in conception
sometimes in terms of masculine action and feminine passivity only, but
also frequently in terms of form and matter. See Bartholomaeus, *De proprietatibus rerum* 5. 48. 61v; Dante, *Purgatorio* 25. 46–48; Gulielmo Lynd-
wood, *Provinciale, (seu Constitutiones Angliae)* . . . (Oxford: H. Hall
and Ric. Davis, 1679), p. 272; Baldassare Castiglione, *The Book of the
Courtier,* trans. Sir Thomas Hoby, book 3, p. 199; see also Natalis Comes's
rationalization of Dionysius nursed by the nymphs, reported by C. W.
Lemmi, "The Symbolism of the Classical Episodes in *The Faerie Queene,*"
PQ 8 (1929) : 276, and Sir Kenelm Digby's comment on Spenser's Castle of
Alma in *Observations on the 22. Stanza in the 9th Canto of the 2d. Book
of Spencer's Faery Queen* (London: Daniel Frere, 1644), pp. 14–15. The
form-matter antinomy, without excluding the personally sexual reading,
provides a more spacious background for the scene. On the episode as a
sexual allegory see John W. Schroeder, "Spenser's Erotic Drama: The
Orgoglio Episode," *ELH* 29 (1962) : 140–59. For a criticism, see Donald
Cheney, *Spenser's Image of Nature: Wild Man and Shepherd in The
Faerie Queene* (New Haven: Yale, 1966), p. 34. For some strictures on
overreading of this episode, see Paul J. Alpers, *The Poetry of the Faerie
Queene* (Princeton University, 1967), pp. 137–52.

a quester, a patient. This is also implicit in his attitudes as a
fictional character. Beyond the race's susceptibility to illusion
and passion, the knight has individual attitudes that constitute something like a sufferer's syndrome. In particular situations, the Red Cross Knight evinces uncertainty about what
he should be and do.

He so exemplifies in extreme a characteristic Spenser's heroes generally share: they may behave as if unwillingly aware
that the whole potential of doing and being in the world is
open-ended, problematic. They consciously, it seems, entertain
ideas of conduct which they must fulfill, as if the human da-
tum—body, mind, the energies of both—had in fact possibilities open to it other than those lived out but has focused on
being or becoming holy or temperate or just or courteous.
They are not about to change their minds and loyalties, but
the reader is made to feel that effort sustains them. They feed
upon some inner model of excellence. In contrast, in Chaucer
the reader is aware that *Chaucer* is aware of a norm, a model,
the courtly lover, to which he makes Palamon and Arcite and
Troilus conform—but Palamon and Arcite and Troilus are
not trying to be courtly lovers—they are trying to win ladies.
(Arveragus perhaps *is* trying to be in marriage what he had
been "naturally" in courtship.) Chaucer too projects problematic aspects of existence, but this projection is the result of
an interplay among the author's persona, reader, characters,
and materials of the tale. In Spenser minor characters like
Satyrane may simply exist, effloresce, without much self-
admonition or strain, and Britomart is exceptional; but with
the major heroes, including Arthur, the strain is there. The
reader moves easily to the allegorical level, for, because of
some tension in quester, the real task always seems to be not
the narrative exploit—killing a dragon or Amazons—but real-
izing present-moment-by-present-moment the virtue allegorized. To this end, the fallible heroes seem to be using their
selves—perhaps dedicating themselves—as an actor uses his
physical and psychic endowments to realize a role. Suspense is
therefore diverted toward something like psychology, as C. S.
Lewis has remarked; and this suspense is real because though

final outcomes for Spenser's heroes are more or less assured, we are familiar with that tension, that effort, that fallibility. Even though allegory makes characters other than mimetic, Spenser's protagonists often have a hauntingly familiar consciousness.[5]

The Red Cross Knight is least successfully integrated in support of his virtue, holiness demanding so much. At first he is confident to the point of bravado. His first adventure, though it turns out well, is symptomatic. Seeking shelter from a rainstorm he and Una come upon a cave which the knight proposes to enter. Una advises caution, "Least suddaine mischiefe ye too rash provoke" (1. 1. 12). (Una's estimate of her champion emerges in a syntactically subordinated candor.) She remembers that this is Error's den, but the knight is not only courageous but also a trifle vainglorious:

> Ah Ladie (said he) shame were to revoke
> The forward footing for an hidden shade:
> Vertue gives her selfe light, through darkenesse for to wade.
>
> [1. 1. 12]

That the armor of the Christian gives only faint light is often remarked. Of course the Red Cross Knight is less a personality than an allegorical and legendary identity holding together a few behavior patterns. Still, within this limitation, it can be said that his rashness is characteristic. It is the second quality he recovers (the first is courtesy) after his withering imprisonment, and again it gets him into trouble. He forces Trevisan to tell his story (1. 9. 25) and to accompany him, but he disregards Trevisan's advice never to try the "guilefull traine" of Despair and the hint of relationship Trevisan

5. Although allegory may seem to simplify the problem of characterization and no doubt often does for the writer, it may increase problems for the reader because for vital figures the allegorical identity will seem only to begin, not resolve, definition of character. That the reader's, not the character's, psychology is what is really involved is akin to the central idea of Alpers that Spenser's stanzas are virtually modes of address to the reader. See Alpers, p. 5, where the thesis is succinctly put, and throughout. The tension of Spenser's heroes is explained in quite another fashion than mine by Angus Fletcher, *Allegory: The Theory of a Symbolic Mode* (Ithaca, N.Y.: Cornell, 1964), pp. 25–69.

plainly gives: "like infirmitie like chaunce may beare" (1. 9. 30).[6] The Red Cross Knight persists in his old style: "hence shall I never rest, / Till I that treachours art have heard and tride" (1. 9. 32). But at the plausibility of Despair he "much wondred" (1. 9. 41), and is "much enmoved," thrown into amazement "As he were charmed with inchaunted rimes" (1. 9. 48).

Amazement is a key word for the knight. On the one hand he acts rashly; on the other, events frequently dumbfound, confuse, or astonish him, immobilize him—not mental states associated with the actor (see also 1. 2. 31, 1. 4. 7, and 1. 7. 7). (Sometimes there are good physical reasons for this as when he and Sansfoy charge, crashing head-on, and, "Astonied both, stand sencelesse as a blocke" [1. 2. 16]. Details consonant with the literal event make an exact allegory for the theological encounter of faithlessness and holiness; the impasse would be total.) The Red Cross Knight is sufficiently naive and unstable to fall well within Aristotle's requirements for a tragic hero sufficiently like the audience to elicit home comparisons. Most readers probably do feel akin to the first book's hero. He is sympathetic (sym-pathetic) because we do have like pathos.

This instability makes him a proper victim for Duessa. Note that he exerts himself to meet her. Having killed Sansfoy, he chases after the fleeing witch. (Sensibly, Duessa, although a fanatic, "when she saw her champion fall, / Like the old ruines of a broken towre, / Staid not to waile his woefull funerall" [1. 2. 20].) Overtaking her, the Red Cross Knight orders her to "stay," whereupon Duessa petitions him. She calculates her address delicately to fit a client sometimes rash, often confused, just now, he thinks, betrayed. He has had a surrogate revenge and apparently won a surrogate maiden, one prom-

6. The Red Cross Knight is not quick to pick up such cues. Linwood E. Orange, "Sensual Beauty in Book I of *The Faerie Queene*," *JEGP* 61 (1962) : 559–61, discusses Fradubio as a warning to the Red Cross Knight. Cheney, p. 43, says that the knight's stopping of the tree's wound with clay suggests repression of unwelcome knowledge. Kathleen Williams, *Spenser's World of Glass* (Berkeley: University of California, 1966), p. 11, considers the knight's fatuity when he meets Fradubio to show just how blinded the eye of reason has become.

isingly named Fidessa. He is impressed by her history, which both liken to tragedy ("Deare dame, your suddein overthrow / Much rueth me"; "My dearest Lord fell from high honours staire"); by her clothes ("so ritch weedes and seeming glorious show"); and by her manner of "humblesse low" (see 1. 2. 21, 23). But in view of not only Una's plain garb but also her tendency to offer advice, perhaps most grateful is Duessa's implication that she is the patient, he the actor. She is only a "silly Dame" subject to the reverses of fortune and to his, the knight's, "mighty will," a "wretched woman" now made "thrall to your commandement" and so forth. She tells with conscious pathos how foes slew her betrothed and how like a stricken hind she had wandered until the proud Saracen captured her. Now she asks "of you in pitty of my state, / To do none ill, if please ye not do well (1. 2. 26). The Red Cross Knight is the doer; it is all up to him. Insidious, exact, soothing to a battered ego, no wonder Duessa's demeanor "Did much emmove his stout heroïcke heart." Presently they ride off together, "he feining seemely merth, / And she coy lookes" (1. 2. 27).

Uncertain and gullible, the Red Cross Knight is also subject to wanhope. In all his sojourn he is most helpless in Orgoglio's dungeon and in the Cave of Despair. Both episodes suggest that something like a death wish is deeply a part of the mercurial hero. When Arthur calls through the grate of Orgoglio's dungeon, the knight calls back, greeting, "O welcome thou, that doest of death bring tydings trew" (1. 8. 38). Arthur brings contrary tidings of life and freedom, but the hero is listless. Una mourns when she sees her emaciated champion:

> . . . Ah dearest Lord, what evill starre
> On you hath fround, and pourd his influence bad,
> That of your selfe ye thus berobbed arre,
> And this misseeming hew your manly looks doth marre?
>
> [1. 8. 42]

The reversal from the jolly young man who set out to prove his puissance and learn his force is complete. He has not discovered a heroic self, he has been robbed of himself.

This reunion scene has novelistic qualities which Spenser seldom yields, which he is not fundamentally trying for, a social density and psychological subtlety that comes from furnishing the characters not with the stereotyped response but with one shaded, discrepant. Ironically the meeting is less joyous than Una's with Archimago impersonating the Red Cross Knight. To be sure, Una now again gives her champion a wholehearted welcome; she spiritedly derides fortune—"fie on Fortune mine avowed foe" (1. 8. 43)—and she looks on the bright side—"good growes of evils priefe" (1. 8. 43). But the knight has no relish in this particular conversation, "no delight to treaten of his griefe; / His long endured famine needed more reliefe." In the exact language of the topos Arthur intervenes:

> Faire Lady, then said that victorious knight,
> The things, that grievous were to do, or beare,
> Them to renew, I wote, breeds no delight.
>
> [1. 8. 44]

Manifestly then the reuniting of the Red Cross Knight and Una is not a happy ending but a sobered-down basis for a new, more realistic beginning.[7] (Not that they ever seem to have been a merry couple. The more lightsome conversations are with Duessa, Una's small talk being often confined to advice about getting one's rest, etc.) The Red Cross Knight is too weak to begin his quest; he will at least twice more wish to die.

The definitive exploration of the death wish comes at the Cave of Despair. The temptation there is grounded in action and passion as modes of being. Spenser develops the passage by exploiting antitheses and ironic conjunctions of doing and suffering. The episode has been much discussed, but not from this perspective so far as I know. The pinchbeck spookiness of

7. Spenser handles the reunion of Britomart and Artegall in book 5 in a similarly muted fashion. When Britomart finds Artegall spinning "She turnd her head aside, as nothing glad, / To have beheld a spectacle so bad" (5. 7. 38). She finally speaks candidly and ruefully, "Ah my deare Lord, what sight is this (quoth she) / What May-game hath misfortune made of you?" (5. 7. 40).

the setting (the decor an anticipation of Gothic, with tree stubs, ragged crags, an owl, carcasses, and howling ghosts) vanishes when the knight enters the cave. The "man of hell" begins by trying to persuade the intrepid, indignant intruder to recognize that he really envies the suicide he is trying to rescue:

> Most envious man, that grieves at neighbours good,
> And fond, that joyest in the woe thou hast,
> Why wilt not let him passe, that long hath stood
> Upon the banke, yet wilt thy selfe not passe the flood?
>
> [1. 9. 39]

Generations of *Faerie Queene* readers have marked the next langorously persuasive lines of Despair:

> He there does now enjoy eternall rest
> And happie ease, which thou doest want and crave,
> And further from it daily wanderest:
> What if some little paine the passage have,
> That makes fraile flesh to feare the bitter wave?
> Is not short paine well borne, that brings long ease,
> And layes the soule to sleepe in quiet grave?
> Sleepe after toyle, port after stormie seas,
> Ease after warre, death after life does greatly please.
>
> [1. 9. 40]

(Consider the internalization of Despair; how vivid and congenial the image of dissolution is to the Red Cross Knight.) Spenser lends all his art to Despair.[8] The "deepe delight that is in death" did elicit Spenser's most lyric vein.

8. The art is in simplicity. Most of the words of the stanza are of one syllable, the vocabulary plain. *Eternall* is perhaps its "highest" word. Every verse element progressively augments a sense of relaxation as the stanza proceeds. The plain syntax becomes more plain, freeing the reader from all effort. Faintly ambiguous modifications in a subordinated syntax mark the first three lines; the following questions are more lucidly articulated and the series of parallelisms in the statement of the last two lines—sleep/toil, port/sea, ease/war, death/life—induce the reader to accept also the parallelism of Despair's meaning. The sound effects of the stanza are never harsh, but the accession of liquids in the final lines is marked. The dulcet movement is furthered by assonance at early and terminal positions in four lines (5, 7, 8, 9), and this also increases. The word "ease" echoes through the lines, even replacing the expected "Peace" of line 9. Nothing is lost, the similar sound leads the reader to feel both the expected and the literal word, and Despair thus evokes not only

But this is early; these lines alone do not bring the knight to the verge of suicide. Somewhat later Despair tempts the knight to the unforgivable sin—despair of salvation. This also appeals to passivity. For the Christian believer, the content of the death wish must be the wish to give up the burden of action. Only to an unbeliever would death promise an end of suffering in either limited or general meaning. The orthodox Red Cross Knight does not dissent when presented that hopeless vista, "The lenger life, I wote the greater sin, / The greater sin, the greater punishment" (1. 9. 43). The knight is *pulled* toward death in appeals to passivity, in discrepant accounts of death as rest (1. 9. 40) and as torment (1. 9. 49).

And midway between these most seductively psychological and most theologically horrific persuasions, he is *pushed* toward it in a thorough attack on action as an illusion, his peculiar, existential illusion. Despair attacks the knightly vocation as not heroic but bloody, sinful, and squalid:

> All those great battels, which thou boasts to win,
> Through strife, and bloud-shed, and avengement,
> Now praysd, hereafter deare thou shalt repent:
> For life must life, and bloud must bloud repay.
>
> [1. 9. 43]

Shortly thereafter, he is pointing out that the knight has not kept faith with "this Ladie milde." Despair impugns the chief subjects of the Renaissance epic, love and war; he puts it that the fierce wars and faithful loves that moralize Spenser's song and make coherent the lives and significant the quests of his heroes are trivial, the wars only fierce, the loves rarely faithful.

With the Red Cross Knight on the defensive, Despair suggests that he is deluded if he thinks he is an actor: he is a patient, a sufferer, one who does not *go* on his pilgrimage, but *strays:*

---

peace but a fuller peace of ease. The analogies are successive, progressing from common daily experience (sleep after toil) to the more intense and particular trials, and the unarguable first three statements make the analogy seem inevitably acceptable. Moreover, as warfare and a voyage were common metaphors for life and as the analogy of sleep and death was a commonplace, their collocation of welcoming resolutions makes the argument seem to be accustomed, to be one with them.

> For he, that once hath missed the right way,
> The further he doth goe, the further he doth stray.
>
> Then do no further goe, no further stray,
> But here die downe, and to thy rest betake.
>
> [1. 9. 43–44]

Then the tempter subdues all the chances of life to a litany of vulnerabilities:

> For what hath life, that may it loved make,
> And gives not rather cause it to forsake?
> Feare, sicknesse, age, losse, labour, sorrow, strife,
> Paine, hunger, cold, that makes the hart to quake;
> And ever fickle fortune rageth rife,
> All which, and thousands mo do make a loathsome life.
>
> [1. 9. 44]

Finally comes the vision of hell (1. 9. 49). As commentators have pointed out, Despair is not consistent about the next life.[9] But he is fearfully consistent in his attack on this life. He reduces all its general claims and this hero's particular experience and deeds to mere passion and suffering.

The encounter is not like a judicial trial nor a duel; it is not like a discussion of theology, though it embodies one. Rather the knight is like a swimmer in shallows who finds suddenly that the tide is in and the water fathoms deep, bottomless, and a strong undertow runs out. The verse urges the sinking toward dissolution as the diphthong *die* whispers through the speech of the man of hell: "did not he all create / To die againe?" (1. 9. 42). The question is transmuted into an incantation:

> Is not his law, Let every sinner *die:*
> *Die* shall all flesh? what then must needs be donne,
> Is it not better to doe willinglie,
> Then linger, till the glasse be all out ronne?
> Death is the end of woes: *die* soone, O faeries sonne.
>
> [1. 9. 47; my italics]

Despair's onslaught, eloquent, varied, wooing, sometimes prodding, grave, almost paternal in tone, finally roughly impera-

9. See Ernest Sirluck in "A Note on the Rhetoric of Spenser's 'Despair'," *MP* 47 (1949): 8–11.

tive, brings the knight to accept inertly the dagger thrust into his hand. In a reversal of tactics, Despair has couched this final move in a suggestion that the knight yet can act—his one valid, voluntary action can be suicide (while the enveloping syntax makes it clear to the reader that the tempter is the actor—see 1. 9. 50). The knight neither rejects the knife nor uses it; he lifts a hand and draws it back, he is absolutely irresolute for death, in a paralysis of will.

Una's argument is short. Like Despair's, hers is based on an appeal to passivity—the knight is elected, which is not his doing. But unlike Despair, rather than attacking she appeals to the ethic of action in a rhetorical reminder of the quest: "Is this the battell, which thou vauntst to fight / With that firemouthed Dragon, horrible and bright?" (1. 9. 52). Una does not answer directly the attack on the heroic claim but countermatches it and dismisses him. "Ne let vaine words bewitch thy manly hart, / Ne divelish thoughts dismay thy constant spright" (1. 9. 53). Significantly, she also acts. She snatches the knife; this is the salient countermove to Despair's thrusting it upon the hero. Despair's contempt of life and action cannot match in ardor practical Una's contempt of death, of passivity, of letting go. The topos *agere et pati* defines the climax. Gestures compose into a psychomachia: the action of Despair thrusting the knife, the countering action of Una snatching it, between them the total passion of the hero. (The knight is, of course, at one allegorical level, simply the psychic terrain in which Una and Despair dispute.)

The word *psychomachia* signalizes that we have moved away from a quasi-novelistic discussion of character. A note on the placement of Una as an allegorical figure, as an aspect of the hero's psyche, and on her action and suffering, may close our consideration of book 1. Una lingers in memory in a poetic integrity time does not wither. She is the stellar image in an iconographic grouping of creatures—Una with her white ass, with her lamb, her lion, her dwarf, with, above all, her knight. Secondarily she emerges from the memory in incongruously appealing situations: ruefully crowned among satyrs, perhaps, or befriended by Satyrane, who, rather better than her own knight, provides a foil for her girlish quality. I should like to begin discussion of her action and suffering more capriciously and abstractly than with these felicitous contexts, to note that Spenser places Una firmly as regards Ignaro, Contemplation, and the House of Wisdom so as to show that ignorance, wisdom, and contemplation bear different relations to truth—respectively, privative, contextual, and teleological. If Ignaro is the total deprivation of the activity Una represents and Duessa is her depraved opposite, Contemplation is truth in an action directed toward highest wisdom.[10]

Una directly encounters neither; she points the way past Ignaro and leads the Red Cross Knight to the House of Wisdom, toward, not up, the hill of Contemplation. Unlike Ignaro, whose passive noncognition *is* his total relation to Una (truth), defining exactly his moral squalor, listlessness, and haunting repulsiveness, she acts; and unlike Contemplation, she acts in the human realm.[11] Most of her advice is strikingly pragmatic, though presumably the instruction given the satyrs is doctrinal. She is human truth in a human world, the quotidian need of everyman if he is to stay in touch with himself and reality. As human truth, Una acts and suffers, too, and her tribulation as a deserted girl matches her allegorical identity much of the time, for truth sometimes is abandoned in the world, consigned to unprestigious wilderness places to shift for itself with unlikely appreciators and defenders. Under this suffering her bravery and initiative as a fictionally independent character and the active power of truth to stay the course, to overcome, shine out. At the worst, thinking her knight dead, she goes on with an appropriately mundane, arithmetical conviction that "Who hath endur'd the whole, can beare each part" (1. 7. 25). Plot makes Una a patient, the befriended one. But she very nearly continuously acts.[12] This

10. Ignaro is a deglamorized version of those in Dante's Limbo.
11. Jones, *Spenser Handbook*, p. 159.
12. In the cantos that give their separate stories, while the knight has "strayed" (1. 3. 8), Una "seeks" her love and journeys forward (head verse to canto 3, 1. 3. 8, 1. 3. 21, and 1. 7. 28). She does suffer; he leaves her, the woods people rescue her; she has no power over Sansloy; she suffers, perhaps with allegorical inconsistency, the impersonation of Archimago.

is because any but the most primitive narrative complicates the division between action and suffering. But it is also because as an element in the Red Cross Knight's character, truth is an active force even if sometimes working submerged, at a frightening distance from conscious dalliance with the supposed Fidessa.[13] No one, not the most gullible, wishes to be lied to; we wish pleasant statements to be true, we court Fidessa, not Duessa. Daughter of a king, Una shows truth's royal face in even dingy circumstances and its persistence as an ideal in even a deluded human being.

Una is persistent and strong; and she is lightly touched with a severity that seems appropriate to her allegorical character. Hard good sense comes when she is under pressure: "Strangle her, else she sure will strangle thee" (1.1.19); "Come, come away, fraile, feeble, fleshly wight" (1.9.53). (In such moments, if we wish to take Una as an aspect of the Red Cross Knight, we would say that crises make him more astute.) The satyrs find Una charming with her pathetically "ruffled rayments,

---

But she also awes the lion and teaches the satyrs. (See Rosemond Tuve, *Allegorical Imagery: Some Mediaeval Books and Their Posterity* [Princeton University, 1966], p. 123, on the nature of the encounter between Una and the lion and the allegorical pictures of virtues exacting submission.) Reunited with her knight, until the final canto Una preserves active ascendance over him: she sets Duessa's punishment (1.8.45–46); delays their "forward course" until he is more fully recovered (1.9.20); she snatches the knife from him in the Cave of Despair (1.9.52); she brings him to the house of Caelia (1.10.2–3), introduces him there, and places him under the tutelage of Fidelia (1.10.18). When he has passed through his training, Una reminds him "Of her adventure mindfull for to bee" (1.10.68). As they near the battle, St. George reassumes fully his initial relation of agent, champion, protector, ordering her to withdraw to a hill. Holiness is active, truth is patient as the poem's climax comes. The Red Cross Knight's and Una's interchange of agent and patient roles contributes greatly to book 1's satisfying design.

13. Harry Berger, Jr., points out in "At Home and Abroad with Spenser," *MLQ* 25 (1964): 106, that many of Spenser's characters lead double lives determined by an allegory "whose reference is primarily psychological. Una, Archimago, Duessa, and the Sans-brothers, for example, exist simultaneously outside the hero in the fictional landscape, and within him, as permanent or transient aspects of his psyche." This is more acceptable with Una and the Sans-brothers than with Archimago. It is too strange to think of St. George projecting an Archimago in order to deceive himself. The basic notion, however, is sound and helpful.

and faire blubbred face" (1. 6. 9), but the carlin hag and her daughter who live off Kirkrapine entertain in Truth a costly guest. Some critics have not liked Una's treatment of Duessa, but I doubt that we are to react as to a woman who, knowing another's deformity, orders her to be stripped. Truth is the harsh, stripping virtue.

The baring of Duessa's misshapen self is an instance of a peculiarity frequent in Spenser's description of evil, of inauthenticity—the presentation of nether and hindsides of things and people in obscene contrast to their fronts. These rear views seem not to balance, but to invalidate, the front ones. The Echidna shows the face of a fair maiden, "But all her hinder parts did plaine expresse / A monstrous Dragon, full of fearfull uglinesse" (6. 6. 10). The gods hate the Echidna not for her ugly rear, but for her "so dreadfull face" (6. 6. 11); that is, for the abnormality, the perversity of the rear with the lovely face. But Una, unveiled, and Britomart, disarmed, shine. Still this is not enough to certify truth in Faerie Land, where light and perspective may deceive judgment, and so Una is not only brightly beautiful but "true as touch"—a reference to the touchstone test for coins, an emblem book motif.

With deeds so heroic performed by an uncertain hero, it is difficult to attach the label of either agent or patient to St. George. When Archimago tries to interrupt the wedding, St. George explains in language the book has made familiar. In his mishaps, he says, "unwares," he "strayd" out of his way. As he tells his prospective father-in-law of meeting the witch, he corrects his syntax, assigning himself the role of patient: "There did I find, or rather I was found" by the false woman who "Unwares me wrought unto her wicked will" (1. 12. 32). The poet has interposed reminders that most aspirants to Christian gentlemanliness would not emerge with more panache over such foes (see 1. 7. 1. and 1. 10. 1). The reader is to refrain from taking the self-congratulatory stance of comedy, though book 1 has a happy ending. Una and her knight set a pattern that is varied, but not essentially different, in the other books—alternately vincible and victorious, alternately acting and suffering. That is how it is.

Guyon at Sea

Sir Guyon is less disaster-prone than St. George. More consistently and perfectly the doer, he remains an agent through the whole of his book apart from brief intervals, notably the faint at the Cave of Mammon. Because reason controls his passions, he may usually opt to do or to refrain. In reverses which limit his physical action, he exercises the choice of taking a positive stance; in minimal situations where it must be "patience perforce" (2. 3. 3), he persists in choice and therefore in moral action. Guyon's main adventure gets under way with his vow to avenge Mordant and Amavia which he couches biblically (e.g., 1 Kings 3 : 17, Ruth 1 : 17), as vows of vengeance often are phrased, in the discriminations of *agere et pati:* If I do not *do* this, may I *suffer* that. Guyon the actor does accomplish the vengeance and therefore never becomes subject to the "Such and such evill" that God is to call upon him, nor must Ruddymane bear the "worse and worse . . . paine."

As a fictional creation he is somewhat numb beside the volatile knight of the red cross, and even though Guyon goes from a hell to a perverse earthly paradise, resisting the one, destroying the other, bearing and doing in model fashion, he does not remind us of the extremes of our plight and scope in suffering and action, as St. George does. This is because Guyon is so much in command of himself and of his terrain. In the last fifteen years or so several stimulating readings of book 2 have appeared, and most take account of what I am here describing as Guyon (or Guyon-cum-palmer) figuring as the agent of his tale.[14]

14. For instance, Harry Berger, Jr., in *The Allegorical Temper: Vision and Reality in Book II of Spenser's Faerie Queene* (New Haven: Yale, 1957), p. 16, writes that "Guyon is not the Christian relying upon God but the megalopsychos relying on himself." He sees, p. 64, the design of the book as twofold, hinged at the Mammon episode; the first part of the book offers a classical world view, the second a religious one; "Tyche" rules over the first part of the book, a more Boethian concept of fortune over the second. Hamilton, pp. 116–23, offers as a model for the structure of book 2 that the first half imitates the *Iliad,* the second the *Odyssey.*

Though the hero seems so preeminently an agent, the antithesis of action and endurance touches the book at important points. Guyon's experiences divide between those which require him passively to bear a testing and those which require him to act. The antinomies of doing and enduring defined the virtue of courage from classical times. A locus was Cicero: "Fortitudo est considerata periculorum susceptio et laborum perpessio" (*De inventione* 2. 54. 163; "Courage is the quality by which one undertakes dangerous tasks and endures hardships"). Livy's story (2. 12. 9–10) of the Roman youth threatened with torture who thrusts his hand into the flames and says, "facere et pati fortia Romanum est," became a popular emblem motif. In St. Thomas, aggression and endurance are the two acts of fortitude ("fortitudo . . . habet duos actus, scilicet sustinere et aggredi"); and endurance rather than attack is the chief act of fortitude; though endurance may be a passion of the body ("passionem corporis"), it is an action of the soul ("actum animae").[15] Boccaccio in Il Filostrato 1. 8 distributes the two acts of courage respectively to attackers and defenders of Troy; Calchas learns which is to conquer, "la lunga sofferenza / De' Troiani, o de' Greci il grande ardire" ("the long endurance of the Trojans or the great daring of the Greeks").

A. C. Hamilton's observation that the first part of Guyon's book is modeled on the *Iliad* and the second includes an *Odyssey* prompts the recollection that some Renaissance critics al-

---

Nelson, pp. 182 ff., sees the division between the "forward" and the "froward" passions as important to the book's design, the first in some senses more active, the second more passive. Alastair Fowler, *Spenser and the Numbers of Time* (New York: Barnes & Noble, 1964), pp. 9–17 and 80–121, remarks on book 2 as the book of the dyad and the book of the moon. A. S. P. Woodhouse's argument that book 1 is governed by the concept of grace and book 2 by that of nature in "Nature and Grace in *The Faerie Queene*," *ELH* 16 (1949): 194–228, has prompted several articles of corroboration and reservation. A review of main interpretations of this (or any) book of *The Faerie Queene* between 1937 and 1960 may be found in Waldo F. McNeir and Foster Provost's *Annotated Bibliography of Edmund Spenser, 1937–1960* (Pittsburgh, Pa.: Duquesne, 1962). As the annotation is thorough, the bibliography is in fact a digest of Spenser criticism within the dates indicated.

15. *ST*, Dominican Fathers, pt. 2-2, q. 123, art. 6 (2 : 1711); see also art. 10 (2 : 1714).

legorized the *Iliad* as a model of action, the *Odyssey* as a model of patience.[16] One may even say that the *Iliad*-like parts of book 2 and the Odyssean sections respectively display the two acts of courage and that Guyon in his doing and enduring is as much the model of courage as he is of temperance. If the book had appeared under the title "The Legend of Sir Guyon, or of Courage," it probably would not have been spotted as a mistake, though a discovery that it also dealt with temperance would not have been avoided. Even the burlesque mock-knight, Braggadochio, who lacks courage, fits in.

But although Guyon is an actor and a courageous one, his story seems to demand less derring-do than is asked of some other heroes. In fact, one critic finds Guyon passive:

> Guyon in the deeds of temperance was meeting dangers that were not so much monsters as phantasms, the dreams of the senses. . . . his journey became not so much a marching against enemies as a transport through a series of dreams. This passivity contrasts with the aggressions of the Red Crosse Knight. . . .
>
> Guyon's endurances are often only in the sight of things: of the child playing in his mother's blood; of Furor's fierce attack on Pyrochles; of Mammon's wilderness of wealth. The passivity of his progress is witnessed, too, by this, that more often than other heroes he is likened to a boat. . . . borne on ships, sometimes unaccompanied, sometimes at the mercy of the wind.[17]

This is well observed, although it refers chiefly to Guyon's lack of *aggressive* action. Guyon does more than view Ruddymane playing in his mother's blood. He tries to wash him up, he buries his parents, he finds him a home. Guyon rescues and lectures Phedon, he tries to befriend Pyrochles, he calls on Mammon. As I see it Guyon remains the moral agent because after a brief outing as patient to Archimago's agency, he selects his options.

One way of expressing this command Guyon seems to possess, usually so surely, is to put it that he is a kind of case study of Renaissance mental health. And if a proper analogy for book

16. Hamilton, pp. 116–23; see above for allegorization of the epics, pp. 35–36.
17. Arthos, pp. 185–86.

1 is theology, particularly redemptive history, the comparable allegorical subject of book 2 is psychology. This retreats from recent approaches to the book to an older and more obvious one. (The *Variorum* editors in recognition of the psychological lore informing book 2 provide an appendix on Renaissance psychology.) The vegetal, sensitive, and rational souls (or principles of the soul) are points of reference throughout. The famous places of book 2 involve all three. Although this is most clear at the Castle of Alma, I think it may also be that the strain Guyon undergoes at the Cave of Mammon, the temptations to eat and to rest, and the faint when he emerges, indicate a design to include a threat to the vegetal soul there. (Growth and nourishment come under the vegetal soul.) Reason and will are clearly in tension as between Guyon and Mammon throughout the episode from their initial discursive argument, accounting for the rational soul. The personifications in the passageway to the Cave (Revenge, Despight, Hate, Gealosie, Feare, Sorrow, Shame, and Horrour [2. 7. 22–23]) bring the passions of the sensible soul into the canto.[18] At Medina's castle, the lecture of the hostess (2. 2. 29–31) to her sisters' bellicose friends enacts the reasonable soul governing the perturbations of the sensible soul, in this canto, wrath, melancholy, and love. The vegetal soul is less in evidence, though Medina provides "meete satietie" (2. 2. 39) for her guests, irrepressible Perissa flows "In wine and meats . . . above the bancke" (2. 2. 36), and the company's going to rest ends the canto. (Housekeeping necessarily caters to the vegetal soul.)

The main plot line, the contest of Guyon and Acrasia, exemplifies the proper, temperate functioning of the rational soul as against its disorganization. Acrasia is developed in

---

18. Berger's treatment of the Cave of Mammon in *The Allegorical Temper* may be found on pp. 15 ff.; the discussion of Alpers, pp. 235 ff.; that of Frank Kermode, "The Cave of Mammon," in *Elizabethan Poetry,* ed. John Russell Brown and Bernard Harris, Stratford-upon-Avon Studies 2 (London: Edward Arnold, 1960), pp. 151–73, is also of special interest. Remarks on these and other interpretations of the episode may be found in Patrick Cullen's "Guyon *Microchristus:* The Cave of Mammon Reexamined," *ELH* 37 (1970) : 153–74.

terms of specifically erotic possibilities and owes much of her style and presence to Armida. But her name indicates a more general riot. Kitchin's edition glosses the name: "the Aristotelian ἀκρασία, that condition of man in which the due government of the appetites, or the combination of the elements of human nature, is neglected. She is the self-indulgent opposite of self-ruling Temperance." [19] The second account of how Guyon comes to go on the quest, that the palmer, Reason, drew him forth from the court to oppose Acrasia, renders in narrative this significance.

Thus the great places of the book gather together themes assignable to rational, sensible, and vegetal souls or principles of the soul, and the overarching action records the triumph of the rational soul's reason and will over passion's anarchy in the sensible soul. Most of the book's episodes deal with the sensible soul, especially as it desires—the varied enactments of forward and froward passions, the stories of Pyrochles, Cymochles, Verdant, Amavia, Phedon, belong here.

Renaissance theory assigned to the sensible soul, however, not only the passions, but cognitive powers. They were not the spiritual reason and will of the rational soul, but a more physically related apparatus, an exterior one, the five senses, and an interior one, internal senses located in the brain (and in some accounts given exact stations in its lobes). Arthur's fight against Maleger brings threats against the exterior senses under control. The reader meets the interior senses—common sense, imagination, and memory—within the Castle of Alma (see 2. 9. 47–58).[20] I should like to suggest that Guyon's voyage embodies a threat to these interior senses and that what the prince has suffered and achieved for the exterior senses, Guyon suffers and achieves, on his voyage preserving the sensible soul's inward life. Here he must endure; "Therefore the prin-

19. *Book II of The Faery Queene*, ed. G. W. Kitchin, 1867 (Oxford: Clarendon, 1961), p. 182.

20. Phantastes is imagination, Eumnestes is memory. But the man of middle years in the room with walls displaying "all that in the world was aye thought wittily" (2. 9. 53) is not so clearly common sense, which was merely a power that received and recognized forms sent to it by the external senses.

cipal act of fortitude is endurance, that is to stand immovable in the midst of dangers rather than to attack them." [21]

Further, Guyon's odyssey furnishes a narrative recapitulation of earlier events. The Castle of Alma in canto 9 has defined and placed the psychological assumptions of the whole book; in canto 11 comes the Maleger-Arthur contest; finally we have Guyon faring forward, and his voyage is both a repetition and a development.

For with the voyage Spenser reviews his own book and he pays his respects at old epic ports of call, with Tasso particularly well in mind; but he also introduces something new in the perilous flux. The imponderable sea becomes a suggestive symbol for obscure, threatening devastations. The differences with Tasso are more instructive than are the resemblances. For Tasso was interested in the sea of legend and of history; one could map the geography of the first part of the voyage. But Spenser's sea has no such mark as the pillars of Hercules. Guyon, most prosaic hero in Faerie Land, undergoes a haunting, uncertain adventure about which only the outcome is certain: clearly, he reaches land.

Exactly what threats Guyon undergoes we do not know fully. The mode of assault is in part like that on Arthur in canto 11: Guyon's senses of vision and hearing are under siege. But the target is behind the eyes. One might sort out more specific correspondences with Renaissance anatomies of the soul and label the odyssey's first perils an attack on the memory; the next, culminating in the sea monsters, an attack on the imagination; and the third, ending with dark and fog, an attack on the common sense. But this schema seems inappropriately rigid. Better to say that something like this, something this fundamental, seems to be at stake.

In a notable contrast to his previous stance, Guyon survives these radical terrors not by meeting them face on, as he does Phaedria, the overwrought brothers, and Mammon, and as he is to face Acrasia, but by avoiding them. In the Cave of Mammon, Guyon coolly seeks to know. "What art thou man?" (2. 7. 7). "What secret place . . . can safely hold / So huge a

21. *ST*, Dominican Fathers, pt. 2-2, q. 123, art. 6 (2 : 1711).

masse . . . ?" (2. 7. 20). "What meant that preace about that Ladies throne?" (2. 7. 48). Wondering about the black waters of Cocytus in which souls endlessly wail, "to behold, he clomb up to the banke" (2. 7. 57). Seeing Tantalus labor vainly, Guyon "Askt who he was, and what he ment thereby" (2. 7. 59); spying "Another wretch," Pilot, "The knight him calling, asked who he was" (2. 7. 62).[22] Guyon is in the Cave of Mammon because he has asked to be, and he explores every aspect of its temptations even as he refuses them. But on his odyssey, because the hero does not confront and test the perils, the reader does not come to know them. Possibly, as in the First Garden, to know what the threats are would imply that the knower had already succumbed to whatever temptation they figure forth. Although unknown precisely (this because they are *from* the unknown), the new threats all pose a direct attack on Guyon's mind, his identity, his sanity.

Three such drastic trials, mounting in intensity, mark the voyage. They provide stress peaks framed by other perils that recapitulate book 2's own themes and/or the epic tradition Spenser is transmitting. Divagation may be the subject of canto 12, but a dense concinnity is its method, a rondo-like interweaving of old and new themes. The opening referring episodes combine motifs of Mammon and lust in the Gulf of Greediness and the Rock of Reproach. Then Guyon first falters before a more problematic trial, a feint, as it turns out. He descries land and directs the ferryman to steer for it. The ferryman refuses; despite fair, fruitful aspect and grass of "delectable hew," the islands "Are not firme lande, nor any certein wonne"; they are "straggling plots, which to and fro do ronne / In the wide waters" (2. 12. 11). They threaten an extraordinary loss: "whosoever once hath fastened / His foot thereon, may never it recure, / But wandreth ever more uncertein and unsure" (2. 12. 12). Then might even competent Guyon be made a wanderer, "uncertein and unsure," like Ruddymane a "Poore Orphane in the wide world scattered"

22. Guyon's consistent, pertinacious questioning in part prevents Kermode's interesting reading (see n. 18), or else indicates that Spenser's own attitude toward vain knowledge was unorthodox.

(2. 2. 2)? The hint of wide alarm dissolves into the familiar when Phaedria launches her little boat from one of the islands, continuing, thus, the remembrance of things past. This time it is only Phaedria and her island.

The Quicksand of Unthriftyhead and the Whirlpool of Decay constitute a refrain; then in a churning, windless sea, Guyon sees the horrific shapes of sea monsters. A litany of fabulous marine exotica includes the sea-shouldering whales that Keats later admired; it insists upon their abnormality, their formal monstrosity. "There are many most ouglie monsters and strange-formed creatures in the sea (thought indeed to bee much more then on the land)," Linche's *Fountaine of Ancient Fiction* reports.[23] Three times in Spenser's descriptions, variants of the word "deformed" appear (2. 12. 23, 24, 25). The creatures are "defects" from *de + facere:* the etymology targets the failures in their making).

> Most ugly shapes, and horrible aspects,
> Such as Dame Nature selfe mote feare to see,
> Or shame, that ever should so fowle *defects*
> From her most cunning hand escaped bee;
> All dreadfull pourtraicts of *deformitee.*
>
> [2. 12. 23; my italics]

Spenser uses the dark vastness of the sea as a mythic and geographic zone where inner terrors may be consigned and objectified. And now Guyon *is* afraid:

> Ne wonder, if these did the knight appall;
> For all that here on earth we dreadfull hold,
> Be but as bugs to fearen babes withall,
> Compared to the creatures in the seas entrall.
>
> [2. 12. 25]

The palmer smites the sea with his staff, and the creatures recede "Into great *Tethys* bosome, where they hidden lye." They are laid, hidden; not quelled. The inner sea produces bubbles less radiant than Aphrodite.

23. Richard Linche, *The Fountaine of Ancient Fiction* (London: Adam Islip, 1599; trans. from Vincenzo Cartari, *Imagini delli dei de gl'antichi*), p. 49ᵛ.

The antique male and female deities of the ocean serve the one to introduce (2. 12. 22) and the other to close the passage (2. 12. 26); Neptune and Tethys at once sponsor and submerge the terrors. The placement of the oceanic parental divinities along with the reference to "bugs to fearen babes" hints that Spenser was aware of the survival of childhood terrors rooted in the parental situation. If this may be farfetched, in any case the poetry guides the reader to consider the possibility of fissure in the mental structure of even the rational, temperate man, to glimpse imagination as a hostile vitality that, left ungoverned, can disgorge its own hallucinatory leviathans. Against that, an adult is again a child in his own dark.

The next recapitulation imposes more subtle strains than did Gulf and Rock, Whirlpool and Quicksand. The seemly woeful maiden sitting by the shore and the sirens initially assail the sense of hearing. The sound of weeping reaches the mariners, "a ruefull cry / Of one, that wayld and pitifully wept, / That through the sea the resounding plaints did fly" (2. 12. 27). It may remind us, it may remind Guyon, of another song:

> . . . sad *Celeno,* sitting on a clift,
> A song of bale and bitter sorrow sings,
> That hart of flint a sunder could have rift.
>
> [2. 7. 23]

The sad girl on the shore draws Guyon powerfully. Not only is he a knight and she a damsel evidently in distress and thereby particularly eligible for his professional chivalry—and Guyon is a consummate professional—but pity has been the most prominent response in what is a comparatively impoverished gestalt. Pity led him to the ill-judged attack on the Red Cross Knight; it was his response to Amavia, to Ruddymane, to Phedon, even to Pyrochles. The cry appeals to the strongest of Guyon's passions; he needs the palmer's caution that the maiden is "inly nothing ill apayd" and her cry a "womanish fine forgery."

The sirens, like the maiden, embody the temptress archetype which pervades the book from Duessa's fallacious appearance in the first canto as a ravished lady to Acrasia's as a ravishing one in the last. "Their song was not all in one strain," Bacon wrote of the sirens, "but they varied their measures according to the nature of the listener, and took each captive with those which best suited him." [24] And the sirens do sing to suit Guyon. Phaedria had no success with him. She plainly had shown her careless contempt for the life of action, her hostile sense of it as pretension and irrelevance:

> Who shall him rew, that swimming in the maine,
> Will die for thirst, and water doth refuse?
> Refuse such fruitlesse toile, and present pleasures chuse.
>
> [2. 6. 17]

But the sirens greet Guyon in his chosen, often reaffirmed persona as the man of action who has spurned Mammon's offers proudly: "I in armes, and in atchievements brave, / Do rather choose my flitting houres to spend" (2. 7. 33), and who has with ironic politeness besought "leave to follow mine emprise" (2. 7. 39). The sirens begin:

> O thou faire sonne of gentle Faery,
> That art in mighty armes most magnifide
> Above all knights, that ever battell tride,

—their specific offer is of ease, of *otium,* a retirement more refined than Phaedria's but the exact opposite of the heroic action Guyon has so far been steadfast in choosing and pursuing—

> O turne thy rudder hither-ward a while:
> Here may thy storme-bet vessell safely ride;
> This is the Port of rest from troublous toyle,
> The worlds sweet In, from paine and wearisome turmoyle.
>
> [2. 12. 32]

They tactfully imply that the choice of staying is revokable, that they offer only an interlude. The bass of the rolling sea

24. Francis Bacon, "The Sirens; Or Pleasure," in *Of the Wisdom of the Ancients, The Works of Francis Bacon,* ed. James Spedding, Robert Leslie Ellis, and Douglas Denton Heath (London: Longman, 1858), chap. 31 (6 : 762).

and the treble of the winds measure a mean to their song. No wonder that Guyon, his "senses softly tickeled" wants to hear "some part of their rare melody" and the solemn harmony of the sea and wind behind it. When the sirens sing to Guyon, they offer a version of the death wish that St. George found so tempting. To yield is to be beguiled to death, to become one of the "weake travellers, whom gotten they did kill" (2. 12. 31).

The third assault on Guyon's interior senses is most drastic and least defined in terms furnished either by Spenser or by literary tradition. When the travelers are in sight of the land they seek, light, which Spenser usually equates with good and with order, vanishes:

> . . . suddeinly a grosse fog over spred
> With his dull vapour all that desert has,
> And heavens chearefull face enveloped,
> That all things one, and one as nothing was,
> And this great Universe seemd one confused mas.
>
> [2. 12. 34]

If Guyon's odyssey constitutes a battle for the preservation of the interior senses, the power under attack here is "common sense"—not our kind of everyday prudence, but a power that received forms sent to it by the external senses. In a world where "all things one, and one as nothing was" there is nothing for this "common sense" to grasp or it has lost capacity to grasp. With terrific speed, the fog seems to have uncreated the world (from "all things" to "one" and from "one" to "nothing"), to have returned it to primitive chaos. The travelers fear to wander "in that wastfull mist" and "darkenesse wide." Suddenly, from out this "griesly night," strange birds shriek. Wings strike at them, a "nation of unfortunate / And fatall birds" (2. 12. 36). The champion endures through an enveloping fear, and Spenser's starched rhythms and exactly proportioned caesuras in lines 3 and 4 of stanza 37 embody Guyon's rigidity:

> All those, and all that else does horrour breed,
> About them flew, and fild their sayles with feare:
> Yet stayd they not, but forward did proceed,

> Whiles th'one did row, and th'other stifly steare;
> Till that at last the weather gan to clear.
>
> [2. 12. 37]

They land. Then, an agent even in his patience, having repeatedly shown his power to suffer, to endure, Guyon acts.

Guyon is chiefly an actor. His uniform courage may even irritate readers who feel that claims of flesh and heart are more insistent than his steadfastness makes them out to be. But his success, though virtually continual, is not the whole of his story. He is not only the strong hand that wrecked the Bower but also the imperiled soul who voyaged toward it, a sufferer and a pilgrim, who passed by the wandering islands, the illusory hosts of the sea, and the denuding night of chaos without certainty, without penetration, with eyes averted. Spenser suggests that that is wisest. Guyon acted in the mode of aggression, destroying the Bower. He also endured and so survived the threat of being perpetually homeless in his own being, a wanderer without memory, without the power to make the most rudimentary discernments, accompanied only by a disturbed imagination and its giantesque fears, his selfhood dissolving into a vague and lunatic landscape.

Pyrochles: The Limits of Rage

One of the often-canvassed disadvantages of allegory is that it may seem to separate the good characters from the bad too obviously, such a demarcation being a condition of a form which externalizes in one narrative, but with a multiple cast of characters, the state of the single soul. Presumably the greater the rigor of the allegorical analysis, the greater the number of allegorical characters, the more pure and patent their simplicity, and the more obvious the tale.[25] Spenser, how-

25. In his stimulating general study of allegory, Fletcher, p. 35, writes, "The allegorical hero is not so much a real person as he is a generator of other secondary personalities, which are partial aspects of himself." He comments, p. 195, specifically on Sir Guyon as divided into partials of himself and therefore called upon to fight identical wars against each evil. My own view is that neither the evils nor the wars are exactly identical, although at root related.

ever, complicates his allegorical analysis by presenting related characters with overlapping, but not equivalent, allegorical identities. The case studies of love in books 3 and 4 are a prominent example of this procedure. Furor, Phedon, and Pyrochles in book 2 are another grouping; all relate to the epic subject, anger, but only Pyrochles could have part in a conventional epic.

Although it is in Spenser's Faerie Land that all these figures live, they have different degrees of life. Furor's provenience may be the emblem book, Phedon's is romance, and Pyrochles, with his epic reminiscences, with an eclectic persona from various sources, makes up for his hodge-podge of origins and inconsistency of behavior by consistent brilliance as a fiction, as an image, whether of a capital sin, a rampant humor, a hero manqué, or a sufferer. Furor exists in flat simplicity. Though he has a mother, he has no biography.[26] Phedon's simplicity is qualified by an asserted vita, though not a plausible one. If he does not act quite like a real criminal or suffer like one, he has a criminal record and a wan verisimilitude (a verisimilitude not to "real" life but to "real" romances, that is, ones existing as ends in themselves, not as parts of a larger literary intention). The account of Pyrochles lies somewhat between the simplicity of Furor and the vita of Phedon. He does not exist for the reader outside of his flamboyant entrances and exits as, for instance, Timias seems to go on living when the reader is attending to someone else or as it seems that Florimell must flee through the forests even when we are not following her. Pyrochles vanishes off scene, but the theatricality of his literary construction works during his convulsive movement across Guyon's horizons.

Guyon's adventures in cantos 4, 5, and 6 take him directly from encounters with Furor to Phedon to Pyrochles. Only Pyrochles will occupy us, for he offers ample room to see the emphasis that *agere-et-pati* configurations give to Spenser's treatment of anger.

26. M. Pauline Parker, I.B.V.M., in *The Allegory of the Faerie Queene* (Oxford: Clarendon, 1960), p. 55, writes that characters like Furor and Occasion owe their being to crisis. More solid are those who represent fixed habits and permanent dispositions.

The first and second appearances of Pyrochles in Faerie Land serve nicely as companion pieces of action and suffering. Here is his entrance:

> . . . on the plaine fast pricking *Guyon* spide
> One in bright armes embatteiled full strong,
> That as the Sunny beames do glaunce and glide
> Upon the trembling wave, so shined bright,
> And round about him threw forth sparkling fire,
> That seemd him to enflame on every side:
> His steed was bloudy red, and fomed ire,
> When with the maistring spur he did him roughly stire.
>
> [2. 5. 2]

Without pausing "to greete, / Ne chaffar words," he strikes Guyon; his blow speaks, he acts. (His discourtesy will typically include contempt for words.) Set this brilliant start against his next entrance:

> . . . he [Atin] saw from farre
> An armed knight, that towards him fast ran,
> He ran on foot, as if in lucklesse warre
> His forlorne steed from him the victour wan;
> He seemed breathlesse, hartlesse, faint, and wan,
> And all his armour sprinckled was with bloud,
> And soyld with durtie gore, that no man can
> Discerne the hew thereof. He never stood,
> But bent his hastie course towards the idle flood.
>
> [2. 6. 41]

This is a reversal indeed: enveloping light glancing from "bright armes" as against bloodied, unrecognizable armor; the proud, mounted figure controlling his horse with "maistring spur" as against the gasping, dirty runner; the knightly challenger against the hard-pressed fugitive. But in both, a characteristic impetuosity. Both the agent and the patient exhibit the sweeping extravagance of Anger, the passion personified, and of Pyrochles' personal, headlong style.

The riddling, cryptic shield of Pyrochles with its flaming fire in a bloody field and the motto "Burnt I do burne" epitomizes, in a version of *agere et pati,* the strait limits of Pyrochles and his fate. The root *to burn* shifts from participle to verb, but whether the passive meaning has been changed remains ambiguous—"I do burne": "I burn others"? "I am burning"? Probably Pyrochles wears it as a warning boast of his power to act, to avenge, but the reader notes it as an epitome of defeat. An agent when he rides up, swinging out at Guyon, he is soon a captive, a patient. Freed by Guyon, he takes the initiative again and liberates Furor and Occasion, but soon they have him dirty and bloodied.

The place of Pyrochles may be more fully seen by considering how he fits into Spenser's treatment of anger; then how he is related to the medieval and Renaissance treatment of anger in psychomachia and iconography; and finally by considering means through which Pyrochles transcends his allegorical identity with rage.

Earlier Spenser depicted Wrath in the pageant of the Deadly Sins (1. 4. 33–35). His steed is a lion, his instruments a burning brand and a dagger, his eyes shoot red sparks. And he is a self-frustrated, driven figure with clothes rent to rags because he has "woxen wood" and "of his hands he had no governement." In book 3 a feminine Fury appears in the Masque of Cupid. She too is a self-destructive patient, pathetically like an embost deer:

> . . . from her backe her garments she did teare,
> And from her head oft rent her snarled heare:
> In her right hand a firebrand she did tosse
> About her head, still roming here and there;
> As a dismayed Deare in chace embost,
> Forgetfull of his safety, hath his right way lost.
>
> [3. 12. 17]

A third avatar is Furor, whose "mickle might" does not help him for he fights like a blindfolded bull, dashing at random. In Faerie Land only the "salvage" man—and he possesses a magic invulnerability—succeeds when he fights without caution or art (6. 4. 4–8).

Spenser's treatment of anger is not the result of a stray flash of insight but his individualization of a common view. Anger and patience offer a limited version of action and suffering. Anger is a specialized moral (read immoral) source of action. (This may be because anger spurs large actions, the epic subject.) Anger opposes patience, the moral version of suffering. But if patience can turn the base stuff of its experience, imposed suffering, into a kind of action, anger lets action (in its full sense of exercising rational choice) deteriorate into suffering.[27] This basic opposition and paradoxical reversal informs the tradition Spenser could lay under tribute. In that double tradition, images divide between those that show anger as a power and those that display it as a patient. Anger is invariably one of the seven sins; and its opposite, its remedy, is usually patience. There are variations. Morton W. Bloomfield gives one: in the partially preserved thirteenth-century frescoes at Westminster Palace, "Debonerete" treads down "Ira"; [28] "Debonairetee" also, along with "Pacience," is opposed to "Ira" in the Parson's Tale. Patience might also play a more general role in moral organization. John Cassian (d. ca. 435) speaks of patience as a medicine for all sins; the patient man cannot be perturbed by anger, consumed by "accidie" and sadness, distended by vainglory nor by the tumor of pride.[29] Approaching this notion from an opposite direction, Tertullian had spoken of Impatience as the womb of all sin.[30] Shakespeare was no doubt thinking of patience as such a panacea when he has Gertrude advise Hamlet to sprinkle cool patience upon "the heat and flame of thy distemper" (3. 4. 124).

But these are the exceptions. Regularly on cathedral portals, in windows and monumental art, the Patience-Anger pair is repeated.[31] Of particular interest for the suggestion that anger is allied to action and patience to suffering is a thirteenth-century grouping of roundels at Canterbury Cathedral. Anger, an enthroned figure with a scepter, clubs at the head of a

27. For the victory of patience, see above, pp. 33 ff.
28. Morton W. Bloomfield, *The Seven Deadly Sins* (East Lansing: Michigan State College, 1952), pp. 102, 353, n. 197.
29. *Collatio* 12. 6, as noted by Bloomfield, p. 71.
30. "Of Patience," *Apologetic and Practical Treatises* (trans. Dodgson, 1 : 334).
31. Emile Mâle, *The Gothic Image*, pp. 102, 104, 109; see also Adolf Katzenellenbogen, *Allegories of the Virtues and Vices in Mediaeval Art* (1939; New York: W. W. Norton, 1964), pp. 1–21.

sprawling Patience.[32] In the sixteenth-century *Nova Iconologia* of Ripa, Anger is a threatening figure, an armed young woman with great shoulders, "la faccia gonfia" (swollen face), sword, brand, and a helmet with an animal, possibly a wolf, from whose mouth issues fire. "Patienza" in *Nova Iconologia* is a static figure, a woman of mature age seated on a stone with a yoke on her shoulders, hands arranged "in modo, che mostri segno di dolore" ("so as to show signs of sadness") and with her feet bare, on a fasces of thorns.[33] Ripa's book was published without cuts in 1593; the first edition with engravings was that of 1603. He did not, then, influence Spenser; the same conceptions influenced both.[34]

The images at Canterbury and in Ripa stress anger as active; but the self-destructive, suffering Anger also is found in art. In a window at Lyons, Ira pierces herself with her sword in front of Patientia.[35] This variant owes much to the *Psychomachia* of Prudentius, the fifth-century poem so important in the history of allegory.[36] The poem puts forth vividly that to suffer in patience is an action and that to act in anger is to become liable to suffering. An anonymous eighteenth-century translator describes how

> . . . infernal *ANGER* stood,
> Her *mouth* with *foam,* her *eyes* suffus'd with *blood;*
> So swell'd with *rage,* that each distended vein
> Could scarce the driving flood of life contain;

Anger launches an attack on Patience who has been standing about without engaging in the melee:

32. These roundels are blurred; charts identify them. The figures in the Anger and Patience pair were still distinguishable when I saw them in 1965. Though often the supine figure in such pairs in the vice, the object being to show the victory of the virtue, the typical passivity of patience makes this unlikely here.

33. Cesare Ripa Purugino, *Nova Iconologia* (Padua: Pietro Paolo Tozzi, 1618), pp. 270, 398.

34. Rosemary Freeman, *English Emblem Books* (London: Chatto & Windus, 1948), pp. 79–80.

35. Mâle, p. 115.

36. C. S. Lewis, *The Allegory of Love* (Oxford: Clarendon, 1936), pp. 66 ff. See Katzenellenbogen, pp. 1–13, on the influence of illuminated MSS of the *Psychomachia*.

> Undaunted *PATIENCE* still maintain'd her ground,
> Still in the same *inactive* posture staid,
> And *unconcern'd* the work of fate survey'd;
> Heard, round her head, the darts, unnumber'd, fly,
> Without a *groan,* a *trouble,* or a *sigh.*

When personally attacked, Patience does not fight or groan. She has, however, an effectual suit of armor, and Anger is soon in a bad way, "with *furious passion,* tir'd in vain, / And every arrow scatter'd o'er the plain." Eventually the *barbara bellatrix,* her strength spent in frenzied raving and dart-hurling, stabs herself. Patience claims her victory mildly:

> From discipline, like this, we never part,
> For *hardy suff'rance* is our *martial art:*
> Unmov'd we stand, and let the *blast* go by,
> For *Passion* always, like a *blast,* will die.[37]

Illuminations of the psychomachia varied greatly. In one from the ninth century reproduced by Katzenellenbogen, Patience is a massive warrior in Roman armor standing with feet planted and arms akimbo, looming over tiny, variously armed figures who attack her. In a late eleventh-century illumination, the characteristic dishevelment that appears in Spenser's figures of wrath is in part repaired by an assistant: rather like a dresser helping an actress, she combs Ira's hair while Patience, impeccably draped, her back turned on her rival, holds a square with an air that can only be called nonchalant.[38]

The sins and virtues were not an exclusive avenue for the idea of anger as self-restrictive. The *Sententiae Pueriles* of Leonard Culman, from which many a Renaissance schoolboy and perhaps Spenser himself learned his first Latin, included not only "Praeceps ira, multorum malorum autor," but "Ira tormentum sui ipsius," "Consilio melius vincas, quam ira-

37. Prudentius, *Psychomachia; The War of the Soul: Or, the Battle of the Virtues, and Vices.* Translated from *Aur. Prudentius Clemens* (London, 1743), pp. 15–18.

38. Patientia in the midst of the Vices, *Psychomachia* MS., 9th century, Leiden, University Library, Cod. Burmanni Q 3, fol. 125ᵛ, reproduced by Katzenellenbogen, plate 2; Ira and Patientia, Moissac MS., late 11th century, Paris, Bibliothèque Nationale, MS. 2077, fol. 168ʳ, reproduced by Katzenellenbogen, plate 5.

cundia," and "Irati nihil rectè faciunt." [39] The simile comparing an angry man to a lamp with too much oil which yields no light but puts out its own flame was a homely "memorable conceit" on the theme.[40]

Psychomachia, the sins, and Renaissance tags, although they clearly relate to Pyrochles, do not confine him. Spenser provides him with an ancestry going back to "Aeternitie." His forefathers join him to other characters of the poem who owe their ultimate allegiance to night, death, and evil. He and Cymochles share a primitive pre-Jovian paternity including the fiery river of hell:

> The sonnes of old *Acrates* and *Despight*,
> *Acrates* sonne of *Phlegeton* and *Jarre;*
> But *Phlegeton* is sonne of *Herebus* and *Night;*
> But *Herebus* sonne of *Aeternitie* is hight.
>
> [2. 4. 41]

Spenser has laced classical figures with personifications through two generations. Thus Pyrochles issues from fathers of a remote, horrific, vaguely apprehended time, from pre-time. Harry Berger, Jr., comments on this paternity partly in terms of action and passivity:

> The coupling of abstract personifications (Despight and Jarre) with mythical or quasi-mythical names (Acrates and Phlegeton) reinforces the partly human, partly elemental, partly spastic and automatic qualities with which the brothers impress us. Furthermore, the fathers (the active principles) are in a way more passive than the mothers (passive principles). For akrates, the quality of the incontinent man, is not only self-indulgent but impotent; one who is akrates has lost control of his actions. Phlegeton is an inanimate mixture of elements. Thus the malice

39. [Leonard Culman], *Sententiae Pueriles* (London: Eliz. P[urslowe], 1639), pp. 25, 5, 18, and 12. See Charles G. Smith, *Shakespeare's Proverb Lore* (Cambridge, Mass.: Harvard, 1963), pp. 5–8, for information on the use of Culman's *Sententiae*.

40. Giles Corrozet, *Memorable Conceits of Divers Notable and Famous Personages of Christendome, of this our moderne time* (London: James Shaw, 1602), pp. 319–20. This translation from the French is so organized as to support the continuity of the pairing: a chapter on patience follows that on wrath.

and discord (Despight and Jarre) in Pyrochles' being are not motivated originally by gratuitous evil in the will, not by intemperance, but by a condition of incontinence (akrasia, akrates) which has neutralized the will. And how has this impotence been brought about? Through a submission to the elements, the humors, the accidental temperament of the physical being. Pyrochles is tyrannized by the fiery, Cymochles by the watery, humor. . . . [Pyrochles] is, in short, a model of the adust choleric found in the Renaissance handbooks of psychology. [*The Allegorical Temper,* p. 60]

Humors psychology, moral theology, and classical etymology converge to indicate that Pyrochles is a patient.

He and Cymochles are also Moslem knights, "paynims"; Pyrochles betrays this (and his ruling passion) when he swears by "Termagaunt." As Saracens, they are in Spenser's Faerie Land per se bad, but share with the questing heroes a chivalric commitment. Atin can shame Cymochles by demanding,

> What is become of great *Acrates* sonne?
> Or where hath he hong up his mortall blade,
> That hath so many haughtie conquests wonne?
> Is all his force forlorne, and all his glory donne?
>
> [2. 5. 35]

They have heroic claims. Pyrochles transcends the vice tradition of Anger and is more than a case study of the adust choleric; he is given, fitfully, an epic context. His simplicity and single-mindedness, so exactly caught in the image of the stuck unicorn (2. 5. 10), constitute a critique of simplicity and single-mindedness, a heroic condition that Homer's Achilles himself admitted to and one that Shakespeare satirized in *Troilus and Cressida.* Spenser does not precisely satirize it in Pyrochles, but he presents it. Few have considered Guyon complex, but compared with Pyrochles, what range and flexibility he has. He takes advantage of his own experiences and those of others; *listening* to the palmer is one of his most characteristic acts. He can take advice. Pyrochles, however, is strikingly unable to make use of advice and warnings, whatever their source.

Pyrochles is the victim of fixed ideas. He is unable to modify chivalric preconceptions about poor, aged women to fit the facts of Occasion's reality, and so he frees his enemy. Impatient of qualification, he cuts short the debate. Before he joins battle with Prince Arthur, Pyrochles handicaps himself because he will not listen. He seizes an enchanted sword that will not harm its true owner, the prince, and scorns Archimago's warning: "Foolish old man, said then the Pagan wroth, / That weenest words or charmes may force withstond" (2. 8. 22). Pyrochles does not learn. Neither his spasmodic accessions of chivalry nor his vengeance knows discretion. His predilection for passionate extremes continues until his final choice of destruction.

This account contrasts him with Guyon, but he also displays qualities that resemble Guyon's. One critic thinks that there is something of nobility about him and his brother so that one feels that, had they had palmers, they might have escaped their fates.[41] This puts it strongly, but consider how much more contempt there is in Spenser's treatment of Braggadochio. In some respects, Pyrochles does parallel the hero. Pyrochles' devotion to "derring do, and bloudy deed" (2. 4. 42) makes him Guyon's professional peer, although whereas Pyrochles is grossly eager for "bloud and spoile" Guyon is more formally said to delight "all in armes and cruell warre" (2. 6. 37). (So Phaedria sees him.) Vanquished Pyrochles is attracted to Victor Guyon, which indicates some generosity of mind on the loser's part (2. 5. 14). Pyrochles has Guyon's own moralistic style, for if Guyon has the last word on the dreadful war "That in thy selfe thy lesser parts do move," Pyrochles has first expatiated on the dishonorable practices of using guile and wreaking vengeance on innocence (2. 5. 5). Pyrochles' succor of Occasion is a foolish gesture, but one that duplicates Guyon's tender pity for Amavia, her husband, and the bloody-handed babe. The literal death of Pyrochles outside of Mammon's Cave corresponds to Guyon's death-like swoon there.[42]

41. Nelson, p. 193. But Robert Hoopes, "'God Guide Thee, *Guyon*': Nature and Grace Reconciled in *The Faerie Queene*, Book II," *RES*, n.s. 5 (1954) : 19, calls the brothers "two snivelling libertines."

42. Judith H. Anderson, "The Knight and the Palmer in *The Faerie Queene*, Book II," *MLQ* 31 (1970): 178, in a suggestive treatment of Arthur in canto 8, indicates that Arthur's proffer of life, which Pyrochles refuses, is fulfilled in Guyon's instant revival upon the beheading of Pyrochles. Her reading is not, however, directed toward their resemblances.

To be sure, the character of Pyrochles seems to have deteriorated in his last appearance, when with his brother he attempts to despoil Guyon.[43] Even here, however, Spenser gives an epic cast to the verse. To the palmer's remonstrance that to despoil a dead body is sacrilege and that Guyon's arms should "decke his herce, and trap his tomb-blacke steed," Pyrochles responds with a savage motif from Anglo-Saxon battle poetry: Guyon should "But be entombed in the raven or the kight" (2. 8. 16). Pyrochles' death has a gloomy dignity. He fights on after his brother is killed, "all desperate as loathing light, / And with revenge desiring soone to dye." In his earlier encounter with Guyon he asked for life. Now he spurns Arthur's offer of it, making shift at his end to reverse his casting as a sufferer and make himself the doer:

> Foole (said the Pagan) I thy gift defye,
> But use thy fortune, as it doth befall,
> And say, that I not overcome do dye,
> But in despight of life, for death do call.
>
> [2. 8. 52]

The prince, angry yet sorry that Pyrochles "so wilfully refused grace," complies: "His shining Helmet he gan soone unlace." The helmet still shines—down to his wrong-headed end, Pyrochles keeps some glitter.

The epic pretensions of Pyrochles can be accommodated within an emphasis on heroic anger that was chronologically parallel with but distinct from anger considered as a sin or as a humor. For after Achilles anger was the great epic subject and after Plato anger had its place in political and ethical theory as the energy, the resource of the warrior. Plato (*Republic* 4. 439–41) associated anger with the *thymos* or high spirit, corresponding in the state with the guardians, which might ally itself with reason. Aristotle in *Nicomachean Ethics* (esp. 3. 8. 10–12) takes up the suggestion, although with qualifications. St. Thomas quotes Aristotle to the effect that "anger

43. Berger, *The Allegorical Temper*, pp. 61–62. Berger also puts Guyon and the passionate brothers together in that they are "all knights, and must therefore rely heavily on their 'high spirit,' the irascible power which is the appetite most susceptible to the influences of fire" (p. 61).

helps the brave" and affirms that the brave man makes use of anger (moderate, not immoderate, anger) in his actions.[44] This is the tradition Tasso enlisted when he allegorized (true, to mixed response) his characters in *Gerusalemme liberata.* Rinaldo is the *"Irefull* vertue" which

> amongst all the powers of the minde, is lesse estranged from the nobility of the soule, insomuch that *Plato* (doubting) seeketh whether it differeth from reason or no. And such is it in the minde, as the chiefetaine in an assemblie of souldiours: for as of these the office is to obey their princes, which do give directions and commandements to fight against their enimies: so is it the dutie of the irefull, warlike, and soveraigne part of the minde, to be armed with reason against concupiscence.[45]

Not all the classical sources make this placement of anger; Seneca's *De Ira* and the *Commentary* of Macrobius on the *Dream of Scipio* are important exceptions. Spenser, though treating his limited personifications of Wrath as impotent, evil, pathetic, or contemptible, includes the alternate view in Pyrochles and with his heroes. For like Pyrochles the heroes of *The Faerie Queene* become angry. Guyon and Arthur, the Red Cross Knight, Britomart, Calidore, and Artegall feel rage in battle.[46] Guyon and Arthur in book 2 manage rage as a resource, something like a shot of adrenalin. Guyon tempers "passion with advizement slow" (2. 5. 13; so also Calidore in 6. 1. 30 and 6. 1. 40). It is not thus for Pyrochles, whose initial, dashing entrance betrays his difficulty in a telling detail: both horse and rider nearly choke in their own heat and dust. Pyrochles loses to cooler men (see 2. 5. 8–9 and 2. 8. 47–48). Henry Peacham's emblem book comes later than Spenser's epic. His verse on "choller" and his lion, however, echoes the ambiguity that marks Pyrochles, the limiting rage and the potential of nobility:

44. *ST*, Dominican Fathers, pt. 2-2, q. 123, art. 10 (2 : 1713).
45. "The Allegorie of the Poem," in *Jerusalem Delivered:* The Edward Fairfax translation newly intro. by Roberto Weiss (London: Centaur, 1962), unpaged.
46. Some examples: the Red Cross Knight (1. 11. 39); Britomart (3. 12. 33, 5. 7. 34, 5. 6. 38); Artegall (5. 5. 10); Calidore (6. 1. 36).

> That Lion showes, he seldome can refraine,
> From cruell deede, devoide of gentle ruth:
>   Or hath perhaps, this beast to him assign'd,
>   As bearing most, the brave and bounteous mind.[47]

Spenser's most spectacular verse on Pyrochles owes little, however, to any traditional affiliation. In the final section of canto 6, Spenser does his best for Pyrochles; there the riddling prophecy of his coat of arms comes to pass. In ten stanzas (41–51), Spenser tells how the knight runs desperately across a plain, plunges into the Idle Lake in an effort to put out the flames that consume him, tries to drown himself, and is succored by Atin and Archimago. Spenser conducts the episode almost elegiacally. First, he lets the reader see Pyrochles through the eyes of his squire, who does not immediately recognize him. Atin watches some frantic being coming swiftly and from a distance. As he comes closer, Atin sees him leap into the lake and duck his "loftie crest." Though "all the bloud and filth away was washt, / Yet still he bet the water, and the billowes dasht." Merely curious, Atin draws near and recognizes "His owne deare Lord *Pyrochles,* in sad plight."

Spenser then begins the elegant and plaintive dialogue between Atin and Pyrochles. Exaggerated rhetorical repetitions, stylized paradox, an eloquence unexpected from the abrupt boor that Pyrochles seems elsewhere, distinguish these exchanges. The poet makes no attempt to keep Pyrochles in character; rather the language universalizes and poses the sufferer like a painting of a sorrow. "Harrow now out, and well away," Atin cries out—already in Spenser's time *harrow* is archaic—"*Pyrochles,* O *Pyrochles,* what is thee betyde?" Pyrochles takes up this style, his answer gonging out in rising iambs like a dolefully tolling bell:

> I burne, I burne, I burne, then loud he cryde,
> O how I burne with implacable fire,

47. Henry Peacham, *Minerva Britanna* (London: Wa: Dight, 1612), p. 128. Compare Horapollo's hieroglyphic of the lion that destroys its cub: "If they wish to show unmeasurable anger, as if the spirits were in a fever from it, they draw a lion tearing its cubs to pieces. The lion, because of anger. And tearing its cubs to pieces, since their bones when struck emit fire." *The Hieroglyphics of Horapollo,* trans. George Boas, Bollingen Series 23 (New York: Pantheon, 1950), book 2, no. 38 (p. 92).

> Yet nought can quench mine inly flaming syde,
> Nor sea of licour cold, nor lake of mire,
> Nothing but death can doe me to respire.
>
> [2. 6. 44]

As Atin struggles to save Pyrochles and Pyrochles struggles to drown, Archimago passes. "What hellish furie hath at earst thee hent?" Archimago asks. "Furious ever I thee knew to bee, / Yet never in this straunge astonishment." Pyrochles' answer again repeats the central experience of burning, with liquids and long vowels whining sadly through the line: "These flames, these flames (he cryde) do me torment." Archimago's crisp response, no doubt in part because of an internal rhyme made abrupt by a late caesura but also because of the sudden interjection of common sense, comes with a partially comic effect: "What flames (quoth he) when I thee present see, / In daunger rather to be drent, then brent?" Pyrochles answers fully, locating his difficulty in a swollen liver and hot entrails without losing lyric tone. He also answers the colloquy's opening query: his *"Furor, oh Furor* hath me thus bedight" corresponds exactly with Atin's line, *"Pyrochles, O Pyrochles,* what is thee betyde?"

The section reminds one of a recitative or perhaps of an oratorio. The dramatic differentiation of principal, squire, and wise eld, the devices of recognition and the casual bystander who finds he is closely involved, the emphasis on reversal in the fortunes of the principal, the decorativeness and flow of the verse, just skirting monotony and absurdity in the blatancy of its formalities, blend into one. In this uniquely Spenserian medium, keening Pyrochles is fixed, an eloquent sufferer, a reminder that whatever flames upon the night man's own resinous heart has fed.

5

Cupid's Scene:

The Faerie Queene, Books 3 and 4

Critics have variously described what every reader observes when he comes to books 3 and 4 of *The Faerie Queene:* here the narrative, relatively linear in the earlier books, becomes harmonic, interwoven, "Gothic," as Bishop Richard Hurd put it.[1] There are complaints about but also explanations for the discontinuous technique and some of its inconveniences which may leave characters permanently dangling from psychic cliffs. Spenser is relying more upon Ariosto.[2] He is insufficiently reworking materials that he designed earlier.[3] He is growing fatigued with his original design, finding it troublesome or confining. He is using the multiple plotting that Shakespeare and the Elizabethan dramatists generally were to prefer. Or,

1. *Letters on Chivalry and Romance* (1762), ed. Hoyt Trowbridge, Augustan Reprint Society no. 101–102 (Los Angeles: William Andrews Clark Memorial Library, University of California, 1963), letter 7, pp. 56–57.

2. Ariosto's influence is a staple of Spenser criticism. For some modern, widely spaced examples see R. E. N. Dodge, "Spenser's Imitations from Ariosto," *PMLA* 12 (1897) : 151–204; Jones, *Spenser Handbook*, pp. 220 ff., 242 ff.; Alpers, *Poetry of the Faerie Queene*, pp. 160–99.

3. Josephine Waters Bennett, *The Evolution of the Faerie Queene* (University of Chicago, 1942), pp. 164–77.

having ordered the early books after the formal structures of comedy, tragedy, and epic, Spenser moves on to the more episodic Psyche myth as a model in narrating the trials of Britomart.[4] Consideration of numerology and astronomical symbolism yields accustomed results for structure:

> Evidently the poem is not to develop consecutively, by seriatim concentration on one planetary sphere after another. Instead, it ramifies and burgeons in ever-changing efflorescence, each new mythological influence joining those already present, transmuting and revealing new possibilities in them. As the greater number includes the less, so each book of the poem contains the themes of all earlier books: the structural diagram would resemble a tree's growth rings, not a row of separate globes.[5]

Such critical statements console and some even guide. They furnish the reader formulas that organize his own sense of the books or offer liberating insights, where he before suspected authorial oversights. They seem pleasantly, if not with equal strictness, related to the impression these twenty-four cantos give of a bewildering richness. Here is yet another theory about the "parallel instances" and "case studies" of book 3 and 4, the modes of action and suffering, and the ordonnance of the entire poem.

Spenser changes more than narrative technique when he comes to book 3, though this is what the reader notices with a jolt. From one book to another the poet shifts the *perspective* from which he looks upon his world, Faerie Land, and human life, that for which Faerie Land is an allegory. In book 1 where the events are spiritual and the scope of time universal redemptive history, past and future—from Adam to the Apocalypse, caught *in medias res*—the perspective is theological. There man often appears as a sufferer in spite of his efforts not to be one, but occasionally as, by the grace of God, an actor. In book 2, where the events are moral and the time span a typical lifetime (taking the attempted baptism of Ruddymane and Guyon's visit to Mammon's Cave and its adjoining

4. Hamilton, *Structure of Allegory*, pp. 138–52.
5. Fowler, *Spenser and the Numbers of Time*, p. 122.

hell as allusions to birth and death), the perspective is chiefly classical and ethical and the subject matter is man's moral and psychological organization. Here man appears in various flawed avatars as a suffering failure, but at his possible best, in Guyon, as an independent actor, a moral agent.

In books 3 and 4, Spenser's chosen perspective is racial, his subject, at base, biological, that is, concerned with generation. From this perspective he surveys not a model vita for a redeemed everyman, Red Cross, nor one for a worldly good man, Guyon, but an entire process as it operates among many human lives. We thus may say that Spenser's allegory shifts focus from one of the scholastic categories of causation to the next. If the first book is concerned with man's final cause, the second with his material cause, the third and fourth are concerned with the efficient cause of mankind: that is, with love and appetite as these bear first upon the generation of life and secondly upon its enhancement. (Insofar as book 4 is an anatomy of friendship, it refers to the second theme, the enhancement of life.) To extend this observation over the last books and so fill out the scholastic categories of causation: it may be plausibly argued that books 5 and 6 concern the formal cause of life, embodying, as they do, the great shapes that the life of the social animal takes—polity, the art of administration in the civil order, in book 5, and courtesy, the ordering art of private life, in book 6. (But as this study is minimally concerned with the last books, I offer this speculation in the spirit of what Thomas Warton called "the amusement of conjecture" rather than in an ambition to provide "the satisfaction of demonstration.") [6]

Love as a generative process creating life on the one hand and love transcending this creatural level to manifest itself in the enhancement of life on the other are themes throughout *The Faerie Queene,* but Spenser brings a more intense and exclusive attention to them in books 3 and 4. Here the poem establishes love as the basis of birth, of life itself; and in authorial comment, narrative, and heightened symbolic enact-

6. *Observations on the Fairy Queen of Spenser,* 2d ed. (London: R. and J. Dodsley, 1762), sec. 8, 2. 37.

ments, also asserts that love is the spur for the enrichment of life through significant activity, for what may be called, by synecdoche, the crafts of life (of which poetry is one). Love provides the impetus for culture, for courtesy, for all man's performances and institutions.

The treatment of major characters is of their roles as lovers, with the further innuendo in some cases that they are also, without ceasing to be lovers, something more than this, something not separable from their being mated. The characters illustrate two phases of love: love as a private passion and love as ethical action. Scudamour and Amoret represent love alone, love almost stripped of auxiliary significance. Their names are a cue to their motives and their passion. Amoret's consummate quality is muliebrity, and she is fittingly mated with the unexceptional Scudamour and fittingly threatened by such opposite exotics as the enchanter writing arcane characters in blood, and the wild man who cannot write at all. She figures in both the masque of Cupid, the most elaborate setting for erotic craving, and in the cave of the giant, its barest setting. Love defines the ambit of Scudamour's and Amoret's being.

Artegall and Britomart, however, represent faithful love as a foundation for further values. They are exemplars of the notion that love prompts heroic deeds. Historically, their union founds a dynasty; and their acts include establishing or restoring political order in the places in which they find themselves. Morally, of course, they represent the virtues of justice and chastity, respectively the salient qualities of order in public and private life. Spenser thus discriminates his lovers not only in characters and careers, but also in the human experiences these imply, private and passionate (Scudamour and Amoret) and public and active (Britomart and Artegall). As for Florimell and Marinell, we may place a part of their interest as a couple as having to do with the physical components of the world itself and with medieval and Renaissance theories about it. But while this couple elicit interpretation (see n. 12, below), they also evade it. Therefore, although active-passive reversals are obviously a way of labeling narrative continuities, disruptions, and reversals in their story, it would seem either tactless or redundant to apply them, so I shall say no more about them.

Within the framework of books 3 and 4, when life reaches beyond existence to become quest or culture, it is so transformed because of love. Love motivates magnificence, great *doing,* as Ruskin glossed Arthur's virtue.[7] The ceremonials, festivals, and artistic displays—wedding and tournament, tale, tapestry, masque—exemplify this further relation between love and life and testify to love's forming, active power. Such achievements as Freud attributes to sublimation, Spenser attributes to love. From love "spring all noble deeds and never dying fame" (3. 3. 1). Myth and history testify to love's glorious action:

> Well did Antiquitie a God thee deeme,
> That over mortall minds hast so great might,
> To order them, as best to thee doth seeme,
> And all their actions to direct aright;
> The fatall purpose of divine foresight,
> Thou doest effect in destined descents,
> Through deepe impression of thy secret might,
> And stirredst up th'Heroes high intents,
> Which the late world admyres for wondrous moniments.
>
> [3. 3. 2]

Love is then the source not only of action but of heroic action —and "wondrous moniments" like *The Faerie Queene* itself. In books 3 and 4 a heavy emphasis falls on man as the actor; this is exemplified in the warrior heroine, asserted in authorial pronouncements, and insistently suggested in the continual implication that love is valuable partly because it is a spur to deeds worthy of memory, worthy of poetry. But suffering, enduring, is here too. A closer look at the amorous involvements, the substance of these books, lets us see that although men *act* because of love, it is also *because* of love that they act: in relation to the generative force they are sufferers. Love "leads each living kind" (4. 12. 25).

7. *Stones of Venice,* 3: 205–09, as quoted in the variorum edition of Spenser, 1 : 424.

In relation to the topos of action and passion, doing and bearing, Spenser's depiction of the kindly flame that makes new men and makes men new is complex. Confronted with love—kindly flame—man is initially a sufferer. Thus the hymn in the Temple of Venus bursts forth from an anonymous devotee tormented by "loves constrayning"—the human speaker is only a sort of ventriloquist's puppet. The poet commends Arthur's moderation on the grounds that it is more difficult to abstain from pleasure than for a hungry steed "t'abstaine from pleasant lare" (4. 8. 29). The enamorments of Britomart and Scudamour express helplessness before preferences so immediate and intense that they seem inflicted, not chosen. (So also Arthur's quest for Gloriana is inflicted, though with a difference. Some agency may be involved in dreams and visions. Corflambo would not have had Arthur's dream.)

Further, love is a random and promiscuous energy that may assume grotesque, monstrous, or ludicrous forms. It can be sad. It can be unrequited. It can be an illusion. And it can be sinful. Excepting Belphoebe, desire besets these books' characters. A double wedding crowns even the accord of the knights of friendship. Spenser's Faerie Land is full of ladies fair and lovely knights in various stages of amorous attachment, of yearning oafs and magicians, unrequited, passionate giants, of old men and boys in all states of amiability, civility, and virility longing for unions of almost all descriptions. The variety of relationships and styles of courtship that Spenser encompasses is remarkable. Of the three central couples, only Scudamour and Amoret conform to romance idiom, for both Florimell and Britomart are not at first "daungerous" but take the initiative (though in the final wooing, Britomart is hesitant and both are concerned for reticent decorum). Only the relationship between Timias and Belphoebe accords with the Petrarchan model (that between Prince Arthur and Gloriana being ineffable). Critics cite the historical allegory to explain Timias and Belphoebe, but it is also true that Spenser needed such a relationship to complete his catalogue. In the story of the Squire of Dames and that of Paridell, Hellenore, and Malbecco, Spenser anticipates the life styles embodied in

Restoration comedy, however different the tonality. Passion pulls down vanity, reducing Hellenore, when cast off, to living, and happily, with satyrs. And it transforms unlikely potential, as in the case of Poena. Even incest is not missing from Spenser's anthology of loves, stripped of glamor and pathos in the ugly account of the giants Ollyphant and Argante (3. 7. 47–49).

So despite narrative discontinuity and discrepancy this world is all, all of a piece throughout, a swarming world, fecund in every seam. Love drives this world from top to bottom, from shape-shifting Jove depicted in the House of Busirane down to the hag's oafish son who maddens in lust for Florimell. Acting and suffering are the modes of love, of life's very origin. This may be more particularly demonstrated by a summary consideration of selected motifs of the books and a reading of one episode, the enamorment of Britomart.[8]

Some Motifs of Love's Passion

Recurrent motifs are the mythological celebration of generation, love, and marriage; the magician unfortunate in love; a masterful Cupid; and the iterated sentiment, expressed by characters of diverse backgrounds and morality, that love cannot be consonant with mastery. This last opinion clearly seems to place loving man as an agent, who may not be imposed upon, inviolate at least in the recess of the heart; but the mythic pieces on generation and marriage, the presentation of Cupid, and the unrequited magicians suggest that man suffers his love and is largely ineffectual in mastering passion. The symbolic pivots of the allegory are the account of the creation of life in the Garden of Adonis (3. 6), the courtship at the Temple of Venus (4. 10), and the marriage of the Medway and Thames (4. 11). Whatever their intellectual genetics, these

8. I do not propose a reading of books 3 and 4 as a whole, or even a whole reading of the episodes I do discuss. One thorough and ingratiating reading of the books is that of Thomas P. Roche, Jr., *The Kindly Flame: A Study of the Third and Fourth Books of Spenser's Faerie Queene* (Princeton University, 1964). See also Williams, *Spenser's World of Glass,* pp. 79–150, and Alpers, *Poetry of the Faerie Queene,* pp. 370–405.

three passages all emphasize the most primary genetic process; they treat generation in terms of philosophy (the Garden), courtly love (the Temple), and nature or geography (the river marriage). My addendum is directed not to the well-annotated Garden but to the Lucretian hymn in the Temple episode and to the river marriage.

Spenser placed the Lucretian hymn at the center of the Temple of Venus episode, after Scudamour has won through opposition and has reached the temple itself, but before he abducts Amoret. Though the goddess Lucretius invokes and the goddess of Spenser's poem are both deities of generation, Spenser stresses the sexual process in suggesting Venus may be double-sexed:

> . . . they say, she hath both kinds in one,
> Both male and female, both under one name:
> She syre and mother is her selfe alone,
> Begets and eke conceives, ne needeth other none.
> [4. 10. 41]

In other ways, Spenser's adaptation cannot be rightly judged as a translation, however free; it is an appropriation. For reference, here is the beginning of Lucretius (as altered slightly from Cyril Bailey's translation):

Mother of the sons of Aeneas, delight of men and gods, life-giving Venus, you who beneath the gliding stars of heaven fill with your presence the ship-bearing sea and the crop-bearing land; for through you every tribe of the living is conceived and comes forth to visit the light of the sun: You, you, goddess, turn to flight the winds and the clouds of heaven at your coming; for you the daedal earth puts forth sweet flowers; for you the levels of ocean smile, and the placid sky gleams with spreading light. For when the face of the spring day is revealed and the un-locked, fertile west wind blows strong, first the birds of the air herald you, goddess, their hearts thrilled with your might. Then wild beasts and cattle [*ferae pecudes*] bound over the fat pastures and swim the racing rivers; captured so by delight each follows you in desire where you hasten to lead on. Then through seas and mountains and tearing rivers and the leafy homes of birds and verdant plains you strike fond love into the hearts of all bringing it about that, in desire, they renew their generations. And since you alone guide the nature of things, and nothing without your help comes forth to the bright coasts of light, nothing grows glad nor lovely, I long that you should be my helper in writing these verses, which I try to fashion on the nature of things for the son of the Memmii, my friend, whom you, goddess, have willed always to excell in every grace. Therefore the more, goddess, grant a lasting charm to my words. Bring it to pass that meantime the wild works of war be lulled to sleep over seas and lands. For you alone can bless men with quiet peace, since Mars, who rules warfare, often flings himself upon your lap, conquered by the eternal wound of love; and then pillowing his shapely neck upon you and looking up he feeds with love his greedy eyes, gazing wistfully toward you, while, as he lies back, his breath hangs upon your lips. Great goddess, as he leans resting on your sacred body, round and above him, pour forth sweet petition from your lips for gentle peace for the Romans. For in our country's time of trouble we cannot set to our task with serene mind nor can the noble son of Memmius in such doings fail the fortunes of the state. For it must be the nature of the gods to enjoy life everlasting in perfect peace remote and separated far away from our world.[9]

This is the text of the hymn in Spenser and a part of its context:

> Amongst the rest some one through loves constrayning,
> Tormented sore, could not containe it still,
> But thus *brake forth,* that all the temple it did fill.

> Great *Venus,* Queene of beautie and of grace,
> The joy of Gods and men, that under skie
> Doest fayrest shine, and most adorne thy place,
> That with thy smyling looke doest pacifie
> The raging seas, and makst the stormes to flie;
> Thee goddesse, thee the winds, the clouds doe feare,
> And when thou spredst thy mantle forth on hie,
> The waters play and pleasant lands appeare,
> And heavens laugh, and al the world shews joyous cheare.

9. *De rerum natura,* ed. and trans. with a commentary by Cyril Bailey, 3 vols. (Oxford: Clarendon, 1947). See 2 : 595 for Bailey's comment on *ferae pecudes* which is a textual crux. However, my point holds, whatever reading it is given.

Then doth the daedale earth throw forth to thee
Out of her fruitfull lap aboundant flowres,
And then all living wights, soone as they see
The spring *breake forth* out of his lusty bowres,
They all doe learne to play the Paramours;
First doe the merry birds, thy prety pages
Privily pricked with thy lustfull powres,
Chirpe loud to thee out of their leavy cages,
And thee their mother call to coole their kindly rages.

Then doe the salvage beasts begin to play
Their pleasant friskes, and loath their wonted food;
The Lyons rore, the Tygres loudly bray,
The raging Buls rebellow through the wood,
And *breaking forth,* dare tempt the deepest flood,
To come where thou doest draw them with desire:
So all things else, that nourish vitall blood,
Soone as with fury thou doest them inspire,
In generation seeke to quench their inward fire.

So all the world by thee at first was made,
And dayly yet thou doest the same repayre:
Ne ought on earth that merry is and glad,
Ne ought on earth that lovely is and fayre,
But thou the same for pleasure didst prepayre.
Thou art the root of all that joyous is,
Great God of men and women, queene of th'ayre,
Mother of laughter, and welspring of blisse,
O graunt that of my love at last I may not misse.

　　　　　　　[4. 10. 43–47; my italics, except *Venus*]

What Spenser included or left out is a clue to his own purposes. In *De rerum natura,* the speaker is the poet, and it is
not love for himself but civic peace that he desires, so that he
can compose his poem and so that his audience will have time
enough to read it. Though never averse to erotic heightening,
Spenser deletes the allusion to Mars, and with it goes all trace
of civic and political concerns, any suggestion that Spenser is
here interested in a *pax Britannica.* He thus narrows the
Roman's hymn, keeping it firmly on natural physicality. In the
Roman's poem, personalities bear public identities: there is
the poet himself, there is the son of Memmius, "my friend,"

and Venus is the *Aeneadum genetrix,* the mother of the sons of Aeneas, of Romans, as well as the delight and the creative principle of the universe. Spenser's goddess has less specific identity and more power than the "alma" Venus of Lucretius who is not flatly the first maker of the world, as is Spenser's virtually Jovian "Great God of men and women."

Speaker, address, and occasion are all quite different; thus the whole verbal gesture belongs in its human presentation to the pathic pole of experience. The hymn is wrenched from the unnamed petitioner "through loves constrayning, / Tormented sore." The hymn unites its speaker with a nature whose living members are all subject to the compulsion of Venus Genetrix. The identity of process is accentuated by the repetition of the same verb to describe the celebrating petitioner, nature, and the animals: *break forth.* The song breaks forth from the speaker; living things bloom when they see "spring *breake forth* out of his lusty bowres" and "raging Buls rebellow through the wood, / And *breaking forth*" tempt the flood. The feeling is one of letting loose, but also one of being driven to let loose, like water smashing through a weakened dam, like the force that through the green fuse drives the flower. Lucretius does not use an exactly equivalent verb nor does he repeat his verbs. The radical stress on the instinctual is served by Spenser's changes: by deletion of a persona who asks for poetic inspiration and deletion of all civic appeal; by making the speaker a lover who puts himself at one with other driven creatures; and (the single amplification of Lucretius) by the naming of the animals goaded by desire, which are merely called *ferae pecudes,* "wild beasts" (or cattle), in the original. *Georgics* 2. 323–31 has been cited as an additional source for Spenser,[10] but the effect approaches *Georgics* 3. 242–44:

> Omne adeo genus in terris hominumque, ferarumque
> et genus aequoreum, pecudes pictaeque volucres,
> in furias ignemque ruunt: amor omnibus idem.

10. H. G. Lotspeich, *Classical Mythology in the Poetry of Edmund Spenser* (Princeton University, 1932), pp. 115–16, cites *Georgics* 2. 323 ff. He also gives early sources for the hermaphrodite Venus, p. 115. I use the text in and translation of C. Day Lewis, *The Eclogues and Georgics of Virgil* (Garden City, N.Y.: Doubleday Anchor, 1964), pp. 172–73.

[All manner of life on earth—men, fauna of land and sea,
Cattle and coloured birds—
Run to this fiery madness: love is alike for all.]

The decor of courtly love at the Temple of Venus is a fantastic foil for the naturalism—as much in the nineteenth-century sense of the word as in the Lucretian—of the hymn. The episode is a stunning example of Spenser's consideration of love as a biological and cultural experience.

In the marriage of the Medway and Thames, the celebration of procreation is not so concentrated and framed.[11] Rather, reminders of procreation on a wonderful scale persist throughout the epic catalogue of wedding guests. At the outset, the poet specifies that Proteus gives the solemn feast to the sea-gods and "their fruitfull seede." In the processional, guests are disposed in families, and the numerosity of progeny is a matter of comment—the fifty nereids, daughters of the nymph Doris, close the procession. The Nile's fertility is reported without the dyslogistic cast of many Renaissance accounts. The bridegroom is compared with tower-crowned Cybele, fertility goddess and "mother of the Gods" (4. 11. 28). (Her myth and attributes—fertility and urbanity—make her a ready-to-hand figure for Spenser's treatment of love as biologically and culturally productive.) Guest rivers are endowed with a plenitude of fishes, such as the "Great heapes of Salmons" in the Barrow, whose enforced conception as one of triplets is told in a tiny narrative that the epic catalogue encloses (4. 11. 42–43). The catalogue ends with a tribute to the fertility of the seas and a comment on the birth of Venus herself:

> Oh What endlesse worke have I in hand,
> To count the seas abundant progeny,
> Whose fruitfull seede farre passeth those in land,
> And also those which wonne in th'azure sky?
> For much more eath to tell the starres on hy,
> Albe they endlesse seeme in estimation,
> Then to recount the Seas posterity:
> So fertile be the flouds in generation,
> So huge their numbers, and so numberlesse their nation.

11. See Roche, pp. 167–84, who includes a survey of the river marriage as a type in Elizabethan and contemporary literature.

> Therefore the antique wisards well invented,
> That *Venus* of the fomy sea was bred;
> For that the seas by her are most augmented.
> Witnesse th'exceeding fry, which there are fed,
> And wondrous sholes, which may of none be red.
>
> [4. 12. 1–2]

The birth of Venus is a marvelous allusion with which to close the river epithalamion. Labeled as a fiction and rationalized by the author's own voice (antique wizards made up the myth), the demythification crowns as it explicates. The episode, which closes book 4, comes just before the promise of union between Florimell and Marinell, whose names, redolent of earth and sea, are reminders of the elemental and cosmic scope of Spenser's idea of love.[12] Like a great diapason the

12. It seems to me the union of Florimell and Marinell does convey the concept that love is the elemental bond of the universe, a cosmic force, a view of wide currency recently criticized by Alpers, pp. 119 ff. Florimell and Marinell may not be merely vegetation symbols, but this is surely one aspect of their presentation. Florimell's famous appeal is partly that of Primavera; this most delicate of heroines has both sophisticated and oafish followers, like spring (and like Amoret), and is the only lady whose person is frequently associated with similes drawn from wild life. Belphoebe is a huntress, but she reminds other characters of goddesses, not deer. Pastorella *is* a pastoral image, but as vehicle, not tenor; she is compared to the morning (6. 11. 3), a "Diamond of rich regard" (6. 11. 13), stars, and an angel (6. 11. 21). So far as I know, Janet Spens, *Spenser's Faerie Queene* (London: Edward Arnold, 1934), p. 84, was the first to propose Florimell as a Persephone, an idea many critics have taken up with varying amplifications. Northrop Frye, *Anatomy of Criticism* (Princeton University, 1957), p. 153, refers to Florimell as a Proserpine and Marinell as an Adonis. Cf. his *Fables of Identity* (New York: Harcourt, Brace & World, 1963), p. 83. Williams, pp. 137–45, discusses the couple as cosmic opposites. To Nelson, *The Poetry of Edmund Spenser,* p. 225, Florimell is what her name says, "flower-honey" or the beauty that stirs love or lust and draws all in pursuit, whereas Marinell is money considered as a symbol of power. Roche, pp. 152 ff. explicates the story of Florimell in terms of the chaste Helen, as a symbol of the soul's spiritual beauty manifested through physical beauty. Hamilton, p. 144, finds Florimell represents the cosmic significance of Britomart's story. He also uses the Proserpine parallel and reads the episode of book 3, canto 8 as a drastic erotic allegory (pp. 151–52). The review of Hamilton's book by Waldo F. McNeir in *Comparative Literature* 15 (1963) : 70, corrects this aspect of Hamilton's interpretation. Maurice Evans, "Platonic Allegory in *The Faerie Queene,*" *RES*, n.s. 12 (1961) : 142, suggests that on a philosophical level Marinell and Florimell constitute an image of the

epithalamion rounds out the central theme of fertility in a rich ceremony.

The symbolic centers of books 3 and 4 take their occasion from the narrative line but rise above or stand apart in their ceremonial elaboration to serve much more than the immediate occasion. Spenser might have brought Marinell to Florimell's undersea dungeon on some pretext less epic and less nuptial. Temple, river wedding, and garden are great stages where mythic figures with large gestures enact in a formal dance the frantic and personal preoccupations of the narrative's lovers so that they may be seen as a participation in a destined process. Not the purblind views of Spenser's loving, pleasing, and anxious beings but the infinitely productive and dynamic pattern of the universe is normative.

Spenser's consideration of love's power extends through three levels of being: the gods, magicians and fays, and human beings. The tapestries at the House of Busirane are the most important treatment of the gods. Of the humans something has been said and more is to come. The situations of the magicians are peculiarly ironic, for their powers and immunities contrast with their helplessness in their own cases. For instance, although Merlin can advise Britomart and although he created the magic mirror which occasioned her falling in love, his own love is not fortunate (see 3. 3. 9–11). Wit and wile, gifts and graces, do not avail Proteus in his suit of Florimell, and he turns to "crueltie and awe" with no better effect (4. 11. 2). When finally Britomart confronts Busirane, he has not much presence, but if his castle is the product of his mind, that mind is a resourceful, curious, opulent, and single-track one. Like the other magicians he too finds his formidable powers insufficient.

Cupid in these books frequently appears in strangely emphatic poses. Rarely the cherubic mischief but a matured youth, his oddly mannered, violent attitudes highlight only those aspects of his long convention that show him to be mas-

---

union of form and first matter; and Fowler, pp. 21–22, finds the perfection of *ideales formae* an underlying theme in the narrative allegories in which Florimell is a central figure.

terful and cruel.[13] In one appearance, he is a horse-tamer,
astride Marinell:

> Dame *Venus* sonne that tameth stubborne youth
> With iron bit, and maketh him abide,
> Till like a victor on his backe he ride,
> Into his mouth his maystring bridle threw,
> That made him stoupe, till he did him bestride:
> Then gan he make him tread his steps anew.
>
> [4. 12. 13]

But the most vivid presentations of a sadistic Cupid are in
the House of Busirane, in the tapestries, the golden statue, the
masque. He rules the greatest gods: even Saturn loves in his
saturnine fashion (3. 11. 43). In the arras Apollo rends his
golden hair. In the panels on Neptune all is speed, silver
brilliance, and snorting power, but "The God himselfe did
pensive seeme and sad, / And hong adowne his head, as he
did dreame" (3. 11. 41). Cupid heaps together kings and
queens, lords and ladies with the "raskall rablement" and does
not "spare sometime to pricke himselfe, / That he might tast
the sweet consuming woe" (3.11. 45). On an altar of precious
stone his golden image surmounts that of a wounded dragon,
its eyes through-pierced with shafts; the legend reads: *"Unto
the Victor of the Gods this bee."* Before this statue, devout
and innocent Britomart, amazed, sees the people of Busirane's
house commit "fowle Idolatree." Cupid's is the climactic appearance in the masque which allegorically anatomizes the
career of a doomed, diseased love relationship.[14] Following
Amoret and her torturers, she with her withdrawn heart
bathed in blood in a silver basin, the god rides in on a lion,
unbinds his eyes,

13. In tracing the tradition of a blind Cupid, Erwin Panofsky, *Studies
in Iconology* (1939; New York: Harper Torchbooks, 1962), p. 101, mentions the change of Cupid's portrayal from an infant to a "handsome
adolescent of princely appearance." Cupid on horseback is another theme
which Panofsky traces, pp. 116 ff. See also the discussion of the false Cupid
by C. S. Lewis, *Spenser's Images of Life*, ed. Alastair Fowler (Cambridge
University, 1967), pp. 18–35.

14. The innuendo of this remark is intended to recall the view of Lewis,
Allegory of Love, pp. 340–44.

That his proud spoyle of that same dolorous
Faire Dame he might behold in perfect kind;
Which seene, he much rejoyced in his cruell mind.

Of which full proud, himselfe up rearing hye,
He looked round about with sterne disdaine;
And did survay his goodly company:
And marshalling the evill ordered traine,
With that the darts which his right hand did straine,
Full dreadfully he shooke that all did quake,
And clapt on hie his coulourd winges twaine,
That all his many it affraide did make:
Tho blinding him againe, his way he forth did take.

[3. 12. 22–23]

By and large Spenser does not give his characters those
moments of clear volition that Chaucer gives to most of his in
their love affairs, the instant of dedication when they choose
to love and not to repent of it.[15] But he does pick up a Chaucerian motive to provide one check upon this sadistic Cupid
and the primacy of appetite: love may not be constrained by
mastery. Cupid claps his wings, but Amoret is freed. Florimell
is hard put, but she keeps her faith. Between men and women,
love may not be coerced (the nymph-human unions are exceptional in this respect). Devoted service and brave deeds may
not always win a loving return, but attempts to compel love by
the mastery of physical and psychic force almost invariably
fail. This is true whether the contraint is that imposed by the
lawfully wedded Malbecco or by the physical force of eroto-
maniac monsters and ruffians of the Corflambo type or by the
arcane pressures a magician commands. Britomart speaks very
nearly the franklin's words when she lectures the six knights
at the Castle Joyous who have been fighting to force the Red
Cross Knight to acknowledge Malecasta as his lady:

Ne may love be compeld by maisterie;
For soone as maisterie comes, sweet love anone
Taketh his nimble winges, and soone away is gone.

[3. 1. 25]

15. An exception is the expression in Florimell's complaint (4. 12. 7):
"Yet will I never of my love repent, / But joy that for his sake I suffer
prisonment."

The sentiment attracts less suitable advocates such as Sansloy, who looks upon winning assent as another form of conquest (1. 6. 3), and Duessa, who uses it to justify promiscuity and augment the jealousy of Scudamour (4. 1. 46). The tournament for the false Florimell closes in an ironic tableau on this theme. The lady who only *seems* fair may choose—"Sweete is the love that comes alone with willingnesse"—and chooses the knight who only *seems* brave, Braggadochio (4. 5. 26). In the sequel Arthur reaffirms franchise in love (4. 9. 37). Thus, varying contexts keep the ideal from being merely pious, naive, or libertarian. Britomart defends faith-keeping; Duessa, faithlessness; and Satyrane's tournament suggests that freedom of choice is no guarantor of wisdom in the choice.

Britomart's Enamorment

Spenser's knight of chastity is an Amazonian character—beautiful, brave, aggressive, and above all energetic: a type of action. In Britomart's first appearance in the poem she defeats Guyon himself. Later she leaves Marinell seriously wounded. At the tourney for the girdle of Florimell she bests knight after knight, even Artegall—and these are only a few of her deeds of arms. Her chastity, rare virtue, and valor issue in "goodly deeds."

The poet with heroic precedents and generous praise asserts that women too may achieve great deeds, that the field of action is not merely a masculine prerogative, but the human scene:

> Where is the Antique glory now become,
> That whilome wont in women to appeare?
> Where be the brave atchievements doen by some?
> Where be the battels, where the shield and speare,
> And all the conquests, which them high did reare,
> That matter made for famous Poets verse.
> And boastfull men so oft abasht to heare?
> Bene they all dead, and laid in dolefull herse?
> Or doen they onely sleepe, and shall againe reverse?
>
> If they be dead, then woe is me therefore:
> But if they sleepe, O let them soone awake:

> For all too long I burne with envy sore,
> To heare the warlike feates, which *Homere* spake
> Of bold *Penthesilee,* which made a lake
> Of *Greekish* bloud so oft in *Trojan* plaine;
> But when I read, how stout *Debora* strake
> Proud *Sisera,* and how *Camill'* hath slaine
> The huge *Orsilochus,* I swell with great disdaine.
>
> [3. 4. 1–2]

On the one hand such a frame gives congruity to Britomart's exploits, removing from them the stigma of freakishness; on the other hand it makes her career seem more rich and extraordinary through the resonance of the ancient names. Spenser's first audience would also read these lines with a tacit frame provided by women's position in contemporary society and by the great fact of Elizabeth.

An ideal, not a norm, Britomart's deeds do not lose the distinction of the rare nor, in Spenser's treatment, the charm of the perverse. He never lets the reader forget that it is a girl who is flailing about. The undoing of Britomart's hair discloses her sex three times in these books. The poet likes the golden shining of her unveiled head against the glint of her armor; he works at juxtaposing images that bespeak the warrior with those that betray the woman. Alastair Fowler, who treats book 3 as "The Book of Minerva and Venus," relates the prominent treatment of Britomart's helmet in these disclosure scenes to the helmet's being a familiar attribute of Minerva.[16] And surely the juxtaposition of masculine and feminine subserves a sense of awe as if Britomart were a goddess walking the earth. References to Minerva follow one such passage (3. 9. 22), one to Bellona enlarges another (4. 1. 13–14), and, by innuendo, one to the Blessed Virgin still another (4. 6. 19–24). As creatural need—a stormy night, a helmet hacked open in battle—prompts the disclosures, the ascent from warrior to divinity dazzles in its rapidity; the vision, arising from Britomart's hair, is always refracted through the onlookers who see its splendor and provide the ordinary background that sets it off. Paradoxically, as Britomart puts off her

---

16. Fowler, p. 125; see also Roche, pp. 90–94, on Britomart as the image of God.

armor, she takes on power—the martial image modulates through the girlish one to that of the heavenly being.

Et vera incessu patuit dea. But Britomart who walks like a goddess, despite the crowded acts of her story and all her triumphs, is yet, in relation to her passion, a sufferer.[17] One symptomatic example: when asked why she has come disguised to Faerie Land, her emotion reduces her to speechlessness. Spenser marks her failure to command the distinctively rational capacity:

> Thereat she sighing softly, had no powre
> To speake a while, ne ready answere make,
> But with hart-thrilling throbs and bitter stowre,
> As if she had a fever fit, did quake,
> And every daintie limbe with horrour shake;
> And ever and anone the rosy red,
> Flasht through her face, as it had been a flake
> Of lightning, through bright heaven fulmined;
> At last the passion past she thus him answered.
>
> [3. 2. 5]

The hiatus is temporary, of course. Once she regains her faculties Britomart resourcefully trumps up a false version of her mission that elicits the information she really wants about Artegall.

Spenser uses this conversation to give, in a flashback, the true version of why Britomart is in Faerie Land. She is seeking Artegall, a knight whom she has seen only in a magic mirror. From his account, two emphases stand out: first, Britomart's innocent passivity, the nonvolitional aspect of her enamorment; and second, the double presentation of love as both the beginning of biological life and as the motive for the enhancement of life which transforms and shapes, which gives Britomart an identity as a "mayd Martiall" and as a prospective mother of rulers. With her glance into the magic mirror that "seem'd a world of glas," Britomart's behavior and emotions

---

17. Williams, pp. 91–97, 110–12, discusses Britomart, recognizing her passiveness in enamorment and her almost perfect balance between action and acceptance.

immediately and to an extremity become those of a suffering, lovesick girl.

Britomart is so young she is unaware that "her unlucky lot / Lay hidden in the bottome of the pot" (3. 2. 26), while the false archer who has shot so slyly that she did not feel the wound "Did smyle full smoothly at her weetlesse, wofull stound." The proverbial pot fixes Britomart's situation more convincingly than subsequent comparisons of her sighs to heavings of Mount Etna (3. 2. 32). Throughout, Britomart is quite helpless; her nurse Glauce must take all initiative. At her instance they try prayer, but Britomart is too distracted in church to pray; charms are also insufficient. Britomart is right in her feeling that it is "no usuall fire, no usuall rage" that troubles her, and so is Glauce in her shrewd insight that "love can higher stye, / Then reasons reach" (3. 2. 36). A daring parallel indicates by how much love is a fate, not a choice. Glauce soothes her charge; it might have been worse, a "filthy lust, contrarie unto kind" such as those of Myrrhe, of Biblis, and of Pasiphae, "That lov'd a Bull, and learnd a beast to bee" (3. 2. 40–41). Britomart mournfully answers that however shameful and "unkind" such affections, these women "Yet did possesse their horrible intent: / . . . So was their fortune good, though wicked were their mind" (3. 2. 43).

Britomart is clearly not perverse, but it is also implied that this is luck. And indeed though Spenser always discriminates between the works of lust and the works of love, he implies a fatality about both. The "unkind" union is that between un-equals. His principal couples are strong and / or beautiful young people who mate with one another. There is small pos-sibility of Beauty's transforming the Beast, it works the other way round. (See Pasiphae and Hellenore.) But to love well, to love one worthy of esteem, is highly fortunate.

Spenser's word on Britomart is that "no powre / Nor guid-ance of her selfe in her did dwell" (3. 2. 49). And in the canto's final line he summarizes the nurse's predicament over Brito-mart's wasting and wailing: Glauce "wist not how t'amend [agere], nor how it to withstond [pati]" (3. 2. 52).

At this point Glauce undertakes the expedition to Merlin,

who takes a broader view; not romance, not biology, but history and destiny are on his mind: it was not Britomart's wandering eye but "the streight course of heavenly destiny, / Led with eternall providence" that guided her.[18] She is advised: "Therefore submit thy wayes . . . / And do by all dew meanes thy destiny fulfill" (3. 3. 24).

In a fit of prophecy Merlin gives Britomart an account of her progeny. The future is to be glorious but hard; a catalogue of rule and sorrow amplifies the princess's position as the patient, not the agent, of destiny, strictly at the service of yet unborn generations of sovereigns. Merlin begins with a striking image that brings into synthesis Britomart's position in history on a royal family tree and also her participation in nature's most basic processes. She should not, Merlin tells her, be dismayed by the sharp onset of love,

> For so must all things excellent begin,
> And eke enrooted deepe must be that Tree,
> Whose big embodied braunches shall not lin,
> Till they to heavens hight forth stretched bee.
> For from thy wombe a famous Progenie
> Shall spring . . .

[3. 3. 22]

The image of the deep-rooted tree comes between mention of heart and womb, and the treatment of it not only as a diagram of a royal genealogy in a chronicle but also as a growing seedling restores immediacy to these often poetically perfunctory organs—as if one were seeing the roots thrusting into them. (In medieval illuminations the tree of Jesse is sometimes so treated.)

Not surprising then is the pessimism that marks Britomart's rare philosophizing. She has seen what is to come and mourned the fate of some among her descendants (3. 3. 43); her as-yet-unmet love is to die early (3. 3. 28); and ancient devastations of her line also move her. When Paridell tells

18. The two accounts of Britomart's fatal glance, that which follows her steps and that which Merlin gives, express the roles of the Boethian concepts of common fortune (3. 2. 23), destiny (3. 3. 24), and Providence (also 3. 3. 24).

of the fall of Troy (that is the tale that saddens, while it graces, Malbecco's perturbed, and enforced, hospitality), she speaks in formal elegy of this ancestral example of a present and perennial human woe:

> O lamentable fall of famous towne,
> Which raignd so many yeares victorious,
> And of all *Asie* bore the soveraigne crowne,
> In one sad night consumd, and throwen downe:
> What stony hart, that heares thy haplesse fate,
> Is not empierst with deepe compassiowne,
> And makes ensample of mans wretched state,
> That floures so fresh at morne, and fades at evening late?
>
> [3. 9. 39]

Incongruous only in view of her conspicuous triumphs, her words to Scudamour give a laconic summary of a sufferer's outlook: "who nill bide the burden of distresse, / Must not here thinke to live: for life is wretchednesse" (3. 11. 14).

6

Conclusion:

Action and Sufferance in Spenser

and Chaucer

Spenser the Renaissance poet celebrates action; Chaucer, a medieval poet, sufferance. Are such statements true—or useful? The answer must be a qualified yes, more true than not and useful as a pointer toward where stress falls. But the foregoing discussion has not been designed to establish these bearings. Rather, in passages where the hero as sufferer might be most variously discerned, the topos *agere et pati* has been set against aspects of aesthetic ensemble from plot to image patterns. It helped to locate the crucial tensions of narrative in the Knight's Tale and in book 1 of *The Faerie Queene*. It shed light on development of relations among characters, on the ways in which Theseus is set in opposition to Palamon and Arcite, Una to the Red Cross Knight, Guyon to Pyrochles. Discussion of imagery of the Knight's Tale indicated that a view of man as a patient may be projected not only through episodes and character analysis but also through image, metaphor, and setting. If more subtly, these may more inexorably set man as the suffering protagonist of his own life, and this in relation not to others or to his individual passions and vanities, but to destiny.

A more general inquiry about the themes of doing and bearing in Spenser and Chaucer is appropriate at last. Where they agree and differ can be sorted out by positing a model of man's perception of human life as a sphere within a larger sphere. In the first the human being is the center of an immediately sensed life. Outside there is a circle immeasurably larger, mysterious. The shell of the nearer one we may think of as vague, or porous, so that some interpenetration is possible. In the small sphere of intimate life, people act and suffer on the whole explicably. They make choices and, other things being equal, the choices bring results. The results may not be those counted on; but, though without much assurance in prediction, when looking back one can understand a logic connecting motive and event, choice and result. Looking back, one will consider how much better or how much different it would be or might be now if one had done things differently then. But in the larger area human choices do not seem to count for much even in retrospect. Magic and prayer may seem, or seem not, to avail. Here man seems to be a recipient of disasters and of deliveries beyond his ken, a patient of fortune, or destiny, or God. While what a man does in the immediate sphere may be connected with what he suffers in the larger one or from it, the connections will be tenuous, mysterious, not susceptible to his analysis, however much considered ingenuity he expends in trying to discern links and connections. Because human beings are rational, they will and must restlessly try to understand what happens in that larger circle, too, but it is a realm of faith in the end. Because the poet as maker of an extended fiction (as opposed, say, to a dramatic lyric) almost necessarily imitates a perception of both spheres, as author he may imply as a truth about the second sphere what as a human being he can only hold as opinion, or dogma, or hope. That is, his work will seem to say that God is in his heaven and all is right with the world, or that He is not and it is not, or to make various other combinations of these assertions and negations. (Although the antinovel does avoid mimesis of the larger sphere by excluding phenomena that might be read as intimations from it, still the puritanic lacunae express the opinion that the sphere does not exist. Nothing there is, but all that is I see.)

Both Chaucer and Spenser count man a sufferer in this larger sphere. Both admit enigmatic communications, leakage, gestures, from one sphere to the other. But in the small daily round, Chaucer seems to place value on suffering and Spenser seems to place value on action. Neither denies the alternate as a living mode, but so the stress falls. Spenser's heroes face the ruck of events and strive to order them so as to bring about a better world; and though that world, gallantly new and golden, cannot be imagined as ever achieved, the doing, the fabrication, its *poiesis* (in *The Faerie Queene* itself and in all heroic poetry) is always under way. Chaucer's people, few of whom are heroes, are not making up a new world or restoring a golden one but for the most part coping with one another within the same old world, leaden, but dear and engaging. The Wife of Bath and Chantecleer compound speculation, docility, and initiative in their dealings with common fortune and with destiny.[1] Pluck, mother wit, the posture of action—these are not, in Chaucer, exclusively the qualities of rascally agents. But by and large, when most exemplary—and here Troilus too is an exception, for though admirable he is never, in his *life,* resigned—Chaucer's characters are not shaping events, but submitting themselves to them. In all kinds of accents, with varying purity, they make the patient's radically comic accommodation, resignation. To see themselves as patients is their characteristic moral action. The poets' emphases can best be seen by looking first for the dominant pattern in each and then at how it is qualified.

1. The Nun's Priest's Tale spaciously reviews the destinal problem of necessity versus free will but nowhere brings it to the acuteness with which the problem is posed in the Knight's Tale. This is because of the delightful ending, which is conclusive at the narrative level—Chantecleer's presence of mind, his action, frees him—but not so conclusive about the philosophical question. The priest "kan nat bulte it to the bren" (3240), and therefore leaves "swich mateere" to derive more mundane morals from his tale.

Of Spenser and Agere et Pati

Spenser, then, is the poet of action. In *The Faerie Queene,*
a fair proportion of generalizations offered *in persona auctoria*
declare the worth, the fundamental humanity, of action he-
roically defined. (I am not speaking to Spenser's own views,
though it is improbable that he would give repeated stress to
views at an extreme from his own.) "Brave poursuit of chevalrous emprize" links heroes one to another (1. 9. 1); action is
the medium for the heroes' good golden chain of virtues and
friendships. The noble heart does not rest until it brings forth
the "brood of glorie excellent" (1. 5. 1), a remark which re-
calls Aristotle's that man is "begetter of his actions as he is
of his children" (*Nicomachean Ethics* 3. 5. 5–6). Deeds are a
true index to the man (6. 7. 1). The best are marked for brave
pursuit of honorable deeds, as one may see by the way they
fight, ride, and entertain (2. 4. 1); poetry itself, when the subject is royal ancestry, is a "haughtie enterprise" (2. 10. 1), and
its composition is a labor (3. 9. 1). The "rugged forhead" is
not wrong in devoting himself to affairs of state and commend-
ing instruction in virtue, but does not understand that love
motivates virtuous action and poetry commemorates it last-
ingly (4. prologue). When Spenser says in the Lay of Clorinda
that man's best redress is his best sufferance, notice how qualified the situation: the sentiment is locally dramatic, possibly
bitter rather than resigned, immediately denied for a more
resounding affirmation—and perhaps in the first place was
not his own line but that of the Countess of Pembroke. In
The Faerie Queene, it is expected that when exemplary characters are off-scene, they are seeking hard adventures and
achievements brave in another part of the forest.

Knightly combat, war, is a major Spenserian metaphorical
vehicle, and this inevitably means action. Typically, even the
knight of courtesy who admires the speech of young Tristram
"more admyr'd the stroke" (6. 2. 13). Recurrent gestures, situations, motives, support this metaphor and the authorial inter-
positions. The woods child who betrays his noble heritage in

precocious deeds is one of these. (See Satyrane, the sons of
Agape, Artegall, Sir Calepine's foundling, Tristram.) The hero's renewal of quest is another. After peril or delay, the heroes
set out *again*, perhaps confused or fatigued but no less determined. The heroes "forward fare" as Spenser puts it in
one of the first of these narrative movements that become in-
crementally significant.[2] Herculean allusions abound, not only
in relation to Artegall. One curious situation recurs: the hero
finds himself in a narrow place, in dubious battle, the foe
inclined to retreat; again and again when matters are in such
balance, the hero forces the issue, compelling engagement.[3]

Model action, however, need not be warlike. The heroes
perform menial services. Arthur plods through a dungeon's
filth to rescue the Red Cross Knight: "Entire affection hateth
nicer hands" (1. 8. 40). When Priscilla is at a loss about her
disabled friend, not wanting to trouble Sir Calidore nor to
carry him herself as "thing too base," Calidore instructs her:

> Faire Lady let it not you seeme disgrace,
> To beare this burden on your dainty backe;
> My selfe will beare a part, coportion of your packe.
>
> [6. 2. 47]

And at the House of Holiness instruction is given in the cor-
poral works of mercy, prescribed Christian "doings" on behalf
of passible man's sufferings: hunger, nakedness, captivity, illness, death, and bereavement.

Frequently Spenser indicates that will, attitude, and choice
determine agency or passivity. Perhaps most readers have noticed how often people in *The Faerie Queene* wait out wake-
ful nights. The objective content is that they are not getting
proper sleep. But sometimes they watch, and sometimes they

2. See the Red Cross Knight (1. 9. 2); Guyon (2. 11. 3); Britomart (3. 4. 18
and 5. 7. 24); Artegall (5. 7. 43–45 and 5. 11. 36); Arthur (3. 5. 2 and 5. 11. 35).
For a different explanation of the Spenserian hero's forward thrust, see
Fletcher, *Allegory*, pp. 64–65, 302, 350–51.

3. See the Red Cross Knight and the dragon Error (1. 1. 17); Timias
and the third forester (3. 5. 25); the Prince and the monster of idolatry
(5. 11. 26); Sir Calidore and the Blatant Beast (6. 12. 26). Herculean allusions have been frequently discussed in recent writing on Spenser. Hallet
Smith, *Elizabethan Poetry* (Cambridge, Mass.: Harvard, 1952), pp. 290 ff.,
discusses the background of the Renaissance view of Hercules.

have insomnia. Spenser distinguishes these as actions and sufferings, respectively. The most vivid insomniac is Scudamour with his night at the Cottage of the Blacksmith Care (4. 5. 32–46). Britomart cannot sleep, or dreams fitfully, in her first enamorment (3. 2. 28–29), but she watches at the House of Busirane (3. 11. 55). In the eager early days of his quest, the pre-pastoral Sir Calidore suffers the beast to rest neither day nor night, "Ne rested he himselfe but natures dew" (6. 9. 3). And "wakefull watches ever to abide" (2. 3. 41) is on Belphoebe's list of active life's tasks.[4] "It is the mynd, that maketh good or ill" (6. 9. 30), Meliboe tells Calidore, and his context in this passage is the distinction between agents and patients. The differences between watching and insomnia exemplify this.

So does the small story of Mirabella. In precise touches it brings out issues related to the *agere-et-pati* distinction and expressed through it from the time of Aeschylus, issues of justice, of freedom, and of the willed, chosen essence of action. She is a "scornefull lasse" (6. 7. 35) who callously wreaks such havoc among Cupid's men that the god calls her to account, sentencing her to wander the world, whipped by Scorn and led by Disdain, until she saves as many souls as she has spilled. The story begins with Mirabella's freedom as an agent and her impervious joy in the state: "She was borne free, not bound to any wight, / And so would ever live, and love her owne delight" (6. 7. 30). Until a final plaintive line, her recollection of her heyday pirouettes, chiefly because of short *i*'s, liquids, and repetitions of *list*, capturing the very music of caprice, that trivial expression of choice, will:

4. For other examples compare 1. 2. 6, 1. 5. 1, 5. 6. 24–34, and 6. 4. 40, the last a mixed *agere-et-pati* night. It may also be noted that Guyon refuses not only the golden apples of Proserpina but the silver stool under the tree's branches (2. 7. 63). This is the final temptation in the cave; if Guyon "inclined had at all" to sit, the fiend following him would have rent him in pieces. In general, races are to be run; one is not to be found sitting down in the middle of them. But see Kermode, in *Elizabethan Poetry*, ed. Brown and Harris, pp. 164–65, where the silver stool is related to the stone of Ceres and the penance of Theseus and hence to a temptation to vain knowledge—this being associated with ambition, not sloth.

> But let them love that list, or live or die;
> Me list not die for any lovers doole:
> Ne list me leave my loved libertie,
> To pitty him that list to play the foole:
> To love my selfe I learned had in schoole.
> Thus I triumphed long in lovers paine,
> And sitting carelesse on the scorners stoole,
> Did laugh at those that did lament and plaine:
> But all is now repayd with interest againe.
>
> [6. 8. 21]

Mirabella cannot even imagine that anyone *can* be less than free; she assumes her suitors must "list" to play the fool. She is not only free and uncaring, but absolutely powerful, able to "save, or spill, whom she would hight. / What could the Gods doe more, but doe it more aright?" (6. 7. 31). But tragedy, in the *Mirror for Magistrates* manner, befalls:

> Ensample take of *Mirabellaes* case,
> Who from the high degree of happy state,
> Fell into wretched woes, which she repented late.
>
> [6. 8. 2]

The second part of her story begins with the whilom lady of liberty condemned to suffer for what she has done and so to meet that inner requirement of justice, the felt need that the torturer *understand* what he has done to the victim. Mirabella explains her sentence in the terms *agere et pati:* Cupid in revenge of "wrongfull smarts, / Which I to others did inflict afore, / Addeem'd me to endure this penaunce sore" (6. 8. 22). Bruised, beaten, called unpleasant names, harried so that she cannot rest, she becomes so little callous that for Timias, who tries to rescue her and is himself captured, she is "touched with compassion entire" (6. 8. 3). Her new empathy prepares for her decision after Arthur's intervention, for, when freed, she chooses to act out the full penance. A greater ill betides if she does not, she says. It may be the pending ill is a constraint, but the verse emphasizes the renewal of her options as Arthur repeats her own favorite early words, "list" and "liberty" (6. 8. 29). Possibly the greater ill would be to become again impervious.[5]

Mirabella's story is chiefly Petrarchan hyperbole distended into a mock tragedy complete with hybris and fall but with a comic, qualified ending. Though a paradigm for the subtopics of *agere et pati,* it is slight. But more usually Spenser's sense of man as an actor, the value placed on heroic action, comes with serious urgency. Why this urgency, is a question. A tentative answer might be that the good must act in this world because evil in it is active. The experts among dark's children, when suffer they must, suffer the minimum because they remain total in will to act, constant in contrivance and stratagem. *Their* wills are undivided. The minor children of dark— Pyrochles, for instance—may suffer even to the bitterness of unregarded deaths, but the masters live on potent in spirit when humbled by ludicrous situations.

The ludicrous note is frequent. Possibly this is owing to the same psychological and moral strategy that led medieval morality writers to make a guy of the devil; the theatrical precedent is congruent at any event with Archimago, where the notion of acting in the professional sense contributes farcical tinges to his presentation. He is always doing impersonations and is sometimes unmasked. We first gather he may not be the holy man he seems when the poet hints his overacting: "He told of Saintes and Popes, and evermore / He strowd an *Ave-Mary* after and before" (1. 1. 35). Later he acts the solicitous friend when he runs to wake the Red Cross Knight "with feigned faithfull hast" and display the sprite-Una and sprite-squire abed (1. 2. 4). Archimago is not too proud to take the role of busybody and informer. At the end of book 1 he is again careless of dignity and a little hammy as "A Messenger with letters" (1. 12. 24) rushing in to interrupt nuptial festiv-

---

5. B. E. C. Davis, in *Edmund Spenser* (Cambridge University, 1933; reprinted New York: Russell & Russell, 1962), p. 127, thinks that Mirabella's story ends in much ado about nothing, for she goes on in the same way after Arthur's help, but surely this overlooks a real difference. Williams, *Spenser's World of Glass,* pp. 219–20, discusses Mirabella's story in terms of growth.

ities. Book 2 discovers him once more in amateur theatricals, playing a humble "miser," befriending another damsel.[6]

Of the manipulators of evil, Night most has the presence of a divinity. Old, injured, sulking, she holds formidable residual power. The others arouse fear and wonder chiefly because of their pertinacity, their activity, or because they are grotesque. Night's cordial welcome to Duessa when she learns who the witch is provides an example of another means by which Spenser induces respect for the active power of evil. Duessa and Night are related, and evil agents are always recognizing one another, always turning out to have common kin and acquaintances. So it is that an impression forms of a great network of evil that will always threaten the values of Faerie Land. The alliances they form may be sporadic, but it would be a mistake to think of them as thieves who will fall out when interest dictates. Interest will not dictate this. Unlike the false human friends of book 4, they are fastened one to another in mutual care through a loyalty they share just as the true knights serve one another in serving Gloriana.[7]

Their motivation is not a question. They are simply bad, like the radically inimical characters in fairy tales. Most are irremediable—Poena and Briana reform, but they never quite rank with Ate, Duessa, Archimago, Mammon, and Busirane. The issue and instruments of night may represent some unredeemable, primitive remnant of chaos, a heart of darkness within the psyche, but I think it also likely that they are images of an evil which Spenser felt to have genuine, nonhuman existence, as he felt grace to have an extrahuman source. His imagined world is Manichean.

Evil is volatile and recalcitrant. It may be cleared from a locality long enough so that the hero may proceed on his quest or briefly celebrate its outcome, but it lurks potent in some wild or deep place, the cave of Mammon, the pit in the Garden of Adonis, the rocky defiles of the "waste wildernesse" that harbor Duessa in her nakedness and from which she

6. Cheney, *Spenser's Image of Nature*, p. 46, remarks on Archimago's vitality and lack of dignity and places him as an artist.

7. Ate's impeaching of Duessa (5.9.47) is exceptional.

emerges with a fresh wardrobe and a new story. One cannot imagine these evil figures ruling—they are rovers and raiders, spoilers. One cannot imagine them winning; also, one cannot imagine them definitively beaten. So the hero must act.

Still, Spenser sees that he is also going to suffer. Belphoebe is spokesman for both modes of experience. To Braggadochio and Trompart she declares the ethic of action; to Timias she presents man in all the pathos of his creatural suffering. These scenes, her first appearances, are a diptych, Belphoebe expressing the missing half-truth in each case. To the man who seems to be the heroic doer but who proposes primrose courts, she gives an account of the meaning and right arena of action (2. 3. 40–41); to the sufferer, she offers a sympathy that places his suffering in a wide frame. Assumed by Timias to be a goddess, Belphoebe denies divine identity and immunities:

> We mortall wights, whose lives and fortunes bee
> To commun accidents still open layd,
> Are bound with commun bond of frailtee,
> To succour wretched wights, whom we captived see.
>
> [3. 5. 36]

The aristocratic ethos of deeds which has been upheld throughout the poem and which Belphoebe has severely itemized to Braggadochio loses place for a moment to the universal pathos of suffering. The golden chain that links those "In brave poursuit of chevalrous emprize" (1. 9. 1) is not stronger than the bond of a shared human fragility.

The scenes are supplementary. Belphoebe's first appearance has bearing on man's duty in the smaller sphere. Her second suggests his vulnerability in the enveloping, mysterious one. Her words to Timias come with a comforting sweetness— *comfort* is a word much in use in the sequence—because her very denial of divine exemption is an allusion to an unexampled transcendent largesse. But Spenser could also be bleak about man's exposure to "common accidents," and this is the tone when Mutability claims the passible world. She puts man in negligible place; along with beasts, he is among the tenants of earth in stanzas on the passion of the cosmos—cos-

mic susceptibility to change in the elements. The goddess at-
tends to man's unique dignity only in noting ironically his
pretensions to it:

> As for her [earth's] tenants; that is, man and beasts,
> The beasts we daily see massacred dy,
> As thralls and vassalls unto mens beheasts:
> And men themselves doe change continually,
> From youth to eld, from wealth to poverty,
> From good to bad, from bad to worst of all.
> Ne doe their bodies only flit and fly:
> But eeke their minds (which they immortall call)
> Still change and vary thoughts, as new occasions fall.

[7. 7. 19]

No change is for the better, none is willed. The stanzas on
"Ayre" also hint a tacit, shivering human sufferer:

> . . . O weake life! that does leane
> On thing so tickle as th 'unsteady ayre;
> Which every howre is chang'd, and altred cleane
> With every blast that bloweth fowle or faire:
> The faire doth it prolong; the fowle doth it impaire.

> Therein the changes infinite beholde,
> Which to her creatures every minute chaunce;
> Now, boyling hot: streight, friezing deadly cold:
> Now, faire sun-shine, that makes all skip and daunce:
> Streight, bitter storms and balefull countenance,
> That makes them all to shiver and to shake:
> Rayne, hayle, and snowe do pay them sad penance,
> And dreadfull thunder-claps (that make them quake)
> With flames and flashing lights that thousand changes make.

[7. 7. 22–23]

Early through the hawthorne blows the cold wind. The conclusive and biting placement of man as patient comes through
the rhetorical ostentation with which the titan makes joy as
nonvolitional as pain. The response is mindless: fair sunshine
"makes" all skip and dance; bitter storm "makes" all shiver
and shake. Parallel syntax and the choice of strong bodily
gestures (*smile* and *glaunce* would as well fill out rhyme

scheme, metrical pattern, antithesis, and syntax) give the cheerful response a compulsive, automatic quality. Mutability is beautiful, and Spenser may be half of her party; she offers pleasure—all change is sweet, all that moves does delight in change.[8] Still to the earthly aspirations of individual men and women, she is other or hostile.

"What so is fayrest shall to earth returne," Spenser writes in *Amoretti* 13; and in *Amoretti* 58, "All flesh is frayle, and all her strength unstayd" for "on earth nought hath enduraunce." The ruin poems cannot be dismissed as youthful Weltschmerz, for what Spenser was saying first he said again at the last. One must act now, for none can work in that night.

Both Poets and Agere et Pati

To Chaucer, action simply does not seem to stand in need of so much recommendation. Chaucer's characters do act— especially the less admirable ones like Diomede, like Nicholas, like the canon, like the friar of the Summoner's Tale and the summoner that the Friar tells about, like Pandarus—they are always scheming to *do* something. Their designing hearts are in action. But the substance of their activities carries a devastating criticism. Whereas Spenser's doers fight dragons and paynims, Chaucer's arrange assignations and hoaxes. And certainly Chaucer never seems to be insisting that a man should act, should perform noble deeds, should pursue honor or glory or redress wrongs or even hoist a neighbor's ox out of a slough, though some of his people do these things. Whereas Spenser in his poetic persons praises action, Chaucer the narrator is less expansive in affirmation, in fact is conspicuous for his bemusement, withdrawal, vagueness, and inadvertence.

Less committed, then, and on the whole presenting action skeptically, Chaucer does not find idleness, ease—giving up— the seduction it is in Spenser. Neither sloth nor *otium* has the

8. Cf. Sherman Hawkins, "Mutabilitie and the Cycle of Months," in *Form and Convention in the Poetry of Edmund Spenser,* ed. William Nelson, Selected Papers from the English Institute (New York: Columbia, 1961), pp. 76–102.

same bearing. The Second Nun tells off the conventional condemnations of idleness, and that is that. Possibly only when heavy stress falls on worldly action as ethically admirable will either of the alternatives, *la dolce vita* with Phaedria and its pastoral and approved version, *otium*, have much following. When something acquires power and prestige, alternatives will be also seriously defended, as the retired life came to be in the Renaissance.[9] (That money is not everything would be a dark saying before the advent of a money economy.) Such a recoil as the death urge of the Red Cross Knight suggests that the social context is placing high value on energetic achievement. The overstretched elastic goes limp. When Chaucer's Dorigen considers suicide, it is not out of weariness of life, but because she is in a jam. If she had done away with herself, it would have been as an agent; had St. George done so, it would have been as a patient. The Parson's Tale explains acedia, but Chaucer never embodies it in a fictive situation, with the just possible exception of *The Book of the Duchess* (1–43 passim) in the narrator to whom "nys nothyng leef nor looth" (8).

What a poet ignores is revealing. Toward war, political affairs, history, Spenser is attentive. Apart from some careful lines on war in the Knight's Tale, by and large Chaucer treats these subjects casually. Troilus' deeds of war were immense, but that is not his subject; the curious can look it up in Dares (5. 1765–71). Granted, most of the battles of *The Faerie Queene* are vehicles; the tenor is the moral and inner life. But in poetry choice of vehicle cannot be a slight matter.

That Spenser's work has sustained so much investigation of contemporary political references is evidence of its alertness to politics. Chaucer's work is also held to make contemporary references, but a historical allusion is fully as apt to refer to a royal scandal as to a royal policy. Chaucer and Spenser were both free in their levies on history, but Spenser was more particular. He manipulated myth, and he fabricated allegory that would have a mythic sound; but he did so as a national

9. See Hallett Smith, *Elizabethan Poetry*, on the appeals of the heroic and the pastoral in Spenser, p. 323–24.

poet. An Angela joins Camilla and Penthesilea as precedent for Britomart; Joan of Arc does not. Any history, any legend, would serve Chaucer. A classic tale, one from Late Latin antiquity, current news from the Continent could fit his less rigorous, less patriotic amenity. Above all, history could be ignored, Dido could be chiefly a betrayed lady, Aeneas chiefly a perfidious lover.

Comprehensive metaphors, those that seem capable of completing the statement "Life is a ———," give the same lines of force as regards deeds and pathos. War and quest, straightforward counters for action, are major life images for Spenser and are not so for Chaucer. (It is really curious how rarely the quest is central in Chaucer's romances.) The bargain, which will need to be discussed, and the prison, are Chaucer's alone. (*The Faerie Queene,* of course, describes several prisons. But whether a cave underground or under seas, a castle dungeon or a state of mind, the prison in Spenser is finite. Escape, release short of death, is possible; there are other places to go. The prison may be allegorical, but it is never an allegory of life.)

Spenser and Chaucer share the life image of pilgrimage, the tradition of the Christian wayfarer. They share also a motive associated with action and suffering ever since Demodocus sang for Odysseus, the feast perturbed with crying. The earlier poet made more of it. Its role in the Knight's Tale has been discussed above, and Chaucer also used this motive in the Man of Law's Tale.[10] It appears too in *The Faerie Queene.* St. George's tale of suffering sobers his victory feast, and Archimago's alarm interrupts the marriage feast. The abduction of Amoret disrupts Scudamour's wedding feast. Jeers and quarreling end the great tournament for Florimell's girdle. A variation, the feasting scene qualified by a perturbation recollected in tranquility, is virtually an epic convention, and Spenser provides several besides that for St. George. Guyon tells the story of Amavia's death at the House of

10. See Robert Enzer Lewis, "Chaucer's Artistic Use of Pope Innocent III's *De Miseria Humane Conditionis* in the Man of Law's Prologue and Tale," *PMLA* 81 (1966) : 485–92.

Medina, and Paridell's tale of Troy saddens Britomart at Malbecco's castle (though, more than his story-telling, Paridell's conduct is perturbing at that feast). And of course Gloriana is keeping her annual feast when several wronged sufferers present themselves with injuries to be avenged, woes to be solaced, so the whole officially projected framework for the poem is based upon the theme.

Evidently both poets thought about the unexpected, that of which the perturbed feast is example and mimesis. Both were ambivalent about it, though again Chaucer's reserve and questioning is marked. By definition, we suffer the unexpected; it is not something we plan or choose. Chaucer sometimes issues a cool little warning—watch your step!—as if apprehension may be a talisman. After the butchery of wedding guests in the Man of Law's Tale, the narrator offers, "Upon thy glade day have in thy mynde / The unwar wo or harm that comth bihynde" (426–27).

The unexpected may be rewarding to prodigality. "Hap" and "grace" have place even in the Knight's Tale. In Spenser, rescuing interventions are so regular that they become a structural link among the books. Both poets may heavily mark such rescues with religious innuendo: there is "care in heaven" (*FQ* 2. 8. 1–2); on perilous seas, Constance is saved by Him who saved Daniel, Jonas, the people of Israel, Susanna, by Him who made small David mighty and gave Judith "corage." But to be surprised is to be a patient.

Both poets reflected upon fatality. If man is predestined, he is quite flatly a patient. If he thinks he acts, he is so much a fool. Neither poet arrived at a solution adequate to the occasions his poetry presents. Troilus comes to think foreknowledge excludes freedom, but Troilus may not speak for Chaucer. In translunar excursions, Chaucer offers canceling interpretations of cosmic direction: the close of the *Troilus* opens out in benignity and joy; in the Knight's Tale Theseus hopes for cosmic love, but triviality and malignity reign. The Nun's Priest's Tale returns us to the human sphere, where whatever his theories about possibility and necessity a rooster with wit can outfox a fox, retrieve early losses; where the word about fate and necessity is "Perhaps this . . . , but on the other hand, perhaps that . . ."; and where a clerical teller claims incompetence, he "wol nat han to do of swich mateere" (3251).

Spenser's consideration is said to have a Calvinist accent.[11] Still, he rarely permits us to feel predestination has solved much for his characters or lessened their sense of heavy responsibility. The fates are firm, as Merlin, who can read them, says, "Yet ought mens good endevours them confirme, / And guide the heavenly causes to their constant terme" (3. 3. 25).[12] A pained sense of man's ultimate helplessness and an urgent sense that men ought to act, must take hold—Spenser registers both. The heavens may be hostile or benign, but you may "Your fortune maister eke with governing," with "faire handeling" (1. 8. 28), as Una, truth, says. Chaucer would not, perhaps disagree; but how different the emphasis.

Of Chaucer and Agere et Pati

If one had to give up part of Chaucer, the Parson's Tale and the Tale of Melibee would be least regretted. But a discussion of Chaucer as the poet of patience appropriately begins with them, for their forms let doctrine appear unadorned. The Parson treats patience as the remedy of ire. He defines with an *agere et pati* statement: "Suffrance suffreth swetely alle the anoyaunces and the wronges that men doon to man outward" (655). Like Tertullian, the Parson does not cite Christ's death as itself an example of patience, but Christ patiently bore "foure manere of grevances in outward thynges": "wikkede wordes"; damage to "catel" (his garments); harm in

11. Paul N. Siegel, "Spenser and the Calvinist View of Life," *SP* 41 (1944) : 201–22. However, cf. Virgil K. Whitaker, *The Religious Basis of Spenser's Thought*, Stanford University Publications, Language and Literature, vol. 7, no. 3 (Stanford, Calif., 1950), pp. 7–8 et passim.

12. DeWitt T. Starnes and Ernest William Talbert, in a discussion of the treatment of the Parcae in Renaissance dictionaries, in *Classical Myth and Legend in Renaissance Dictionaries* (Chapel Hill: University of North Carolina, 1955), pp. 379–80, quote Merlin's words as a more positive reflection of the conventional "Ducunt volentem fata, nolentem trahunt" ("The fates lead the willing, drag the unwilling").

body ("That suffred Crist ful paciently in al his passioun");
and "outrageous labour in werkes" (carrying the cross). "If
thow wolt venquysse thyn enemy, lerne to suffre" the Parson
quotes (661). And without any sense of paradox he sets side
by side the Christian and pre-Christian advantages of a virtue
that will make man "Goddes owene deere child" and also dis-
comfort "thyn enemy" (660). (See above, pp. 33–34.) Dame
Prudence picks up other standard themes—patience and self-
mastery, the superior wit of patience, and the bad effects of ire
in counsel. Her husband manages to interject one contribution: "they that been wrothe witen nat wel what they don, ne
what they seyn" (1698).[13]

If these were the only tales in which patience figures, we
might say that Chaucer paid comprehensive, but perfunctory,
respects to popular themes in appropriate forms. But Constance and Griselda prevent this. Unlike the Knight's Tale,
where suffering is the most salient fact of the poem's universe
but has no particular ethical authority, both stories surround
the passions of the heroines with an aura of affirmation, chiefly
through interposition of religious allusion. Much of the conspicuous, the extraordinary, patience of both protagonists
comes from the plots Chaucer found. But not all. Studies of
sources establish that Chaucer altered and added so as to
throw emphasis on the sufferings of the heroines and so as to
heighten religious significance.[14] To be sure, the material lent
itself to the shaping, but in two tales with similar materials,
the story of St. Cecilia and the Physician's Tale, main figures
take a stance only superficially similar.

These also are fundamentally passions, not actions, one in
fact a martyr's legend. But the protagonists are full of initiative. Though few would wish to act at the price, Virginia's

13. The Tale of Melibee offers several variants of *agere et pati,* a
heavier collocation of instances than elsewhere in Chaucer except in the
translation of Boethius. For instance: "And if so be that thou be in
doute wheither thou mayst parfourne a thing or noon, chese rather to
suffre than bigynne" (1216). Cf. 1219, 1291, and 1460–65.

14. Edward A. Block, "Originality, Controlling Purpose, and Craftsmanship in Chaucer's *Man of Law's Tale,*" PMLA 68 (1953) : 587–89; John A.
Yunck, "Religious Elements in Chaucer's 'Man of Law's Tale'," ELH
27 (1960) : 252; J. Burke Severs, *The Literary Relationships of Chaucer's
Clerkes Tale* (New Haven: Yale, 1942), p. 233.

father makes a choice where seemingly he has none, "By resolution simply marvelous / Transforming the disgrace to tragedy" as Jean de Meun puts it.[15] The father's ruthless perceiving of the issue creates alternatives, though dire ones, and his
act brings down his child's enemy. The dialogue of Virginius
and Virginia appears in neither Livy nor the *Romance of the
Rose.* "Ther been two weyes; outher deeth or shame, / That
thou most suffre," he tells the child. He advises her to take
her death "in pacience" and answers, "No, certes, deere
doghter myn," when she asks, "Is ther no grace, is ther no
remedye?" The child is also an actor as well as victim: "Yif
me my deeth, er that I have a shame; / Dooth with youre
child youre wyl, a Goddes name!" (249–50). The tale's appeal
may be a dubious compound of sentimentality, lubricity, and
gore, but to count it only this is to overlook that both father
and daugther behave with stark, superb dignity. Virginia faces
her fate and chooses—the crucially human *act*—as the "litel
clergeon," for instance, is never seen to do.

St. Cecilia, throat cut (a hazard of extraordinary incidence
in the *Tales*), successfully intercedes with heaven so as to
hold up her death for three days while she transforms admirers into Christians, and earlier she not only converts her
husband and kin but scolds the magistrate who demands her
obeisance to idols with so relentless a fluency that the reader's
sympathy goes partly to that beset personage when he says,
"I recche nat what wrong that thou me profre, / For I kan
suffre it as a philosophre" (489–90); even though in this he
overestimates himself.[16]

The crucial, opposing stresses in Chaucer's treatment of

15. "Si change honte pour domage / Par merveilleus apensement, / Se
Titus Livius ne ment" (5632–34); the story is given in *Sources and Ana-
logues of Chaucer's Canterbury Tales* (1941), ed. W. F. Bryan and Germaine Dempster (New York: Humanities, 1958), p. 401. I use the translation of Harry W. Robbins, *The Romance of the Rose,* by Guillaume de
Lorris and Jean de Meun (New York: Dutton, 1962), p. 119.

16. Alfred W. Pollard, in his introduction to *Chaucer's Canterbury
Tales* (London: Macmillan, 1894), p. xvi, counts this "a real contribution
to the much-tried magistrate's character." The magistrate uses an *agere-
et-pati* variant; that he does so would be more obvious and not a greatly
worse rhyme if Chaucer had reversed the position of "suffre" and
"philosophre" in the second line.

St. Cecilia and Virginius and Virginia as agents and Constance and Griselda as patients come about, perhaps, from the character of the antagonists. When the adversary is Providence, the part of virtue is to be patient, to be obedient unto death. But if one suffers because of an unjust human official, that is different; Christian and pagan change what they can before they bear what they must.

Chaucer goes beyond his sources for the Clerk's Tale in another way significant for the topos. He develops more fully Walter's procuring of Griselda's agreement to the marriage.[17] A rereading with Griselda's sufferings in mind makes plain how far Walter's language in the interview goes beyond a marriage proposal and how far also her assent goes (see lines 348–64). He seems ominously, and she perilously, thorough. Some readers see in this episode only further evidence of Walter's sadism, but treaties and bargains enter Chaucer's work so frequently that it may be wiser to conclude that he intends them to be taken seriously.

Certainly Chaucer's characters are often punctilious about one "tretys" or another. For Chaucer one of the enduring shapes of life is the bargain—kept or broken, rarely voided, vividly memorial in its fragments if broken (as at the closing of *Troilus and Criseyde*), sometimes apparently trivial but nearly always turning out to be material, a mainspring of *The Canterbury Tales* framework and of many of its fictions. This theme complicates Chaucer's position as to action and suffering. For bargains do imply agents. At the heart of the love tales, travestied in the fabliaux, obscene or grave, the bargain in Chaucer takes several shapes: promise (Dorigen, Griselda); agreement (the Wife of Bath's Tale and the Second Nun's Tale); sale of services (Aurelius and the magician, the canon and the priest); game (host and pilgrims); union in love (Troilus and Criseyde, Anelida and Arcite).

The General Prologue initiates this theme of promise and game, of word-keeping, in *The Canterbury Tales*.[18] Once

17. Severs, p. 240.

18. Helen Storm Corsa, *Chaucer: Poet of Mirth and Morality* (Notre Dame, Ind.: University of Notre Dame, 1964), pp. 91–95, calls attention

underway that first morning, the Host reminds the pilgrims of their "foreward." The Knight responds to the cut that designates him first player with a gracious alacrity; the narrator approves, and incidentally considers the bargain in its nature as something both freely entered and as having the standing of an obligation:

> And telle he moste his tale, as was resoun,
> By foreward and by composicioun,
> As ye han herd; what nedeth wordes mo?
> And whan this goode man saugh that it was so,
> As he that wys was and obedient
> To kepe his foreward by his free assent,
> He seyde, "Syn I shal bigynne the game,
> What, welcome be the cut, a Goddes name!
>
> [847–54]

And all of the more gentle pilgrims, except the Parson, do keep their "foreward." The link passages frequently advert to the pilgrims' sociable contract. In the main, though Harry Bailly tries sorely the patience of several pilgrims and sometimes seems to want to extend his prerogative, only churls display restiveness about the bargain made at the Tabard.

The exchange between the Man of Law and the Host throws into relief again the proper attitude toward agreements:

> "Sire Man of Lawe," quod he, "so have ye blis,
> Telle us a tale anon, as forward is.
> Ye been submytted, thurgh youre free assent,
> To stonden in this cas at my juggement.
> Acquiteth yow now of youre biheeste;
> Thanne have ye do youre devoir atte leeste."
>   "Hooste," quod he, "*depardieux*, ich assente;
> To breke forward is nat myn entente.
> Biheste is dette, and I wole holde fayn
> Al my biheste, I kan no bettre sayn.
>
> [33–42]

---

to the role of "game" in the structure of the *CT*. See also Richard A. Lanham, "Game, Play, and High Seriousness in Chaucer's Poetry," *English Studies* 48 (1967) : 1–24.

"Biheste is dette." The Host's speech also contains the essence of a bargain, its rationale and proportions of suffering—"Ye been submytted"—and act—"thurgh youre free assent." Similarly the Host reminds the Clerk, "For what man that is entred in a pley, / He nedes moot unto the pley assente" (10–11). The Clerk responds "benignely"; he is under the Host's "yerde," and will obey "As fer as resoun axeth, hardily" (25). Admittedly, this becomes a considerable qualification. Later, the Host peremptorily reminds the Franklin that each must tell a tale or two or "breken his biheste." "That knowe I wel, sire," the Franklin answers (699); and he tells a story that hinges on promises, pacts, and the importance of keeping "trouthe." The Host alludes to the agreement before the last tale when he asks the Parson for his contribution: "Be what thou be, ne breke thou nat oure pley; / For every man, save thou, hath toold his tale" (24–25). Although at first the Parson refuses to keep the bargain, "Thou getest fable noon ytoold for me" (31), his return offer of a bargain of his own perhaps acknowledges the claim:

> . . . if that yow list to heere
> Moralitee and vertuous mateere,
> And thanne that ye wol yeve me audience,
> I wol ful fayn, at Cristes reverence,
> Do yow plesaunce leefful, as I kan.
>
> [37–41]

The company agrees; so at the "thropes ende" unity descends upon the contentious community of Christian wayfarers, no member of which, except the Pardoner, has said or implied that *he* need not nor does not keep his word, though their tales show extensive acquaintance with the fraudulent rest of the world.[19]

In the tales, as in the framework, agreements are important. In the Knight's Tale the human actors respect the game. Palamon must concede defeat not alone because he is weaker than the twenty champions who bring him to the stake but

---

19. Perhaps, however, in their exchanges with the host, the manciple and the cook tacitly admit to somewhat underhanded conduct.

also because those are the rules of the game: "His hardy herte myghte hym helpe naught: / He moste abyde, whan that he was caught, / By force and *eek by composicioun*" (2649–51; my italics). In the churls' tales, the bargain gets a scherzo treatment. Bargains cap the ribaldry of the shipman's and summoner's stories, and whereas the explicit bargain of fellowship is less essential to the plot mechanism of the Friar's Tale, the courteous devil there expresses a superior understanding of a bargain's nature, which he realizes is intent, a consideration that Griselda is not enough apprehensive of, and one which the immune gods in the Knight's Tale ignore: "The carl spak oo thing, but he thoghte another" (1568).

If variety and insistence count, there is reason to say that "trouthe" and patient suffering of what God sends—"Welcome the sonde of Crist" (*MLT*, 760)—form a moral substructure in Chaucer's poetry, anchoring his iridescent themes of human and divine love and forming a bond between his most and his least glamorous people, whose allegiances must be the same. For if we go from the episodes based upon explicit agreements, contracts, bargains, to the general idea of troth-keeping, it is apparent how Chaucer comes back to this and to its opposite, perfidy, treachery, fraud. Fraudulence and treachery are the basic stuff of the Pardoner's Prologue and Tale, the Miller's, Reeve's, Merchant's, Squire's, and Physician's tales, that of the Nun's Priest, the Manciple, and of many of the Monk's tragedies. Most of Chaucer's "Good Women" were famously betrayed. Troilus and Criseyde plight their love in a setting rife with treachery.[20] *Anelida and Arcite* begins with the theme uppermost. Troilus is a hero primarily for his troth-keeping. The lovers Arveragus and Troilus see truth as a part of the integrity, even the identity, of the beloved (see *T&C* 5. 1386, 1414, and 1674 ff.; Franklin's Tale, 1474 ff.). "Trouthe is the hyeste thyng that man may kepe" (1479), Arveragus says, and says it in an extremity.

20. For a consideration of the falseness pattern of the Troilus, and in particular of the part of Calchas in it, see Stanley B. Greenfield, "The Role of Calkas in *Troilus and Criseyde*," *Medium Aevum* 36 (1967): 141–51.

Plighting troth, striking a bargain, making a treaty, and joining a game imply a free agent who will win or pay up, who acts by binding himself to perform certain actions, not others, and thus chooses limits upon his freedom. If life is like a game one may (reductively) explain the myth of the Garden of Eden: it establishes that there was an original choice. If it sometimes seems that Chaucer's patient protagonists pay and pay, they have usually first agreed to play. This will not make Griselda's and Walter's "tretys" realistically acceptable, but perhaps does validate symbolically that outrageously adhered-to compact. Again and again, Chaucer comes back to the point of a first free assent. In the love poems there is a variation. Usually, the lovers choose their destinies, though to be sure destiny first chose them. The lover (wounded by Cupid, by the dart from his lady's eyes) nevertheless separately and deliberately assents to love. There is a double-enamorment. And faithful lovers renew assent, rechoosing to love.[21]

"Lak of Stedfastnesse" may seem to be conventional complaint, but read in consideration of the weight of Chaucer's poetry, it is resonant:

> Somtyme the world was so steadfast and stable
> That mannes word was obligacioun;
> And now it is so fals and deceivable
> That word and deed, as in conclusioun,
> Ben nothing lyk, for turned up-so-doun
> Is al this world for mede and wilfulnesse,
> That al is lost for lak of stedfastnesse.
>
> .   .   .   .
>
> For among us now a man is holde unable,
> But if he can, by some collusioun,
> Don his neighbour wrong or oppressioun.
>
> .   .   .   .   .   .
>
> The world hath mad a permutacioun
> Fro right to wrong, fro trouthe to fikelnesse,
> That al is lost for lak of stedfastnesse.

21. *Troilus and Criseyde*, 1. 379 and 1. 391–92; *The Book of the Duchess*, 791 and 1075 ff.; and "Complaint of Mars," 15–21. Choice and chance both enter into the matings in *The Parliament of Fowls*; Nature tells the fowls that they come "for to cheese" but "as I prike yow with plesaunce" (389).

For the most part Chaucer keeps to the immediate and social aspects of "trouthe." "Trouthe" is keeping the bargain, with the rigor of a child. That man cheats and lies to his fellow man, "by som collusioun, / Don his neighbour wrong," is the biting evil.

Despite these bargains, Chaucer's emphasis falls on the human being as a suffering protagonist in this life. Sometimes patience is urged as a virtue, sometimes, as with Theseus and Canacee, only as the better face in necessity. It escapes from the Franklin, who commends patience in marriage as a "heigh vertu, certeyn," that it is also a necessity: "Lerneth to suffre, or elles, so moot I goon, / Ye shul it lerne, wher so ye wole or noon" (777–78). After a compassionate account of the hope and grief of Troilus, the narrator withdraws from the narrow scene of embattled Troy with a matter of fact note on his heroine and the lover—

> Criseyde loveth the sone of Tideüs,
> And Troilus moot wepe in cares colde.
> Swich is this world, whoso it kan byholde:

—but closes with a sad reason for patience, a widening view, and a reverent disposition:

> In ech estat is litel hertes reste.
> God leve us for to take it for the beste!
>
> [5. 1746–50]

In the more active mode, it is also thus with Spenser's questers and doers. Though frequently not fully armed, either within or without, for the thrusts their quests bring, they never stop trying; and through them the poet seems to say that this is right, this is human, one should keep trying.

Index